The Soul of Education

I0805833

The Soul of Education is a deeply integrative exploration (both spiritual and secular) of what it means to reclaim the moral, spiritual and relational heart of schooling. Drawing together contemporary educational research, insights from Vedic philosophy and lived practice, the book invites readers to re-examine the purposes and possibilities of education in a rapidly changing world.

Through interconnected chapters, the authors present a soul-full vision of education, grounded in teachings from the *Bhagavad Gītā* and Vedic thought. They explore how beliefs, virtues and values shape character, agency and wellbeing in school life, while critiquing the performative pressures and utilitarian aims that have eroded the "soul" of modern schooling. Central to the book is the Tree of Life framework, which integrates Educational Excellence, Character Formation and Spiritual Insight to create a holistic ecology of learning beyond religious designations or traditions. Practical examples and classroom anecdotes illustrate how educators and parents can foster inner growth through listening, reflection, meditation and compassionate action.

This book is ideal for educators, parents, policymakers and anyone invested in the future of education. It speaks to those seeking alternatives to materialism and performativity, offering tools to address the challenges of growing up in a technologically advanced, socially fragmented world.

James Biddulph MBE FCCT is an award-winning educator, researcher and founding Executive Headteacher of the University of Cambridge Primary School. He is now the CEO of Avanti Schools Trust. He is a pioneering leader bridging research and practice in schools to empower diverse communities. His PhD focused on creative learning and, in 2025, he was awarded the MBE for services to education.

Nitesh Gor OBE founded Avanti Schools Trust and has inspired various projects, including a dharma-based endowment fund, equity indexes by Dow Jones and a retreat centre. He has authored three books on Vedic philosophy and its relevance for education, leadership and business. He was awarded the OBE for services to education.

"*The Soul of Education* is a powerful reminder that education is never just about knowledge but about shaping attention, values, and purpose. This book courageously restores depth, compassion and meaning to schooling, offering a vision of learning that helps young people become not just successful, but whole."

Jay Shetty, #1 New York Times Bestselling Author &
Host of Award-Winning Podcast ON Purpose

"As AI threatens to erase out of schools both humanity and caring human relationships, it is refreshing to read this inspirational volume."

Sir Anthony Seldon, Educationalist author

"A scholarly, deeply conceived and landmark contribution to the field of education! Biddulph and Gor open the heart of education by drawing on the deepest wisdom of the Vedic Tradition. Profound educational transformation here lives at the crossroads of guiding children in a value driven, enlivening, foundationally ethical life within the existing challenges of our global community. Presenting an elegant framework for implementation, there is no appeal for a simplistic leap of change, but rather a grounded, clear actionable stepwise ladder towards the ascension of spiritually centered education."

Lisa Miller, PhD, NYT Bestselling Author of *The Spirituality Child*,
Past-President The Collaborative for Spirituality in Education,
and Professor, Spirituality Mind Body Institute,
Columbia University, Teachers College

"*The Soul of Education* bridges ancient Vedic wisdom with modern pedagogy. It challenges us to consider that the intellect without an inner life is half an education. Biddulph and Gor invite us to recalibrate and to teach not just minds, but souls. The wonderful case studies show that it's possible to awaken wisdom, wonder, and human flourishing. A luminous manifesto for the future of learning."

Mary Myatt, Education writer and speaker

"James and Nitesh restore that sense of soul to our classrooms, our communities, and our leadership, so that we may yet raise a generation capable not just of succeeding, but of healing, of building a world where the mind, the heart, and the spirit move together in harmony."

Lord Krish Raval OBE, Member of the House of Lords

"This book is a hugely welcome yet profoundly unusual education text. Most treatises set out to improve the current system, this book, however, seeks to help us rediscover core purposes and philosophy of education."

Professor Dame Alison Peacock DBE DL,
CEO The Chartered College of Teaching

"This is a deeply considered, courageous book that draws on both new and ancient philosophical thinking to propose a radically different foundation for education - one framed by equality, diversity and love, rather than academic, political and socio-economic priorities. James Biddulph and Nitesh Gor present a carefully-argued, discursive journey in which they adopt a transdisciplinary lens to consider cultural, psychological, philosophical and spiritual understandings of the concept of the human soul. They also offer moving examples of classroom practice to illustrate how an education that…" honours the boundless potential of every child" (Biddulph and Gor, conclusion) can transform children's lives, communities and futures. Whilst much attention is currently being given to technocratic visions of humanity's future, Biddulph and Gor's timely contribution invites us to return to the fundamental questions of what it means to be human, to be compassionate, to be wise."

Dr Julia Flutter, Author and Academic Founding
Director, Practical Wisdom Network

"As we live through precarious ecological, economic and geopolitical times, we need an education that empowers agency and guides young people towards more hopeful futures. *The Soul of Education* inspires and challenges - it's a manifesto of hope and possibility."

Professor Emily Shuckburgh CBE, Director
of Cambridge Zero, Cambridge University

"*The Soul of Education* is a thought-provoking 'must-read' which is spiritually informed by Vedic philosophical traditions that light the life of education for human flourishing. This unique and insightful reframing of soul-led education is a call for integrating relational and spiritual dimensions of learning by attuning to the agentic forces that nurture human compassion and empathy, love and belonging. This inspiring and life-giving book will be read and re-read for decades to come for its holistic soul-led educational vision of schools as homes of human flourishing."

Professor Pamela Burnard, Professor of Arts, Creativities
and Educations, University of Cambridge

"I've worked with James for many years. The words in this book align with a practice that he has showed time and time again – bold, innovative and inclusive and there are numerous wonderful examples of values in practice throughout the book. *The Soul of Education* provides a new pathway to enable every child to be valued and included. This isn't a religious book - it's more. It's about the human spirit and how we can develop it. As a member of the teaching assistant community, I see how such a philosophy could engage us in asking even better questions for and about children. The book is challenging in places, but I recommend that you go on the journey - it's one of self-discovery!"

Aimee Durning MBE, Director of Inclusion
University of Cambridge Primary School

"*The Soul of Education* speaks powerfully to a truth I see daily in my work: that human beings do not thrive in cultures shaped by shame, blame, and fear, but in environments that guide, inspire, and awaken a deeper sense of worth and purpose. James (a Hoffman graduate himself) with Nitesh offers a compelling and compassionate reimagining of education as an inner as well as outer journey, one that honours the emotional, moral, and spiritual dimensions of being human. This book challenges the damaging narratives of performance and deficiency that so often dominate schooling, and instead invites educators to cultivate attention, relationship, reflection, and meaning. It resonates strongly with the Hoffman Process understanding that healing, growth, and learning happen when people feel seen, supported, and encouraged to live from their authentic selves."

Serena Gordon, Managing Director,
The Hoffman Process UK

"Having Chaired the Learned Society in Educational Leadership for the past three years - where I have had the privilege to work with scholars from all around the world - I had become downhearted that our education system in England had become overly performative, behaviourist and reductionist. This Soul of Education book does exactly as it is entitled, it offers the soul back to education, so we can learn and move forward generationally together… a must-read for anyone who has had qualms about the direction in which we were going, as this text shows us that there is real hope inside our education system. This should give us all the faith to help enact the changes that are needed - it is a thoroughly beautiful read."

Dr Deb Outhwaite FCCT, Chair, BELMAS 2023-2026

The Soul of Education

Inspiring Spiritually Compassionate Changemakers

James Biddulph and Nitesh Gor

Routledge
Taylor & Francis Group
LONDON AND NEW YORK

Designed cover image: © Getty Images

First published 2027
by Routledge
4 Park Square, Milton Park, Abingdon, Oxon OX14 4RN

and by Routledge
605 Third Avenue, New York, NY 10158

Routledge is an imprint of the Taylor & Francis Group, an informa business

British Library Cataloguing-in-Publication Data
A catalogue record for this book is available from the British Library

Library of Congress Cataloging-in-Publication Data
Names: Biddulph, James author | Gor, Nitesh author
Title: The soul of education : inspiring spiritually compassionate changemakers / James Biddulph and Nitesh Gor.
Description: Abingdon, Oxon ; New York, NY : Routledge, 2026. | Includes bibliographical references and index.
Identifiers: LCCN 2026017061 (print) | LCCN 2026017062 (ebook) | ISBN 9781032783970 hardback | ISBN 9781032783918 paperback | ISBN 9781003487654 ebook
Subjects: LCSH: Education--Philosophy | Transformative learning
Classification: LCC LB14.7 .B497 2026 (print) | LCC LB14.7 (ebook)
LC record available at https://lccn.loc.gov/2026017061
LC ebook record available at https://lccn.loc.gov/2026017062

ISBN: 978-1-032-78397-0 (hbk)
ISBN: 978-1-032-78391-8 (pbk)
ISBN: 978-1-003-48765-4 (ebk)

DOI: 10.4324/9781003487654

Typeset in Optima
by KnowledgeWorks Global Ltd.

The Talking Tree

Roots stretching deep into the earth,
drinking spiritual strength—
silent, steady, unseen,
they draw from the eternal source
never to be exhausted.

The trunk stands firm.
Joy, friendship, and vision
bristle through its rings,
luminous, the hidden life force.
And the heart grows wide and unshaken.

The crown stretches into the vast sky,
offering fruit and shade freely to all.

As you stand beneath the tree,
can you hear the leaves
whispering in the wind:

Tend your own tree of life with care.
Be rooted in spiritual essence,
strong in body,
clear in mind,
and generous in heart—
a giver, not a taker.

Thus, quietly,
you will blossom
and become a guiding light
for all those
who pass through your life.

Written by His Holiness Sacinandana
Swami in celebration of *The Soul*
of Education | April 2026

Contents

List of figures and tables

Figures

Tables

Acknowledgements

This book could not have been written without the support, guidance and encouragement of many people. We would particularly like to thank Aimee Durning MBE, Dr Julia Flutter, Luke Rolls, Dr Molly Warrington, Mike Younger, Jane Wheeler, Professor Pam Burnard and Hari-Vallabhi Raja for their careful review of various iterations of chapters. Also, to Professor Dame Alison Peacock DBE DL and the Right Honourable Lord Raval OBE for their foreword and afterword, respectively – they both captured the essence of the book, its purpose and hopes. Thank you to the many colleagues who contributed their stories and anecdotes. Much gratitude to Federico Baca, artist, who brought the rhizome to life and reminded us of the power of human connection, creativity and collaboration. To His Holiness Sacinandana Swami for his inspiration, enthusiasm and belief – the spiritual guidance for this book was through his words, thoughts and long adventurous walks.

Foreword

The Soul of Education: Releasing the notion of transformative education

Education risks being perceived by politicians as an expensive problem that needs to be continually tinkered with, instead of a powerful means of empowerment and liberation that needs to be unleashed.

This book is a hugely welcome yet profoundly unusual education text. Most treatise set out to improve the current system, and this book, however, seeks to help us rediscover core purposes and philosophy of education. We are shown how to consider and reflect on the very soul of education and what this means as we learn throughout life. We are urged to rethink the place of education within society; to reimagine schooling. The word soul has a double meaning: it is about identifying the 'core,' the 'central purpose,' the spirit of education and its purpose; it is also about education as needing to involve the soul or spirit or inner self of each young person (and indeed the adults who work with them).

I have written and spoken at length about 'Learning without Limits' a philosophy of teaching that refuses to accept notions of fixed 'ability' instead offering the transformative power of social, affective and intellectual growth and understanding. As a school leader, together with a brilliant group of educationalists we set about creating a school where learning was without limits. Children from my teaching career remain with me in my thoughts as I reflect on a life dedicated to education.

One such child is 'Mary' a little girl who was introduced to us by her family as needing a padded room to contain her tantrums. Mary had not attended any playgroups or a nursery before starting school as her family believed she would not be able to cope. The key to understanding Mary was in listening to what she needed to help her flourish. If as teachers, we are full of our own self-importance we might see children's behaviour as a rejection of our own authority rather than providing them the space to self-regulate. Mary was encouraged to make her own choices about activity within our Reception class. She was gently supported by the teaching team in her choice of play; she was invited to participate in small and large group sessions and when she felt able to do so she joined but always on the edge or alongside the group. It was not until February that Mary showed us that she could draw. Until that point, she had not engaged with any form of mark-making in the setting. Staff showed patience and trusted that when she was ready, she would do so. In February, Mary drew this on a white board with black felt pen:

When I was shown this drawing my first response was one of relief that Mary was happy. Happy children learn. Mary's career in our school was a delight. She was different but her difference was celebrated as a strength and her artistic capability continued from that day in Reception to grow and to flourish. Mary's story could have been very different in a school where evidence of performativity is valued more highly than belonging.

Figure 0.1 Self-portrait by the young child, Mary. From Peacock, 2015.

Children taught in this manner are not viewed as participants in a relentless race striving for ever narrower academic goals. Ironically, as soon as pressure to perform is removed, power to find meaning in education is released. Ultimately, this means learners viewed without limits paradoxically are more likely to achieve well in the examination system, as one small part of a much broader notion of educational success.

If we are to unleash, this vision of transformative education without limits our teaching profession needs similarly to be 'unleashed.' In past years, the pressure on governors and leadership teams to participate in the race to prove their worth has meant privileging narrow attainment measures over wellbeing. One has only to glimpse the testimony from young people sharing their GCSE results online to see how performance in tests has become an impossibly high stakes venture. GCSE performance data in 2025 yet again pitches the pass rate at 67% of entrants, meaning that a third of all entrants fail. It is the education system that has failed these young people, and we need to act to redress this. Broader notions of educational success are needed. Recognition that exam attainment is only one part of what it means to engage in education needs to be understood. As adults do we choose people to be our friends based on their CV? Or on the way that they communicate, cause us to laugh, to feel valued?

The skills of craftmanship and of artistic creativity are too often overlooked. In many cases, neurodivergent youngsters may find the constraints of an exam hall problematic but later in life through divergent thinking approach life in an entrepreneurial way. School has been insufficient and too narrow to appreciate diverse skills and talents. Having said all this, it is very difficult for school leaders to truly broaden their approach whilst the accountability system remains all powerful. This leads to schools desperately trying to 'swim against the tide' of a narrow performative culture. Our profession seeks to do well by their learners, but the current system can work against this because as a society we are valuing the wrong things.

In a future dominated by AI, human skills will be needed more than ever. Collegiality, collaboration and collective problem-solving are rapidly becoming ever important. Alongside this, the pandemic taught us that human beings are not built to be isolated, plugged in to machines. Schools are ideal places within our communities to provide opportunities for intergenerational sports, arts, design, theatre, cooking, gardening, ecology, bee-keeping the list is endless. An education with learning about and for the soul at its heart is a compelling alternative vision.

Our children and young people are our future and as such their teachers should be drawn from the very best within society, teachers with a deep ambition for their learners who understand that this is optimally achieved through compassion, guidance and inspiration. Teachers who believe in the art of the possible, providing schools that are full of joy, creating schools where learning is irresistible. Indeed, this book contends that teachers should be revered in the same way as they were within the Ancient World – as Guru, wise, curious, questioners and debaters.

Since the 2019 COVID pandemic, subsequent Ukraine War, conflict in Israel–Gaza and Iran, cost of living crises brought about by global financial disruption, and worsening public health, questions about education, its purpose and vision are vitally relevant. The book is a response to this complex global context. It provides a new, diverse position to foster dialogue about education, rooted in Eastern Vedic philosophical tradition as an antidote to the dominant western perspective. In it, James and Nitesh explore how Vedic philosophy could provide new reimagined responses to the challenges of a modern education system and consider how it might support future-making opportunities. They provide a narrative full of hope and possibility. This optimism draws upon the ancient philosophy and traditions from India, which are timeless and not specifically about one religion, but instead drawing lessons from this time with particular emphasis on the importance of inclusion and kindness.

I am privileged to visit many schools across the UK and encounter hundreds of teachers every year. It is a very unusual school that does not set out to inspire their children and there are thousands of brilliant educators in schools up and down the country. The Chartered College of Teaching is ambitious for educators everywhere. Our vision for education is one where teachers and leaders are empowered through a deep sense of belonging as part of a knowledgeable and respected profession.

So, am I inspired by the narrative of hope presented here? Yes, because the teachers I meet are committed to supporting their learners in the best possible way. With greater self-efficacy, inspired courageous leadership and a vision for education that supersedes the accountability agenda in favour of human flourishing there is much that can be done. At the Chartered College, we seek to support our profession to question, review and mutually celebrate innovation that truly makes a difference to learning. We are committed to building the professional knowledge and agency needed to best respond to every learner and to take a principled, ethically sound approach.

What is vital, and what this book brings to the fore, is that for education to be successful we need to 'find a way through' for all children in order that they have the capacity and the opportunity to contribute meaningfully to our world.

Professor Dame Alison Peacock DBE DL
CEO, Chartered College of
Teaching, London, UK

PART A

Preparing for a Journey

An Invitation

1 An invitation to join us in the search for the soul of education

This book is a meeting point. It aims to be hopeful and positive. It starts a conversation. But why pick up a book about 21st-century education that draws on an ancient Indian philosophy? You might be interested in exploring new ideas to reimagine the purpose of education because you think that the notion of human flourishing is more than it is now. You might have a sense that the current status quo in education is not meeting the needs of children and young people. You might have woken one day, like we did, and thought, 'where has all the joy gone in education?' Or, like neuroscientists Andrew Newberg and Mark Waldmen, you might be searching to understand the self, beyond the self: "having faith in the human spirit is what drives us to survive and transcend" (2009, p. 20). You may be asking how notions of the soul or spirituality might be brought back into an education experience, curious about the benefits of so doing.

We wrote this book because we longed to read it, and it did not yet exist. Too often, conversations about education lean heavily on Western and Abrahamic philosophies, leaving other rich traditions in the margins. Too often, because of constraints of time, statutory responsibilities, structures, systems and policies, we do not pause to consider the questions that matter most; we rarely explore these together as a profession and with those who care about education, young people, their childhoods and futures.

But how could an educator, policymaker or parent possibly connect with a philosophy if it doesn't reflect their own world view or stance on faith, religion or spirituality? Do we really need yet another book on education, in a field already full of research, evidence and opinion?

DOI: 10.4324/9781003487654-2

Hasn't the Education Endowment Foundation (a UK research organisation providing 'trustworthy and actionable information') already have all the answers? Or could this be an opportunity to step into fresh conversations, to see familiar challenges differently and to imagine possibilities that have not yet been considered? What if the real breakthroughs lie in the ideas we've ignored, dismissed or which are so intuitive we have forgotten to see them?

Our aim is to offer a balancing contribution: to explore how Vedic thought could illuminate and enrich modern educational practice and ultimately improve the lives, present and future, for all children, everywhere.

Personal reflections and our purpose

The book is guided primarily by James's voice as an educator and pracademic[1] (Boyer, 1996; Volpe and Chandler, 2001), providing the central structure, argument, theorisation of frameworks and narrative through which the work unfolds. It draws from his reflections and anecdotes from practice (Biddulph, 2020; Biddulph and Flutter, 2021; Biddulph, Shuckburgh and Pearse, 2026). Nitesh's contribution enriches this foundation by offering Vedic concepts and philosophy, which James grappled with and frames in relation to western research, theory and practice to make their meaning accessible for readers who may be unfamiliar with them. There are also invited reflections from others to help to bring the ideas to life, adding texture and lived resonance without shifting the book's overall authorship or direction.

We write from a life shaped by converging worlds: James, white, of British Greek heritage and born in Zimbabwe, raised within the Church of England and deeply influenced by the Greek Orthodox faith of his grandmother. His vocation has been in education and academia, where he has sought to articulate and embody a vision of learning that holds together intellectual rigour, bridging research, practitioner wisdom and spiritual depth. Alongside James writes Nitesh, British of Indian heritage, born in India and raised in London – a social entrepreneur and author growing up within the Hindu Vaishnava tradition. Though our cultural and religious inheritances differ, our paths have drawn us toward a shared commitment: that spirituality is linked with the concept of True Love, as relationship and reciprocal connection with something beyond the self which some and we call the Divine. Together, we share the conviction that human beings are, in essence, spiritual. We believe that life is lived in relationship, experienced and developed differently, dependent on contextual matters including, but not limited to, cultural, ethnic, language, religious, educational experience, family, and personal and childhood experiences.

It is not only our belief. In the *Bhagavad Gīta*[2] (Bhaktivedanta Swami Prabhupāda, 1983), education is understood as a twofold pursuit that unites the material and the spiritual dimensions of life. The first, *apara vidya*, refers to knowledge of the material world: science, arts and worldly learning that help us navigate and contribute to society. The second, *para vidya*, is higher knowledge: the understanding of the self, consciousness and our relationship with the divine. The *Bhagavad Gītā* teaches that true education harmonises these two forms of knowing, cultivating both intellect and inner wisdom. When balanced, they lead to self-realisation and right action. Thus, education is not merely the acquisition of information but a journey towards understanding reality in its fullest sense, material, moral and spiritual. The problem, as we see it, is that our current approach to education is unbalanced and prioritises the former with marginalised effort for the latter.

To be clear, we are not suggesting that contemporary education is without value. We recognise and deeply respect the commitment of educators and school leaders, who work tirelessly within challenging social contexts and pressurised accountability frameworks. However, given that science (what we currently know) cannot yet state with confidence that human consciousness arises purely from physical processes, nor can religion assert with certainty that it is wholly transcendent, reliance on what has been or what we think we know to be true must be critiqued and challenged. It is the 'wide-awakeness' that Maxine Greene (1995) advocates; it is 'being a stranger' in our practice.

A pluralist approach

We take an open-hearted mindset in exploring the soul of education, seeking you, the reader, to suspend beliefs and currently held positions about education and its purpose and to consider: what could be possible? What if? This pluralist way is so wonderfully captured by the holy sage, Bhaktivinoda

Thakura (2017).[3] He urges us to approach difference as opportunity warning against polarities in our thinking or arguments:

> If one goes to another place of worship, one should think, *'The people here are worshipping my Lord, but in a different way; because of my different training, I cannot properly comprehend this system of worship. However, through this experience, I can deepen my appreciation for my own system of worship. The Lord is only one, not two. Therefore, I offer my respect to the form I see here and pray to the Lord in this new form that He may increase my love for Him in the form to which I am accustomed'*. Those who do not follow this procedure, but who instead criticise other systems of worship and who show envy, hatred and violence are worthless and foolish. The more they indulge in such useless quarrelling, the more they betray the very goal of their own religious system
>
> ([Bhaktivinoda Thakura's emphasis], 2017, p. 1)

Translating this into an educational context, we offer this book as an invitation for exploration of different ways of being, thinking, conceptualising in relation to the soul, its role in education and in life, to deepen our comprehension and to minimise polarised criticism. Bhaktivinoda Thakura's teachings build from a well-known and deeply resonant statement that is often used to express the spirit of inclusivity found in the Vedic tradition:

> Truth is one; sages call it by many names
>
> (*Ṛg Veda* 1.164.46; version translated by Schweig, 2010)

This verse offers a radically open, non-sectarian vision of reality. Vedic ideas refuse to fit into neat boxes (Gor, 2025). They avoid extremes and instead embrace pluralities, offering, "insights into the human condition, the nature of reality, and a goal that takes its seeker beyond sectarian limitations" (Gor, 2025, p. xi). Vedic philosophy does not draw boundaries around truth nor does it claim exclusivity for any one tradition. Instead, it affirms a singular, universal reality that is encountered through diverse human interpretations. Such plurality is not a weakness but a necessity: no single voice, culture or tradition can contain the whole. This insight resonates with contemporary scholarship across the social sciences, including post-modern, post-human and trans-disciplinary approaches that recognise multiple ways of knowing and being in the world. It also encourages a healthy scepticism, which "implies open-mindedness and the willingness to suspend judgment until both sides of an argument are considered, and this enhances neural functioning, particularly in the frontal lobes" (Newberg and Waldmen, 2009, p. 142). Open-mindedness seems good for the brain!

While inspired by Vedic thought, this book is not about Hinduism or Hindu education or religious education. Nor is it concerned with scriptural interpretation as an end in itself. Its focus is to draw from the wisdom such traditions carry and present how a universal approach to spirituality might illuminate education for today.

The clarion call for a soul-led education

Throughout western contemporary and historical thinking, as we will present, there is a persistent clarion call for education to think beyond technocratic functionality and to expand its purpose to explore matters of the heart, mind and body – to be transformative. This is not a glib, progressive or a weak call. It is rooted in the insights and attention of many great personalities across history and contemporary culture, from diverse domains including the arts, education, science and more; people who see the world differently and whose creativities and social imaginations offer opportunities for us to pause and ponder:

- How does education empower?
- How do we empower children with agency for democratic social imagining?
- Why is spirituality central to education?
- How do we create a kinder and more generous system?

You will have your own people and sources of inspiration and we invite them on our journey as we explore what a soul of education might entail. What would they say? How might their ideas contribute to our sense making? What divergent views might provide the grit to challenge the system, educational practices and often strongly held assumptions?

As a beginning and to illustrate examples of this clarion calling, we bring together the voices of a poet, an educator, a comedian and a few scientists all of whom have inspired this thesis. This is a deliberate choice. By drawing on diverse voices, we emphasise that the concern for what education is, and what it is for, is not a new preoccupation but a living debate shaped across time and disciplines. These different insights remind us that education has always carried the power to open futures or to narrow them, to cultivate agency or constrain it. As we gather at the outset of this journey, we encounter a shared insight: that humanity needs spirituality for human flourishing.

Drawing from James' own inspirations, to begin, we welcome William Blake, the late 18th early 19th-century British poet, because of his preoccupation with the dangers of materialism and the need for spiritual insight even some 300 hundred years ago. In his poem, *London*, he warns of the dangers of shackling the mind; concerns that we both share in relation to contemporary education. Mark Edmundson's reflections (2010) foreground the consequences for humanity when the mind is imprisoned by narrow forms of thought, what we might now describe as technocratic neoliberalism.

> 'London' is spoken by a poet-prophet wandering through the imperial city, stunned by what he sees and feels. Human misery is everywhere around him: "I ... mark in every face I meet/Marks of weakness, marks of woe." There are a number of sources for this misery, but maybe the main one – or at least the one Blake cites first – is the locking down of human consciousness. The people Blake sees are miserable in large part because their minds are radically restricted by oppressive ways of thinking. They are the victims of "mind-forg'd manacles." That is, they are imprisoned by their own mental limits and by the limits imposed upon them by others.
>
> (Edmundson, 2010)

This is significant. Does our education system 'radically restrict' our children and young people? Does the fast-changing technological world create a new oppression and perpetuate the 'mind forg'd manacles' because increasingly we are invited not to think, but to ask ChatGPT?

In a world in which the pursuit of a hedonistic conceptualisation of happiness is dominant, the main concern we have with materialism, philosophically, is its sectarian nature; it holds that reality is fundamentally physical, explaining mind and consciousness as brain processes *solely*. Beauregard and O'Leary (2007) also critique materialism's reductive interpretations within neuroscience and scientific debates. In essence, materialism states that there is only one Truth and one interpretation of the Truth, which is then scientifically proven. Everything else is folklore, they might say.

When we understand, however, that folklore has considerable relevance in determining meaning, purpose and existential enquiry even in contemporary societies, "that [it] embodies and expresses the spirits of different nations and centuries. Since time immemorial, various traditions and beliefs have been passed down orally in every nation. In it, we find astronomical, meteorological, geological, and ethnographic references, ancient customs, myths, and beliefs" (Kashaka, 2025, p. 32), we see the limitations of a (purely) materialistic view of the world. This raises questions about what we value in education in terms of knowledge, skill, behaviours, diversities, narratives and cultural expressions.

They are the type of questions that Maxine Greene, educator, philosopher and social imaginer pursued in her teaching and philosophical discourses. Her thinking about the arts and the social imagination provokes new sense making about education and teaching, the role of educator and learner. She brings a powerful thesis about broader educational responsibilities in order to enact a more socially imaginative hopeful narrative for education:

> .... Imagination is what, above all, makes empathy possible. It is what enables us to cross empty spaces between ourselves and those we teachers have called "other" over the years. If those others are willing to give us clues, we can look in some manner through strangers' eyes and hear through their ears. That is because, of all our cognitive capacities, imagination is the one that permits us to give credence to alternative realities.
>
> (Greene, 1998, p. 3)

As we walk together in this book, we will navigate new spaces to reimagine the purposes of education, exploring a landscape that brings the whole person to the educational encounter. We will argue that when we raise our consciousness, we can in turn raise our capacities to imagine and to think what might be, which Maxine Greene says is the act of becoming. Through this, we can reimagine society.

The centrality of human collective happiness is articulated by another, albeit unusual fellow traveller, comedian and unlikely social commentator, Charlie Chaplin. In his famous speech from the 1940s film, *The Great Dictator*, acting as a Jewish barber mistaken as an autocratic dictator, he highlights how a world without kindness and gentleness is a world of division and violence. In our current fractured communities and politics of conflict, his words, performed in 1940 at the worsening of the Second World War, chime loudly and are particularly poignant to our search for the soul of education:

> We all want to help one another. Human beings are like that. We want to live by each other's happiness - not by each other's misery. We don't want to hate and despise one another. In this world there is room for everyone. And the good earth is rich and can provide for everyone. The way of life can be free and beautiful, but we have lost the way.
>
> Greed has poisoned men's souls, has barricaded the world with hate, has goose-stepped us into misery and bloodshed. We have developed speed, but we have shut ourselves in. Machinery that gives abundance has left us in want. Our knowledge has made us cynical. Our cleverness, hard and unkind. We think too much and feel too little. More than machinery we need humanity. More than cleverness we need kindness and gentleness. Without these qualities, life will be violent and all will be lost...
>
> (Final speech in *The Great Dictator* (1940) performed by Charlie Chaplin (accessed from https://www.charliechaplin.com/en/synopsis/articles/29-The-Great-Dictator-s-Speech on 30th January 2026))

Such a view still has relevance for our contemporary context. It urges us to ask: how does an education encourage, nurture and value the emotional landscape that allows for beauty, acceptance, empathy and interrelatedness to become core? How do our education systems foster the qualities that lead to a better life for all?

Contemporary research increasingly affirms that attending to the inner life of children is essential. As psychologist and bestselling author Lisa Miller observes, "there is nothing known to science as profoundly associated with thriving and success in our children" than spirituality (Miller, 2015, p. 38). Drawing on decades of longitudinal research, including large-scale epidemiological studies and clinical data, Miller argues that spirituality functions not as a peripheral belief system but as a core dimension of human development. Her findings suggest that adolescents who report a personal relationship with the sacred – however they define it – are significantly less likely to experience depression, substance abuse and high-risk behaviours.

Miller found that in some studies, a strong spiritual life reduced the risk of major depression by up to 60–80%. Beyond protection from pathology, spirituality also predicts positive outcomes: greater resilience, stronger moral reasoning, enhanced purpose and improved academic engagement. Miller proposes that spirituality activates neural pathways associated with meaning-making and attachment, supporting teenagers in navigating identity formation and adversity. Far from being an optional add-on, spirituality emerges in her research as a developmental asset – an orienting framework that fosters coherence, hope and long-term flourishing into adulthood. Other neuroscientists, Newberg and Waldman (2009) also state that thinking about faith and belief is a key part of maintaining a healthy brain. To invest in spirituality, our understanding of it, our personal relationship with it and the value we place on nurturing it within our schools, is to advance a more holistic vision of learning and a more flourishing humanity, both now and for the future. These scientific perspectives strengthen our confidence in the face of any critique that this book is overly intellectual or philosophical.

It is also worth considering the Organisation for Economic Co-operation and Development's (OECD) vision for the future of education systems, which refocuses on the whole person, emphasising the realisation of human potential and the nurturing of healthier ways of living. However, the vision statement notably omits any reference to spirituality or the concept of the soul. While broadly sympathetic to its intentions, we observe this absence as a significant omission.

> We are committed to helping every learner develop as a whole person, fulfil his or her potential and help shape a shared future built on the well-being of individuals, communities and the planet. Children entering school in 2018 will need to abandon the notion that resources are limitless and are there to be exploited; they will need to value common prosperity, sustainability and well-being. They will need to be responsible and empowered, placing collaboration above division, and sustainability above short-term gain. In the face of an increasingly volatile, uncertain, complex and ambiguous world,

> education can make the difference as to whether people embrace the challenges they are confronted with or whether they are defeated by them. And in an era characterised by a new explosion of scientific knowledge and a growing array of complex societal problems, it is appropriate that curricula should continue to evolve, perhaps in radical ways
>
> (OECD, 2018, p. 3)

Building further from this, our hope is for a soul-led and soul-full education: one that weaves together ancient wisdom and contemporary psychological insight, restoring depth, meaning and connectedness to the educational encounter. Such an education depends not only on structures or curricula, but on the dispositions of educators, those who cultivate wisdom, spiritual sensitivity and attentiveness to what lies beneath the surface of learning (Biesta, 2010; Coltman and Rolls, 2021). A soul-led education is not an escape from the world's challenges but a deeper engagement with them. It invites education systems to flex and reimagine in the face of 21st-century fragmentation, division and despair. Where modern schooling often, arguably, trains young people to compete and compare, a soul-full approach cultivates the capacity to connect, to hope and to act from compassion. It teaches that beneath the visible identities of class, culture or creed, there exists a shared (spiritual) humanity. When education is guided by this awareness, that the self is not an isolated ego but part of an intricate web of relationship with others, with the Earth, and with the Ultimate, then the purpose of learning is reoriented towards responsibility, reverence and joy. This is not naïve idealism. And we know that none of this happens by chance.

We write also conscious of the profound inequalities that shape children's lives around the world. The experiences of those in the Global South, of children in conflict zones or communities scarred by poverty, remind us that spirituality must never be a luxury. The relevance of Vedic insights must be tested in the realities of classrooms where hunger, trauma and displacement are daily companions. We write also aware that artificial intelligence (AI) is and will continue to challenge how schools create the conditions within which human relationships flourish and where humanity is not stripped of its capacity for creativity, play and joyful exploration of the richness of life and of living. For this reason, our offering is necessarily inchoate, a beginning rather than a conclusion. We see this work as an opening: an invitation to educators, researchers and communities to explore how these ideas might meet the complex needs of their own contexts. Dialogue, humility and practical wisdom (Flutter, 2022) will be needed to translate soul-led principles into authentic pedagogy.

Throughout the book, we intentionally use a range of phrases – *the soul of education, soul-full education, soul-led education, the sole purpose of education* and other related iterations. This plurality is deliberate. Rather than fixing meaning, we seek to honour the diversity of ways in which the idea of the soul is understood, experienced and expressed across philosophical, cultural, professional and personal contexts. Language both reveals and limits, and no single formulation can fully hold the depth, complexity or vitality of what we are exploring. By moving between these expressions, we invite openness rather than prescription, signalling that the 'soul' of education is not a singular doctrine but a living enquiry. These shifting phrases create conceptual space for resonance, resistance, reinterpretation and dialogue, allowing you/us to locate your/our own meanings, make connections to practice, and remain open to possibilities that are still unfolding.

Navigating the soul of education

This book unfolds in four interconnected parts, each representing a stage on our shared journey towards understanding what a soul-led education could be. For the reader who is unfamiliar with Vedic philosophy, we have included footnotes, where relevant, to give historic or specific knowledge. We acknowledge that there are some difficult and perhaps challenging concepts presented within; we have, however, hoped to have struck a balance by presenting the complexity with stories, anecdotes and reflections to help bridge the eastern philosophy with western contemporary practices and thinking.

PART A: Preparing for a journey: An invitation

We begin by exploring some of the profound challenges facing education as we move through the second quarter of the 21st century. In Chapter 2, we delve into different understandings of the soul and spirituality, weaving together Western psychology, educational research and theory, and Vedic philosophy which proposes that the soul itself is educable. The first step on our journey opens in Chapter 3, on the battlefield of Northern India, some 5000 years ago. From this vivid scene – used as a metaphor rather than a historical argument – three enduring educational preoccupations emerge: equality, diversity and love. These become our constant companions, threading through the chapters that follow. Chapter 4 introduces the Vedic concept of *Kali-Yuga* – an age of quarrel, complexity and confusion – as a powerful lens for understanding contemporary educational and social contexts. Chapter 5 then traces a concise history of systematised education, largely from a UK perspective. Here, we engage with key thinkers to reveal how the spiritual dimension of learning has been overlooked and marginalised.

PART B: Setting out on the journey: Exploring six beliefs of the soul of education

In the second stage of our journey, we move from exploration to articulation. Chapter 6 introduces six core beliefs that shape a soul-led educational worldview – beliefs that serve as the foundations of a soulful approach to human flourishing. Chapters 7 to 12 unfold each belief in turn, deepening and expanding them: realising potential, empowering choice, strengthening interconnection, enriching diversities, expanding purpose and nourishing loving relationships. These beliefs act as orientation points for educators, leaders, parents and young people seeking to navigate a complex and contested educational landscape.

PART C: Walking the journey: Living by virtues and defining what is valued

The third stage of our journey moves from beliefs to lived practice, drawing from practical reflections from colleagues at Avanti Schools Trust.[4] In Chapter 13, we introduce six Vedic-inspired virtues, showing how beliefs take root in everyday educational interactions. These virtues illuminate what it means to teach, lead, parent and learn from a place of soulfulness. Chapter 14 then turns to the wisdom of the Vedas[5] to examine what we ought to value in education. Through this philosophical lens, we explore how virtues, values and beliefs interweave to form a coherent educational orientation – one that honours both individuality and interconnectedness.

PART D: Arriving at a new terrain: Reimagining a soul-full education

Having assembled a framework of beliefs, virtues and values, we arrive in a new conceptual landscape, one in which education can be reimagined. Chapter 15 brings these elements together to envision a landscape for educating the soul. Chapters 16 and 17 turn to the metaphoric gardeners – educators and parents – who together cultivate the inner life of children and young people. Finally, Chapter 18 invites us to consider how we might reclaim the soul of education, inspiring spiritually compassionate changemakers who can shape a more humane educational future. This closing section surveys the terrain we have crossed and looks forward, asking how the ideas explored in this book might inform your own work, life and educational context.

Beginning the journey ...

We welcome you to join us on this journey; to explore what is meant by the soul, how it might be nurtured through education and how it may be thoughtfully integrated within school life. In doing so, we invite critical reflection, scholarly curiosity and dialogic engagement with ideas that reach beyond disciplinary and cultural boundaries. This work is an invitation to think deeply about what it means to educate for human flourishing. Figure 1.1 is a 'rhizome mapping' of the themes and ideas that will arise throughout the book, showing the interrelatedness of the soul of education and illustrating its complexities.

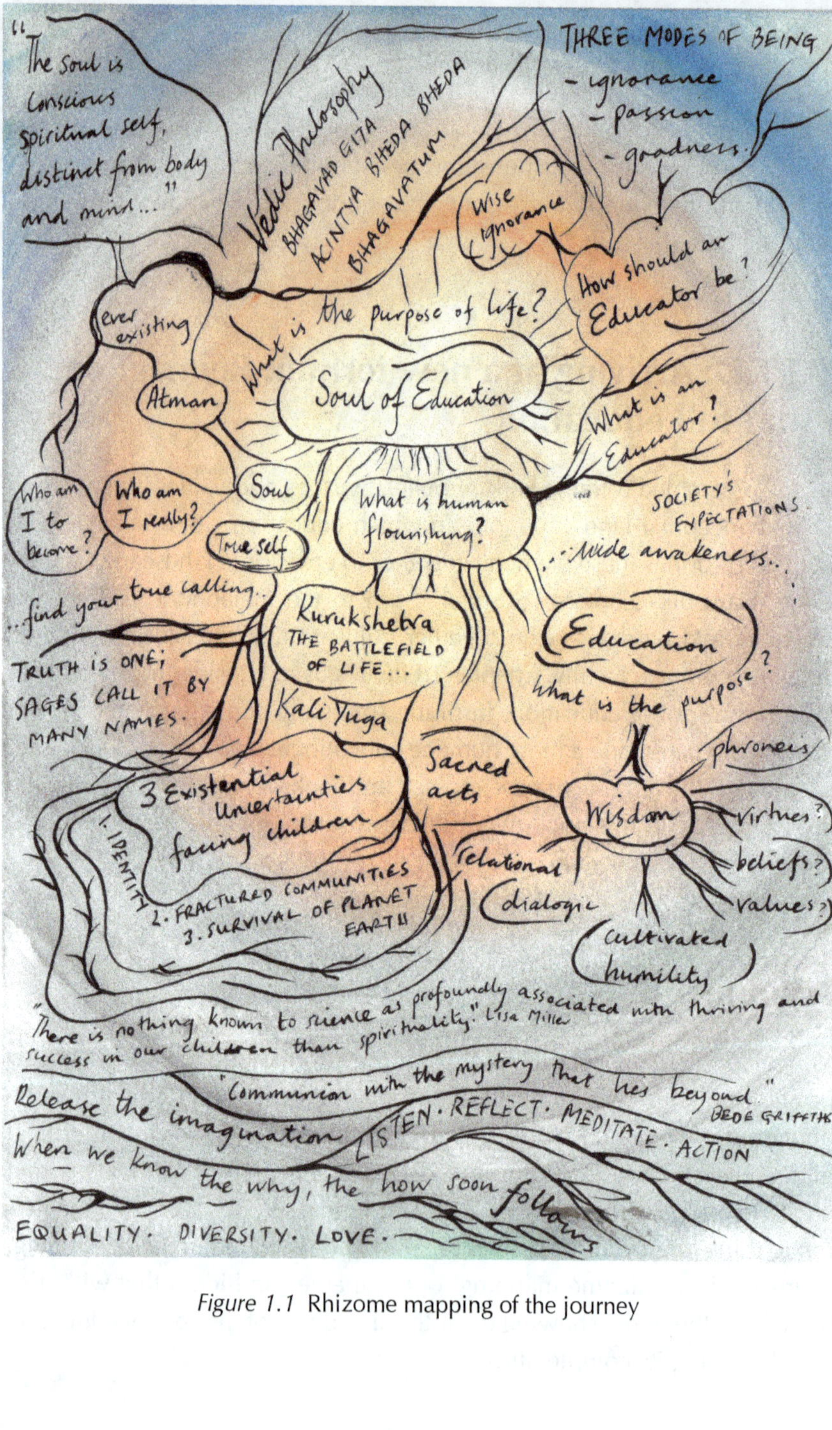

Figure 1.1 Rhizome mapping of the journey

Notes

1 Pracademics are hybrid professionals who simultaneously inhabit academia and professional practice.

2 The *Bhagavad Gītā* appears as a chapter within the epic Mahabharata, the world's longest poem. According to the Hindu tradition, and the text itself, the date it was spoken was in 3137 BCE. It is set on a battlefield (Kurukshetra) where the warrior-prince Arjuna seeks guidance from his charioteer and friend, Krishna, whose divinity is revealed throughout the text. It is widely regarded as the essence and summary of Hindu teaching. All references in this book come from the ISKCON version translated by A.C. Bhaktivedanta Swami Prabhupāda (1983) *Bhagavad-Gītā As It Is*.

3 Bhaktivinoda Thakura (1838–1914) was a pioneering Vaishnava theologian, reformer and scholar who revitalised Gaudiya Vaishnavism in Bengal. A magistrate by profession, he authored over 100 works in Sanskrit, Bengali and English, harmonising devotion and rationality. He envisioned a modern, universalist expression of bhakti (route of love) rooted in compassion and divine love.

4 Avanti Schools Trust – Founded in 2008 it operates the only Hindu faith schools in the UK. Avanti became a multi-academy trust in 2012 and has evolved into a 'mixed MAT' with both faith and community schools. Avanti is founded on the values of educational excellence, character formation and spiritual insight. The centrality of non-sectarian and universal spirituality is a distinctive feature of the trust; its ethos is set out in a document called 'The Avanti Way,' which incorporates the trust's core beliefs, values and virtues. Avanti offers several bespoke curriculum strands, including a unique Philosophy, Religion and Ethics curriculum, *Yoga* and Meditation, amongst others. As of the date of this publication, Avanti's schools are spread across Greater London, Leicester, Bishops Stortford, Frome and Bristol, with 6,000 learners and 900 colleagues.

5 The *Vedas* – Ancient, revelatory texts divided into four parts: *Ṛg*, *Sāma*, *Yajur* and *Atharva*.

2 Making sense of the soul of education

To explore what the soul of education might mean, we must first explore the idea of the soul itself. Like spirituality, the soul is a pervasive concept that resists easy definition, in part because of the ethereal nature of both terms (McMahon and Escarfuller, 2024) and its complexity (Erricker et al., 2001; Mata-McMahon and Escarfuller, 2024; Peterson, Lexmond, Hallgarten and Kerr, 2014). In this chapter, following others who have engaged with this challenge (de Souza and Halahoff, 2018; Scott Webster, 2018), we grapple with the language and concepts of soul and spirit. Beginning with broad, largely Western framings, the chapter then narrows its focus to Vedic conceptions, which provide the primary lens through which the soul of education is examined.

Understandings of the soul and spirit

For our purpose, when we speak of the soul of education, we are invoking not a theological claim but a metaphor for what is most vital, ethical and alive in the human educational encounter. The word soul carries a weight that is at once ancient and elusive. The Royal Society for the Arts research report called *Schools with Soul: A new approach to Spiritual, Moral, Social and Cultural Education (SMSC)* comments, "The word soul has baggage. It might sound too tied to religious traditions, new age, flaky, or connected to the infamous progressive 'blob'. However, we believe that it is highly relevant in meeting the challenges of schooling in the 21st century" (Peterson, Lexmond, Hallgarten and Kerr, 2014, p. 4). In many belief systems, it is the part of a person that is most real, the inner core that connects the self to something greater, be it God, the cosmos, community, or purpose. For many

DOI: 10.4324/9781003487654-3

people, it is the part of who they are that seeks purpose and meaning, in the words of Leo Tolstoy, "without knowing what I am and why I'm here, it is impossible for me to live, and I cannot know that, therefore I cannot live" (Tolstoy, 2000, p. 530). It is the not knowing and the pursuit to find out that engages the soul and why we argue it is a vital component of contemporary education – or should be.

The English word *soul* originates from the Old English *sāwol* or *sāwl*, derived from Proto-Germanic *saiwalō*. Linguists connect it to the Proto-Indo-European root *s(w)e–*, meaning "self" or "of oneself" (Harper, 2024). This etymology suggests the soul was understood as the essential self or life force within a person. The *Oxford English Dictionary* defines it as:

> The spiritual or immaterial part of a human being or animal, regarded as immortal.
>
> (OED, 2024)

And the *Cambridge Dictionary* offers a broader, more psychological definition:

> The part of a person that is not physical and experiences deep feelings and emotions.
>
> (*Cambridge Dictionary*, 2024)

Historically, the soul was seen as the moral and conscious identity of a person, the seat of feelings, conscience, memory and even eternal destiny. In classical philosophy, the soul was conceived as the essence of human life and moral orientation. For example, in Plato's tripartite model, the soul comprised reason, spirit and appetite, with justice achieved when these elements were harmonised under the rule of reason (Plato, 2007). Aristotle (2016), by contrast, located the soul (*psuchē*) not in a tripartite hierarchy but as the form or animating principle of a living body, inseparable from its material existence (Aristotle, 2016). Together, these accounts illustrate the enduring tension between transcendental and immanent conceptions of the soul in Western thought. Building on these, in Christian theologies, the soul becomes the immortal essence to be judged after death.

In modern psychology, particularly influenced by Jungian and archetypal psychology (Hillman, 1996), the soul represents the inner depth and symbolic dimension of human experience; what makes us feel alive, creative and connected. In *The Red Book*, Carl Jung (2009) presents the soul as an inner, living reality encountered through imagination and dialogue, rather than a metaphysical abstraction. The soul is both guide and otherness, mediating between conscious ego and the unconscious. For example, imagine you are stuck in a job where you feel unfulfilled but keep telling yourself, "I should stay, it's secure, my family approve of it, it is good for me to go through challenges." However, one night, you dream of a bird trapped inside a cage, frantically trying to escape. What does each aspect of the self say? What are the intuitive unconscious messages? The ego (the conscious "I") wants safety and rationalises staying, the unconscious holds your deeper longing for freedom and purpose, and the soul, as Jung describes it, mediates between the two: the dream presents itself with a voice and imagery that feels "other," yet it is also *guiding you* towards recognising what your deeper self knows: that you need freedom. Here the soul shows up as both *guide* (revealing the truth you're ignoring) and *otherness* (it doesn't feel like "you" talking, but like a message from beyond).

The words soul and spirit are often colloquially interchangeable, but is there a difference? The word spirit comes from the Latin *spīritus*, meaning breath, air, or life force, derived from *spirāre*, "to breathe" (Harper, 2024). This aligns with the Greek *pneuma* and the Hebrew *ruach*, both of which also mean breath, wind or spirit. The Oxford English Dictionary defines spirit as:

> The non-physical part of a person regarded as their true self and as capable of surviving physical death or separation from the body.
>
> (OED, 2024)

And the *Cambridge Dictionary* defines it as:

> A particular way of thinking, feeling, or behaving, especially a positive and determined attitude.
>
> (*Cambridge Dictionary*, 2024)

In both secular and religious traditions, spirit often refers to a universal, animating force; whether divine (as in the Holy Spirit), metaphysical (as in Hegel's *Geist*), or psychological (as in the human spirit). It tends to express transcendence, vitality, or essence, often beyond individual identity (see also Miller, 2000, pp. 13–29). Phrases such as, 'that's the spirit', or she is in 'high spirits', or, 'I can't come to your party but I will be there in spirit' have colloquial meaning and reveal something of the inner nature of ourselves: "spirituality is increasingly seen as an inner process of connectedness with what a person considers sacred, a psychological process internal to the individual" (Friedman, Krippner, Riebel and Johnson, 2024, p. 150).

Jung (2009) did not consider the soul and spirit as interchangeable. Instead, he saw that they represented distinct dimensions of human experience. He describes the soul as the personal and relational principle, encountered in dialogue with the unconscious and expressed through symbols and myth. By contrast, spirit (*Geist*) represents abstraction, rationality, and the drive towards transcendence. While spirit elevates consciousness towards universals, soul grounds the individual in lived, inner depth. For example: When you hear a song that reminds you of heartbreak, it can bring back memories, images, and strong feelings, almost as if the music is speaking directly to you. This is the work of the soul. But you might also step back and notice how music expresses love, loss and joy in ways that connect people across cultures and generations. This is the work of spirit. These are subtle distinctions and defining the difference is not the core scope of this book.

A sense of spirituality, therefore, emerges when soul and spirit are held in creative tension, spirit providing direction and meaning, while soul offers intimacy, embodiment and psychological integration. This distinction was vital for Jung's notion of individuation, as one-sided identification with spirit risked detachment from psychic life, whereas soul work enabled transformation through encounters with the unconscious. This is complex psychology and there are differences of opinion.

What does seem consistent is that humans seem to search for a sense of self and from that, a sense of purpose and meaning. It is echoed throughout the literature and in different faith traditions (Erricker et al., 2001). For example, across Christian mysticism, Sufism and the Bhakti (loving devotion) tradition, a strikingly convergent understanding emerges of the soul as fundamentally oriented beyond itself, drawn by love towards reunion with its Divine source. In the Christian writings of Julian of Norwich (c. 1342–after 1416), the soul's persistent yearning is not evidence of divine absence but of forgotten intimacy: God remains continuously present, while human awareness of God has dimmed. Similarly, within Sufism, Jalāl ad-Dīn Rūmī (1207–1273) describes the human condition as one of separation, in which suffering arises from forgetfulness of origin. His famous image of the reed flute, sounding its sorrowful music because it has been cut from the reed bed, echoes Rūmī's insistence that longing is a form of remembrance. This same longing of the soul is articulated with devotional intensity in the philosophy of *Sri Caitanya Mahaprabhu* (1486–1534), who gives voice to the soul's aching desire for *Krishna* (a name for God) as its highest fulfilment. In the *Śikṣāṣṭakam*,[1] longing is not a failure of faith but its deepest expression, purifying the heart and drawing the self beyond ego towards loving surrender.

In these understandings, love is not merely affective but transformative; spiritual growth is understood less as the acquisition of knowledge and more as remembrance, of a relationship that already exists yet must be consciously lived into. It is spiritual growth that is open to all, therefore as we explained in Chapter 1, diversity is fully embraced. It is a view that every living being is equal, spiritually, even though materially there remain inequalities. The soul's restlessness, whether named as longing for the Ultimate Truth or search for purpose, thus becomes a shared philosophical insight into the meaning of human life: an invitation to return, through love, humility, and compassion, to what has always been our deepest truth.

As do we, Jung points to the primacy of the soul, the inner voice, the unconscious, that compels us to seek meaning:

> I am weary, my soul, my wandering has lasted too long, my search for myself outside of myself. Now that I have gone through events and found you behind the farrago...I wandered for many years, so long that I forgot that I possessed a soul. Where were you all this time? Which Beyond sheltered you and gave you sanctuary? Oh, that you must speak through me, that my speech and I are a symbol and expression for you! How should I decipher you?
>
> (Jung, 2009, pp. 130–131)

The language differs, but the soul's longing for depth, connection and purpose remains universal. Increasingly, spirituality is associated with experience, with an emphasis on the activity of sense making through and within spiritual practices which form part of the meaning making. Watts (2024) explains,

> Experience is probably even more important in spirituality than in religion. For at least some religious people, there has recently been an increasing emphasis on the experiential side of things, but spirituality probably goes further in prioritizing experience. There is a correlation between having powerful, spontaneous spiritual experiences and

> thinking that the spiritual side of life is important (Hay, 1982). It seems likely that such experiences are more common among people who are SBNR [spiritual but not religious] than among religious people
> (2024, p. 54)

Being aware that we are "ignorant to the mystery" (Jung, 2009, p. 131) is the spark which strengthens the pursuit of knowledge, not only of the material world but of the inner world, "I shall learn that my soul finally lies behind everything, and if I cross the world, I am ultimately doing this to find my soul" (p. 132).

While these are laudable sentiments, how do they apply to state funded education? Is all this purely fantastical philosophising and not useful for the practitioner in her classroom or the leader in their office? Throughout the book, we hold this critique in our minds and seek your support to explore how the messages we present might translate or be evolved in your own situation. Remembering that this book is not a religious text promoting one religious view or secular beliefs, what can be understood by these visions of the soul's searching? Even for those without religious belief, these perspectives speak to a shared human experience: an inner restlessness, a search for meaning, coherence and belonging beyond the ego.

Soul searching from western psychological research

To make sense of spirituality in education, we turned to the research within the domain of health psychology (e.g. Domash, 2021; Newberg and Waldman, 2009) because it offers valuable insights for education, particularly in relation to holistic development and the interplay between psychological well-being (PWB) and spirituality. Lisa Miller's research in psychology of religion and spirituality has significantly advanced understanding of the link between spirituality, mental health and human flourishing.

In *The Spiritual Child* (2015), she argues that spirituality is not merely a cultural or religious overlay but a natural, hardwired capacity of the human brain, particularly visible in childhood and adolescence. Drawing on longitudinal and neuroscientific studies, Miller demonstrates that young people who cultivate a spiritual life, whether through prayer, meditation or a sense of connection to the transcendent, show greater resilience against depression, substance abuse and risk-taking behaviours. In adults, too, spirituality correlates with lower rates of anxiety and a deeper sense of meaning and purpose; with spiritual growth, positive psychological assets can be seen, "thriving, optimism, grit, and the relational assets of forgiveness, intimacy and commitment" (Miller, 2015, p. 75).

There is also Rodrigo Riveros and Mary Helen Immordino-Yang (2023) who bring together neuropsychological research, settling on the view that spirituality is in essence a profound search for self, especially during adolescent development:

> Spirituality has often been defined as the personal search, experience, and response to the perception of the transcendent, sacred, or divine. As such, the experience of spiritual transcendence requires mentally connecting concrete perceptions and actions with broader explanations that invoke sacred values relevant to God, space, nature, the arts, politics, or other domains. These connections elicit transcendent social emotions such as awe, gratitude, admiration, compassion, and moral elevation.
>
> (Riveros and Immordino-Yang, 2023, p. 113)

It is important to note that a counterargument is that some practices of spirituality might cause harm, especially if associated with judgement and a hierarchical process of ascension and descension (heaven and hell) (Friedman et al., 2024). We should note this concern and keep our assumptions in check. However, it does seem a compelling argument from the world of neuroscience – spirituality is good for you!

As well as guiding the search for the soul, the literature also highlights the importance of fostering compassion as the expression of the soul *in action*. For example, Ryff's (1989) multidimensional model of psychological well-being includes six dimensions: self-acceptance, personal growth, purpose in life, positive relations, environmental mastery and autonomy (Ryff and Keyes, 1995). Moreover,

> Clearly, spirituality is a diffuse and multifaceted construct. MacDonald (2000) analyzed a number of spirituality measures based on varying underlying concepts of spirituality, and found factors: cognitive, experiential/phenomenological, existential well-being, paranormal beliefs, and religiousness.
>
> (Friedman et al., 2024, p. 151)

We know that higher levels of well-being are associated with lower depression, reduced engagement in risk behaviours and enhanced resilience (Yonker et al., 2012). From a neuroscientific perspective, spiritual practice appears to strengthen neural pathways associated with empathy, self-regulation and positive affect, supporting not only psychological wellbeing but also healthier interpersonal relationships. Importantly, Miller frames spirituality as distinct from formal religion: it is an innate human capacity for connection, transcendence and purpose, which can be nurtured across traditions and contexts.

All this seems intuitively obvious – treat people well and they do better (Layard, 2011; Layard and Hagell, 2015). And yet, wider education systems continue to separate efforts to develop spirituality from the reified process of knowledge acquisition and achieving academically – as if that is the sole purpose of education. However, such scientific findings invite us to consider the conditions under which schools might actively promote psychological flourishing, not simply academic performance. This resonates with critiques of narrow accountability cultures (Biesta, 2010), which he says marginalises dimensions of education that address meaning, belonging and ethical formation (Biesta, 2017, 2020).

For education research, the key challenge lies in translating health-based models of psychological well-being and spirituality into pedagogical frameworks without reducing them to easily measurable competencies. Whilst constructs such as spirituality and the soul are complex, context dependent and resistant to simplistic operationalisation (and contested), they nevertheless offer promising directions: educators might explore how learning environments can foster experiences of connectedness, reflection and wonder, or how curricula can integrate personal growth and purpose alongside knowledge acquisition. In this way, insights from health psychology can help education move towards a more holistic vision of human flourishing, one that positions psychological well-being and spirituality as core dimensions of learning and not peripheral concerns.

The soul as Ātman: the eternal self in Vedic thought

Having explored scientific-research-informed ideas of soul and spirit, we now turn to the Vedic concept of the Self, which is called the *ātman*. The *ātman* is the key to understanding human identity, destiny, and liberation.

In this Indic tradition, unlike the temporary body, which perishes, and the mind, which is fickle and changing, the *ātman* is regarded as eternal, indestructible, and divine in origin. This term is rich and multifaceted.

In some contexts, *ātman* simply denotes 'self,' the embodied identity, mind or even the vital breath that animates living beings. Yet, within the Vedas, particularly the *Upaniṣads* and the *Bhagavad Gītā*, *ātman* takes on a deeper, metaphysical meaning. It signifies the eternal, indestructible self. The *Kaṭha Upaniṣad* articulates this principle with striking clarity (2.18):

> *na jāyate mriyate vā kadācin nāyaṁ bhūtvā bhavitā vā na bhūyaḥ*
> *ajo nityaḥ śāśvato 'yaṁ purāṇo na hanyate hanyamāne śarīre*
>
> He[2] is never born, nor does he ever die; nor having once existed does he ever cease to be. He is unborn, eternal, ever existing, and primeval. He is not slain when the body is slain
>
> (*Kaṭha Upaniṣad* 2.18)

It is the philosophy that inspired Mahatma Ghandi to mobilise non-violent civil disobedience in India; knowing that whatever great physical force the British Empire might impose, his inner self, his true core self, was indestructible; realising that throughout any hardship, no external factor could diminish who he truly was – a soul. This realisation gave him enormous physical and spiritual strength.

As with Ghandi, the verse establishes a foundational insight of Vedic philosophy: the *ātman* cannot be destroyed by death. Just as a driver is distinct from the car they operate; the soul is distinct from the body it inhabits. When the car ceases to function, the driver remains untouched. The driver of a car is not the car. Similarly, the soul of a body is not the body. With this in mind, the *ātman* – the true Self – departs when the body perishes, remaining eternally conscious and unaffected by physical decay. Our body is constantly changing, from infancy, childhood, youth, middle age, old age, and finally death. But we, the unchangeable soul, witness this "virtual reality" from within. That's why, even though our body changes throughout life, we always keep our sense of personal self. Why do elderly people often say, "I may be 80 years old but I still feel like I am 21"?

In contemporary terms, this teaching suggests that beneath the layers of personality, circumstance, and conditioning, the deepest "you" is already luminous, conscious, and joyful. This essence is not something to be created or achieved but rediscovered through self-knowledge and spiritual practice. In the *Bhagavad Gītā*, Krishna declares (15.7):

mamaivāṁśo jīva–loke
jīva–bhūtaḥ sanātanaḥ
manaḥ–ṣaṣṭhānīndriyāṇi
prakṛti–sthāni karṣati

> "The living entities in this conditioned world are My eternal fragmental parts. Due to conditioned life, they are struggling very hard with the six senses, which include the mind."
>
> (*Bhagavad Gītā* 15.7)

In these texts, the *ātman* (often translated as "Self") refers to the deepest part of a person; their enduring, conscious core. It is described as coming from the Divine in the same way a spark comes from a fire: it shares the same nature but remains distinct. Another image is a drop of water from the ocean – it has the same qualities as the ocean, yet it is still a drop.

Taken together, these teachings present a consistent view of the human person. The *ātman* is not just our thoughts, feelings or personality. It is the unchanging awareness beneath them. It is distinct from the body and mind yet connected to the ultimate ground of reality (often called *Brahman*). The aim of life, in this tradition, is to recognise this deeper identity – to realise that we are more than temporary physical beings, and to live in alignment with that deeper truth.

In many ways, questions about the purpose of life, linked with concepts of the soul and spirituality are not divorced from questions about death. Even very young children are curious about what happens when someone dies, as if seeking to understand the answers to that question, gives some direction about the purpose and quality of living. Wayne Muller (1992) provokes the point that at the end of our lives what will we have considered to be the most important parts of our lives? Will it be what we bought, how much we earned or what we did as a career? Will it be how much we contributed to others? Will it be passing on wisdom, culture and ideas? Or something else:

> When we come to the moment of our death, it is likely that a few questions will arise in our hearts: Did I love well? Was I generous and kind? Did I allow myself to be loved? How did I share that love with

> others? Few people facing the end of their lives worry that they didn't spend enough time at work: not many wonder if they made enough money or went to enough meetings. Instead, as they prepare themselves for death, they become focused on the deep love they have for their family, their children and their friends.
>
> (Muller, 1992, p. 172)

As well as ensuring academic standards are improved for all children to thrive and achieve, if we adopt a spiritual mindset during the process of education, realignment or refocus on what truly matters for a flourishing life might guide our decisions. All of this is deeply philosophical and never features on initial teaching education courses or in professional development in staff rooms, but it does raise questions relevant for education.

Educability of the soul

In *Before Religion* (2025), Nitesh Gor draws on the *Srimad Bhagavatam* to describe four key dimensions of the soul that are relevant to education.

- ***Finding identity*:** This is about understanding who we really are. It is like peeling an onion – gradually moving beyond labels, roles and external achievements to a deeper awareness of self. In schools, this means helping young people explore identity in ways that go beyond exam results, social media profiles or peer approval.
- ***Raising consciousness*:** We all know that our awareness fluctuates – some days we are focused, calm and thoughtful; other days we are distracted or reactive. Spiritual development, in this sense, is about cultivating habits that help us access our 'higher' capacities: clarity, compassion, self-control and insight. Practices like meditation can support this as a technique and as a way of being more present and attentive.
- ***Reducing the grip of materialism*:** Modern culture often tells us that reality is only physical matter (physicalism) or that happiness comes mainly from pleasure and consumption (hedonism). Spiritual education challenges these assumptions. Through reflection, self-discipline and asking deeper questions about meaning and value, students can learn not to be defined solely by possessions, status or immediate gratification.

- ***Discovering purpose:*** Finally, spirituality points towards purpose beyond the self. It encourages young people to contribute to something larger than their own success – to serve, to create, to belong.

Seen this way, soul work in education is not about promoting a particular belief. It is about supporting identity, awareness, depth and purpose, helping young people to grow in knowledge and skills *and* in wisdom and meaning. Our thesis, therefore, is that the soul is essentially educable.

However, the thesis is also that the soul cannot be educated in the technocratic predefined certainties of current curricula and pedagogies. The question remaining is how? Patrick Mahaffey's (2019) engagement with integral theory offers a language through which the soul can be understood. He insists that human development is uneven and multidimensional. Drawing on the Integral AQAL framework, he notes that individuals develop along multiple "lines of development," including cognitive, emotional, moral, interpersonal and spiritual capacities (Mahaffey, 2019, p. 186). We found this also in the research evidence provided by neuroscientists and psychologists. These soft qualities are not simply traits but existential questions that shape how a person lives and learns: "What am I aware of?" "Who am I?" and, crucially, "What is of ultimate concern?" (p. 186). That final question places the soul firmly within the educational horizon. If learners can be supported to deepen awareness across these questions, then the soul itself becomes educable.

For Mahaffey, spiritual/soul education is not about belief formation but about awakening. Similarly, Maxine Greene refers to wide-awakeness and bell hooks to teaching as transgression, where love teaches against fear, alienation and separation. Mahaffey describes "waking up" as "a growth process that leads to what is variously known as awakening, enlightenment, realisation, and freedom" (Mahaffey, 2019, p. 182). This awakening involves a profound shift in identity, in which the learner becomes "identified with reality in a state the Sufis call 'the Supreme Identity,' the realisation that the individual and the ultimate reality are one" (p. 182). Education, from this perspective, is not complete if it addresses only skills and knowledge while leaving untouched the deeper structures of consciousness that shape identity, meaning and purpose.

Crucially, Mahaffey emphasises that such states of consciousness are not accidental or reserved for a spiritual elite. They are taught through *disciplined practice*. He explains that contemplative traditions across cultures identify multiple states of consciousness, including "the waking state; the dream state; the deep dreamless state; the empty witness state; and the nondual or unity state" (Mahaffey, 2019, p. 183). While most education systems operate exclusively within the waking state, Mahaffey argues that "to gain access to these states, one must engage in contemplative practices" (p. 183). The implication is clear: educational environments can either ignore or actively support this deeper cultivation of awareness and thereby educate the soul.

Rachel Kessler, who writes about emotional learning, argues that when soul awareness enters the classroom, "masks drop away" and learners dare to show their authentic selves, revealing both talents and vulnerabilities (Kessler, 2000, p. xxi). Moreover, when the soul is present in education, the quality of attention shifts. We begin not only to hear what learners say, but to listen to "messages between the words" and attend to the emotional and existential currents expressed through gestures, silence and presence (Kessler, 2000, p. xxi). In such a paradigm, questions become as important as answers, and the deeper longings, fears, hopes and wonderings of learners move to the heart of the curriculum. Rather than focusing solely on cognitive attainment, a soulful education honours meaning making, belonging, compassion and the shared human search for purpose.

To speak of educating the soul is to advocate for a form of schooling that cultivates diverse spiritual expressions and fosters conditions in which children and adults alike may explore their "spiritual longings," develop vision and approach life with greater humanity (Kessler, 2000, p. xxii). Our thinking builds on an ongoing pursuit to challenge the 'standards and structures' rhetoric of education towards a third 's' – to that of the soul,

> The mantra for the last twenty years of education in England, said too often but not done often enough, has been 'standards not structures.' It may be time to reintroduce a third 's', the soul of schools, into this mix. Then we may begin to see more clearly the young people behind the standards and think more clearly about whether their long-term needs are being met. We believe that now is the time to put back the soul and spirit into our schools and begin to create a clear vision about the purpose and goals of education and schooling in the 21st century.
>
> (Peterson et al., 2014, p. 4)

In an era of fragmentation and pressure, the education of and for the soul offers a counter-narrative: one that centres what makes us most deeply human, and asks not only how we learn, but who we are becoming (Domash, 2021).

Summary

As this chapter has demonstrated, the yearning for meaning is inherently human. Paraphrasing Frankl (2004), it is the 'why' to life after the 'what,' 'who' and 'where' have been worked out. Meaning, therefore, is a core aspect of making sense of the soul. As Piedmont and Wilkins assert (2020),

> The reason is simple: Meaning is not only seen as the basic defining element of spirituality but also as an essential quality of the human experience. Frankl (1969) has asserted that the will to meaning is what drives the human experience. Park (2013) believes that individuals create an entire meaning system in an effort to organize personal experiences, to evaluate and appraise them, and to eventually construct a global sense of meaning that provides coherence, direction, and purpose. Theologians, too, also acknowledge the central role of meaning in the spiritual process and experience (Tillich, 1951, 1952/2000). How we create meaning says much about who we are as individuals and how we see the world. Meaning provides us with the overall template for organizing our experiences of the world and for creating our anticipations for the future. Meaning arrives as a consequence of our efforts at addressing core existential questions, such as "Why am I here?" "Where am I going in life?"
>
> (Piedmont and Wilkins, 2020, p. 161)

To speak of the soul in education is to return to something fundamental about human life and learning. Across cultures and philosophies, learning has been understood as the shaping of the self in relation to others, to meaning and to the world. The pressing question, then, is not whether the soul belongs in education, but how an education that attends to the whole human being might learn to teach *to* and *for* it and what such an education would need to offer.

Vedic philosophy contributes powerfully to this conversation by suggesting that realising the true self involves a movement beyond narrow self-interest: first into deeper, more ethical relationships with others and ultimately into a felt sense of connection with the wider living universe. When translated into contemporary educational practice, these insights point towards forms of learning that cultivate reflection, service, self-discipline, relationship and reverence for life.

Questions for the journey

As educators, parents or teachers, what questions might deepen our own reflections on the Vedic processes of learning to improve how we make meaning and understand our own sense of soul, before we start working with young people:

- When I pause and turn inward, where do I sense the source of meaning in my life – in achievement, relationship, service or something deeper still?
- In moments of challenge, personal suffering or hardship or stillness, what helps me remember my connection to something larger than myself?
- What practices of listening, reflection, meditation or devotion draw me from self–focus towards openness and wonder?
- When I truly listen to another, to the world or to silence what becomes possible in me that was not there before?
- How might learning itself become an act of awakening: a movement from information towards insight, from doing towards being?
- How might our collective work serve something beyond us, a greater harmony, a more compassionate world, or what the Vedas might call the unfolding of the Self?

Notes

1 A text of eight Sanskrit verses composed by *Sri Caitanya Mahaprabhu* which encapsulates the essence of bhakti-yoga, emphasising the chanting of the holy names of God (*Hare Krishna, Hare Krishna, Krishna Krishna, Hare, Hare, Hare* Rama, *Hare Rama, Rama, Rama, Hare Hare*), humility and pure devotion to Krishna (a name for God which means 'all attractive'). The words surrender and humility are often problematic in western philosophical contexts because they imply weakness. However, in an Eastern philosophical context, surrender does not mean giving up but rather giving in to a higher purpose or Divinity. Humility does not mean 'meek and mild' but rather is a courageous stance to acknowledge that we do not know everything and indeed that we cannot know the fullness of life, both material and spiritual. Both positions allow for curiosity and soul journeying to continue.

2 Often in the scriptural texts and English translations, the language is gendered in favour of male pronouns. However, in reality 'He' refers to all living things, including not only humans and not only men.

3 Viewing the battlefields of education and life

This chapter introduces three key dilemmas that have journeyed through and circumambulated education for decades: the challenge of equality, the challenge of diversity (as well as inclusion and belonging) and the third, the place of love in education. As we continue our journey to consider what an education attentive to the soul might entail, we begin with a story: it is a story that views the personal, collective and education battlefields with which we are faced (Figure 3.1).

Figure 3.1 The battlefield of Kurukshetra. Photo taken of *Bhagavad Gītā*[1] mural on 24th October 2025 by James Biddulph in the Sandipani Muni Ashram, Ujjain, India.

DOI: 10.4324/9781003487654-4

Over five millennia ago, on the plains of Kurukshetra in northern India, dawn broke over the battlefield. Two vast armies stood poised for war; warriors armoured in steel, elephants draped in crimson and gold, horses restless in their harnesses, steam bellowing from their wide nostrils and chariots lined in endless rows. It was to be the battle of all battles.

Yet, beneath the thunder of armies and conch shell trumpets was a quieter, more piercing tension: this was not only a clash of kingdoms but a conflict within a single family. On one side stood the Pāṇḍavas, led by the mighty archer Arjuna.[2] On the other, the Kauravas, his cousins, commanded by the proud and unyielding Duryodhana.

Into this silence, the warrior Arjuna asked his charioteer, Krishna,[3] to drive him between the two armies. From this vantage, he surveyed the enemy: uncles who once held him as a child, companions who once laughed with him, masters who once guided him. His bow grew heavy. His limbs trembled. His heart collapsed under the weight of anguish and anxiety. The moment was unbearable and existential.

And his questions: how can I fight those I love? What is my purpose? How am I to act?

Re-told by James Biddulph from *Bhagavad Gītā (1.27–31)*

This opening scene begins the *Bhagavad Gītā*, a central text in the Vedic philosophical tradition, and is arguably a representation of the human condition. The battlefield of Kurukshetra is not merely a geographical site in northern India but a metaphor for the struggles of the heart and mind. It symbolises the conflicts we each carry within us: between duty and desire, love and obligation, fear and courage, despair and hope, acting or not acting. It is the same dilemma that Shakespeare's Hamlet felt: to be or not to be, that is the question.

Whether 'tis nobler in the mind to suffer
The slings and arrows of outrageous fortune,
Or to take arms against a sea of troubles
And by opposing end them. To die—to sleep,

No more; and by a sleep to say we end
The heart-ache and the thousand natural shocks
That flesh is heir to: 'tis a consummation
Devoutly to be wish'd. To die, to sleep;
To sleep, perchance to dream—ay, there's the rub:
For in that sleep of death what dreams may come,
When we have shuffled off this mortal coil,
Must give us pause—there's the respect
That makes calamity of so long life.

(William Shakespeare, *Hamlet*, spoken by Hamlet)

Like Hamlet, Arjuna's paralysis at the threshold of battle is profoundly human; who among us has not felt torn between competing loyalties, or weighed down by choices that pit principle against relationship? It is an inner struggle that burdens his mind. Trying to make sense of our purpose in life and its meaning is both the human endeavour and the cause of suffering, and "it is well known how many have lost the will to live, and have stopped trying, because such meaning has evaded them" (Bettleheim, 1976, p. 3). The 2025 education survey conducted by Edurio presented a worrying status quo: that only 45% of young people in secondary school felt physically and mentally well with this falling to 31% by the time they are 18 years old. When asked how interesting they find lessons, 53% of children at the end of primary school said they did and a persistent 20–21% of young people during most of their secondary school experience (Edurio, Pupil Experience Report, 2025, pp. 17–21). How can we inspire children and young people to not lose the will to live (through boredom and disengagement from learning) and instead to feel engaged with the exploration of themselves, others, belief systems and the world to co-construct meaning and purpose? We return to the question at the outset: where has all the joy gone in education?

So too for educators and school leaders (Favors, 2002), the battlefield is both inward and outward: the inner wrestling with personal values, hopes and commitments, and the outer pressures of systems that demand performance, compliance and measurable outcomes. To teach is often to negotiate between conscience and curriculum, between what one believes children need and what policy dictates. In this sense, the teacher's classroom becomes a Kurukshetra, a contested space where ethical purpose and institutional expectation meet. It becomes a mirror upon which the dilemmas of existence are laid bare; for us educators, the dilemmas and choices with which we are faced daily and strategically. Kurukshetra therefore is not only a family at war but also the inner war that each of us must navigate; the tension between who we are and who we are called to become – as individuals and as professionals.

By opening with this scene, the *Bhagavad Gītā* speaks across centuries and cultures, reminding us that education (as in life), growth and transformation are often forged in the crucible of conflict, doubt and questioning. In this sense, the *Bhagavad Gītā* offers not only a spiritual text but also a profound meditation on leadership and learning. Leading schools is hard work. It is complex because it involves navigating the hopes and convictions of diverse stakeholders (Biddulph and Gilbride, 2025), each with distinctive beliefs about children, childhood, education and the kind of world we wish to create. Leadership, then, is not simply about direction or decision-making; it is a deeply relational and moral undertaking that involves holding tensions, listening to competing truths and acting with compassion amid uncertainty. It requires the learned ignorance or wisdom of unlearning (Chia and Holt, 2007).

Learning, too, is demanding work. It challenges us to stretch beyond what we know, to unlearn as much as to learn. At its most basic level, learning involves the brain taking on new knowledge or skills, such as mastering reading or mathematics. Yet, on another level, learning requires letting go, relinquishing familiar patterns of thought, revising assumptions or adopting new frameworks of understanding. In this process, our sense of self can feel unsettled. We are confronted with our own ignorance, a state the ego resists, but which is necessary for a soul-led approach to come to light. It is in these moments, whether in the practice of leadership or in the experience of learning, that we encounter, often unconsciously, the deeper human questions:

- *Who am I?*
- *Who am I becoming?*
- *What is the nature of this life, and what lies beyond it?*
- *Why am I here?*
- *What is this Universe?*
- *What is beyond this Universe?*
- *How do I know?*

Though philosophical in form, such questions are lived and felt in practice because education is, obviously, an intensely human practice. The questions surface in the quiet anxieties of decision making, in the vulnerability of admitting not knowing, in the tension between ideals and realities, or in the awe of witnessing genuine learning take place.

In leading, as in learning, the ground of certainty shifts, and what emerges is not simply a cognitive challenge but an existential one (Biddulph and Gilbride, 2025). These moments call us, whether we recognise it or not, to reflect on identity, purpose and belonging. They remind us that education and leadership are not merely technical or managerial acts, but profoundly human and, ultimately, we suggest, are spiritual endeavours. Why does it mean so much to a Headteacher or class teacher when a child does not understand a lesson? Or when a complaint is received by a parent, why does it feel so painful and personal? One could argue it is because the endeavour to educate well goes to the heart of the educator – it is almost a sacred act.

Seen in this light, teaching becomes more than the transmission of knowledge; it becomes a process of awakening, an invitation to examine who we are and how we act in the world. For example, we learn about a period of history and we also learn about how we might act in the world given the historical personalities we meet. Leadership, likewise, becomes not merely the coordination of systems but the cultivation of practitioner wisdom, compassion, and courage amid complexity (Flutter, 2006, 2025). The personal and philosophical, the practical and the spiritual, are thus not separate domains but different dimensions of the same enquiry: how to live well, and how to help others do the same. Sir Anthony Seldon articulates the magical possibilities of the educational experience and yet, for many young people, he warns, *"the joy is squeezed out of school"* (Ean, 2024) replaced by fear and anxiety, a situation that we agree is *"terribly sad and completely unnecessary."* Education, he reminds us, means *"to lead out"*: to discover and nurture the gifts within every child, *"All young people have gifts, intelligence and aptitudes that schools should be actively nurturing"* and a flourishing education builds resilience, character and well-being alongside knowledge.

This is the concern we have with current education approaches. What makes a life truly good and worth living and how does education help children and young people to get there? In *Human Flourishing* (Briggs and Reiss, 2021), the authors argue that human flourishing, an idea with roots in Aristotle's notion of *eudaimonia*, offers a richer and more holistic framework for understanding wellbeing than narrow economic or biological measures such as GDP or life expectancy. A flourishing life, they suggest, involves more than mere survival or material success; it is one marked by dignity, purpose, relationships and a sense of connection to something greater than oneself. Briggs and Reiss position flourishing as a bridge between scientific insight and spiritual wisdom. The social sciences, including psychology and sociology, can illuminate the conditions that foster wellbeing (such as belonging, autonomy and meaning), while spiritual and religious traditions invite reflection on the transcendent dimensions of life. The transcendent, they note, is not confined to religion: it may also be encountered through art, nature or the contemplation of our place in the cosmos. Later in this book, we explore frameworks to make sense of the movement from individualism to community, from materialism to transcendental ways of engaging in the world. The experiences Briggs and Reiss mention awaken a sense of awe and connectedness that deepens human experience and contributes to flourishing. The question: how does education prepare children and young people for a flourishing life in its fullest sense? Does it? Can it? What would need to change to enable this aspiration?

Underlying their discussion is the conviction that every person possesses equal dignity and worth, a principle affirmed both in secular humanism and in religious worldviews. This aligns with the Vedic concept of the soul. By grounding flourishing in this shared human dignity, there is an invitation for us to reflect on what we truly value and aspire to, both individually and collectively. In an age dominated by consumerism and metrics, they call for a renewed attention to the integration of science, spirituality and ethical reflection. Human flourishing, in their view, is not merely about happiness or success, but about living meaningfully, cultivating relationships, and nurturing the transcendent capacities that make us most fully human.

Further to the existential dilemma, Arjuna's huge personal crisis can also be read as a symbol for the crises of our times: insecurities about identity and purpose, fractured communities, both at a local context and on the world stage, and deep concern about the survival of planet earth. Most recently, Biddulph, Shuckburgh and Pearse (2026) foreground the fears and anguish that so many feel in our post-COVID, conflict-full world, in which society is in flux and unsettled by so many uncertainties, untruths, divisions and deceptions. How do we navigate through and make sense of our individual and collective purpose? How do we, as parents and educators, empower young people's sense of agency, and ability to act upon it, as well as grow with a sense of interconnectedness and belonging? How do we enable them (and us all) to feel less lonely, with mental agility and confidence to act for the greater good, not for hyper-materialistic gain but for spiritual advancement and long-lasting contentment?

The questions are many. Like Arjuna, our 'education bow' falls and we tremble, paralysed by the enormity of the task ahead, perhaps? Or is there hope and opportunity in the learning Arjuna receives from his friend that could capture our own hearts and minds to craft new possible possibilities? Is this a moment of unlearning?

Three education dilemmas

In seeking to explore how else Kurukshetra might play out in contemporary classrooms, we saw three initial framing preoccupations:

- the challenge of equality,
- the understanding of diversities and
- the cultivation of love as an educational value.

Structural inequalities, whether economic, social or cultural, continue to shape educational access and outcomes, making equality an ethical and political (and in our view spiritual) imperative for educators. At the same time, classrooms are increasingly diverse in terms of language, culture, identity and worldview, requiring pedagogies that do not erase difference but embrace them as a source of learning and growth. Both equality and diversity are now linked with more dynamic understandings of identity, belonging and community. Beyond structural (in)justices and cultural responsiveness, education also demands a grounding in love – understood not sentimentally, but as a commitment to care, compassion and the recognition of shared humanity.

These preoccupations resonate deeply with the *Bhagavad Gītā's* teachings: equality is described as a spiritual discipline and way of seeing beyond external distinctions; the embracing of diversities reflects the *Gītā's* vision of the divine manifesting in manifold forms (BG 9.15–16); and love (bhakti) is celebrated as a supreme path toward wisdom and unity (BG 12). In this way, the struggles of Kurukshetra (ethical decision, recognition of plurality, and the grounding of action in love) can be re-imagined as critical frames for navigating the challenges of contemporary education.

Dilemma 1: confronting inequalities

Despite rhetorical commitments to equity, inequalities continue to pervade contemporary education systems (Flutter, Biddulph and Peacock, 2023). Herculean efforts are made by teachers, head teachers, school systems' leaders and support staff to change the life chances of children and young people, in small acts and in system decisions. For instance, when a class teacher provides breakfast and second-hand clothing for children, such acts of compassion highlight both the immediacy of children's needs and the teacher's frustration at their inability to effect systemic transformation.

Even with the vision of meritocracy, the UK system continues to reward those already familiar with the hidden 'rules of the game.' The book *Seven Children* (Dorling, 2023) offers vivid testimonies of this perpetuation: young people navigating poverty, precarious housing, and limited access to enrichment opportunities. The accounts of seven imagined children, drawing from big data, reveal how aspiration so often collides with structural barriers, where so called 'ability' (Peacock, 2015) is not the issue but rather circumstance. Diane Reay (2017) argues that dominant education models are symbolically violent in the way they impose middle-class assumptions about what education is for and which aspirations are given legitimacy. Her work builds from Pierre Bourdieu (1977) who demonstrates that schools rarely disrupt structural inequalities but instead reproduce them, valorising the language, cultural capital, and dispositions of the middle classes – without intention, we should add, but because of the habitus or ways of being/thinking/doing that form our practice. This can be seen, for instance, in the regulation of language where non-standard dialects or home languages are corrected or marginalised, and in behavioural expectations that privilege middle-class norms of compliance and self-expression, both of which can disadvantage those whose cultural resources diverge from these norms.

Furthermore, UK national examination data reveal that white working-class boys perform less well than many other demographic groups (FFT Education

Datalab, 2025). Recent evidence that our education system continues to fall short of what young people need, particularly those already facing social and economic disadvantage, is evidenced from The King's Trust and the Learning and Work Institute (2022). A recent report (2025 https://www.kingstrust.org.uk/about-us/our-research/the-power-of-potential-supporting-the-future-of-young-people) (Learning and Work Institute and The King's Trust, 2022; OECD, 2017) shows a sharp rise in mental health conditions among young people who are not in education, employment or training (NEET), increasing from 11 per cent in 2011 to almost a third by 2022. Nearly half of NEET young people report mental health difficulties, disability or caring responsibilities as reasons for being out of work, while others cite low confidence, repeated rejection and difficulty navigating application processes. These patterns point to an education system that rewards narrow attainment outcomes while giving insufficient attention to wellbeing, confidence and relational support. As Reay argues, such systems routinely misrecognise structural inequality as personal deficit, leaving many young people to internalise failure.

A school-based example of how this perpetuation of inequality arises is within the widespread practice of grouping and setting children by so-called ability demands closer scrutiny. Research by Susan Hallam (2013) suggests that while attainment grouping can offer short-term curricular pacing benefits for some learners, these gains are uneven and often achieved at significant emotional cost to those placed in lower sets. There is new research (Taylor and Hodgen, 2026) which suggests an alternative view regarding maths setting. However, in relation to developing identity and soul, we align with Alison Peacock's work on 'learning without limits' (Swann et al., 2012), which highlights how fixed ability labels restrict teachers' expectations and children's self-belief, narrowing both aspiration and effort. While responsive differentiation or adaptation remains important as an inclusive strategy, conflating 'ability' with 'potential' risks foreclosing futures. At a time when almost half a million young people want to work but feel locked out, and about one third of eleven-year-olds do not pass end of primary school assessments, education must move beyond sorting and ranking towards practices that cultivate belonging, confidence and adaptability as core outcomes.

Bringing soul into education is difficult because hearts and minds need some convincing. During the writing of the book, one of us (James) had a conversation with another educator that struck at another complexity of the journey to develop spirituality in education. It was related to its inclusivity. It is an issue that we need to hold throughout the book and indeed into our own schools, classrooms and staffrooms. The remembered comments continued something like this:

Pondering whether spirituality is inclusive

> I came from a working background. *She said.* It was hard. *She said.* We lived in relative poverty and most of the time our parents just focused on getting the next meal onto the table. We played out in the yard. We had good times, but it was harsh. Food. Winter fuel. Getting through school. It's all they could think about. *She paused.* We never had time for thinking about the soul or spirituality, I don't think, although maybe they did in quiet times alone…Church…sometimes at Christmas, but not much else. That's what middle class people did. It is not so much about class, actually, but about the Maslow triangle, you know, 'physiological safety, social, self-esteem, self-realisation'.

Her question has stayed with me. How do we invite children into reflection, interiority, spiritual depth, when home life is shaped by precarity? How do we speak of transcendence when parents are thinking about rent and dinner? And yet I wonder whether such framing risks misunderstanding spirituality as an optional extra – something added once the basics are settled. What if the inner life is not a luxury good but a quiet resource? Not separate from survival, but a way of making sense of it. The challenge for education, perhaps, is not to impose spirituality as a programme, but to create spaces, however small, where even those simply trying to reach dinner time can breathe, reflect, and know themselves as more than their circumstances.

A remembered conversation between James Biddulph and a colleague not at Avanti (August 2024).

The Vedic way has a different view. The concept of spiritual equality is deeply rooted in the Vedic tradition, as illustrated in the *Bhagavad Gītā* (Chapter 2); the notion of "equal vision" (*Bhagavad Gītā* 5.18; 9.32) gestures toward an alternative horizon of justice beyond hierarchies of class, caste, gender, status or any other material identity. Equal vision means seeing beneath and beyond the ways we categorise our differences in favour of seeking our similarities.

At the heart of the Vedic philosophy is the conviction that all living beings – whether human or nonhuman – share the same essential identity as eternal spirit beings, parts and parcels of the Ultimate reality. It's why many people who follow this or similar philosophy choose to be vegetarian – in recognition that all have the same individual internal spark called the soul. From this standpoint, material distinctions of body, birth, or intellect are superficial; they are separate from the essence of the living being. For example, in his lessons to Arjuna, Krishna (*Bhagavad Gītā* 5.18) says, "the humble sages, by virtue of true knowledge, sees with equal vision a learned and gentle *brāhmaṇa*, a cow, an elephant, a dog, and a dog-eater." The sameness here is obviously not physical but spiritual. Though the external bodies vary, the essence is the same: each is a spiritual spark covered by a particular body (whether dog or elephant, etc.).

Typically, from a purely materialistic or physicalist perspective, only difference is seen – by definition, no two things can be the same – but this perspective, while useful in many fields of application, has its limitations when considering spiritual matters. It seems so hard for us humans to see beyond the physical body, or in categorising people's thoughts and beliefs, to identify the differences of colour, gender, sexuality, age, culture, language, religion, political persuasion, etc. It is our typical way of being, perhaps? Such a mindset separates rather than unites us and leads to behaviours that perpetuate inequalities.

How we see others is linked with how we see ourselves; indeed, identity is an important contemporary theme, "identity matters for all of us. Who we are, what we will become, and how we develop character, become citizens, experience belonging, and learn to be inclusive of others who are different from us, these purposes of education and schools are fundamental" (Shirley and Hargreaves, 2023, p. 5). Krishna's message to Arjuna reinforces this theme of identity and equality not least because it has such profound spiritual, ethical and social consequences.

What would happen if we could develop our young people to see beyond the external physical body and see the unique and yet similar spiritual spark in all living beings? Inclusion would cease to be a bureaucratic process and instead become an ethical and spiritual commitment, a recognition that belonging is a birthright, not a privilege. Limiting thinking about so called ability, learning needs, disabilities, disadvantage could be transformational because, taking Alison Peacock's example of Mary in the foreword of this book, she saw beneath the external and instead saw her soul – the enormous potential of possibilities laying within. Social justice, too, would be grounded not only in fairness or equality but in the awareness that each person is sacred, that harming another diminishes oneself and that equality is vital for human flourishing and because, as Charlie Chaplin pointed out in his film, "we want to live by each other's happiness – not by each other's misery."

Dilemma 2: embracing diversities

The concept of diversities reinforces the idea of spiritual equality among all living beings. A simple analogy to help us understand our relationship to the Divine, Ultimate Reality or Ultimate Truth is as sunshine to the sun. When we see the sun streaming through the window and we say, "The sun is here," we are of course referring to the sunshine, the rays of the sun. But are the sunrays the same as the sun? Yes and no. They are the same in terms of quality (the same 'stuff') but of a completely different quantity (thankfully!). Similarly, we are like individual sunrays, and the Divine, or Ultimate Reality, is like the sun. We are the energetic emanation. There is no such thing as just light without the sun. We are, in this very real sense, part and parcel of the Ultimate Reality.

In making this claim, we are prompted to reconsider how we understand diversity and how we respond to difference (Black-Hawkins and Grinham-Smith, 2023). What might it mean to see one another as distinct yet interconnected, each a unique expression of a shared spiritual essence? If we accept that we are spiritual beings, equal, particular and interdependent, like rays of one sun or in another way, as drops within a vast ocean, our worldview begins to reorient. Such a perspective invites deeper compassion and curiosity, encouraging us to engage with diversity not as a challenge to overcome, but as a vital condition for mutual growth and understanding. It is a similar message to that of Bhaktivinoda Thakura, in his exploration of the diversities in religious traditions; diversity within oneness, "there are countless philosophies which although attempting to reach the truth are all incomplete and mutually conflicting" (Thakura, 2017, p. 1).

As we have mentioned, in schools, children are often categorised before they are seen (Walton and Marais, 2023). They are labelled according to need, attainment, or background. But what if we began with the understanding that every child carries within them an unchanging essence, a consciousness that witnesses their thoughts, emotions and circumstances yet remains untouched by their physicality, body etc? Seeing others through this lens would change the moral atmosphere of education. A child with autism, for example, might be approached not through a deficit model but as a unique expression of divine creativity, one whose perspective expands the collective understanding of what it means to be alive. Difference, then, becomes not a problem to be solved but a manifestation of life's abundance.

In the Vedas, difference is important and valued. Similarly, in contemporary research, leading voices of inclusion, like Peacock's *Learning Without Limits* (2016; Swann et al., 2012) or Black-Hawkins and Grinhaw-Smith (2023) echo this liberating possibility. In both Vedic and contemporary educational thinking, the message is clear: to recognise and cultivate uniqueness is to affirm the dignity of every learner, enabling an education that is expansive rather than reductive. And what of other forms of disadvantage and diversity? For learners who are neurodiverse, LGBT+, exposed to gendered bias, refugee, or feel that the system does not speak for them? For all those who struggle to fit in and those who stick out (Biddulph and Burnard, 2022; Biddulph and Hewitt-Clarkson, 2023; Goodall and Ward-Sinclair, 2023)? The tension here is that while on an individual level difference may be valued, at a school and systems level, the propensity is to lean towards standardisation and uniformity. This is probable and understandable given the system is for the mass. In the Vedic view, diversity references the spiritual identity (who we truly are) and therefore, the uniqueness of that spiritual identity and the belief that we are unique and same at once, means that diversity is celebrated as unity and as difference simultaneously.

These are important matters with which to wrestle because diversity in the contemporary world increasingly relates to division, conflict and fear. Unlike the current polarised discourse in the West, the Vedic system allows all truths to co-exist. The ancient Indian story of six blind men touching different parts of the elephant and being unable to understand that they are simply 'touching' different parts of the same truth is a famous illustration of the multifaceted nature of truth.

Dilemma 3: grounding in love

I was interviewing prospective teachers for a role in the school. At the end of the interview, as is common practice, the panel asked, "do you have any questions for us?" The interviewee paused and then asked, "in your opinion what makes the very best teacher?"

What a question, I thought! I pondered and my gut answer came quickly:

> It seems contrite, but the best teachers are those who really like children. The ones who enjoy children's company, who find them curious, who suspend their own assumptions, their beliefs based on their own experiences of schooling and do everything possible to connect with the child, right in front of them. While the children are in the building, they deal with the children and everything else is for after.

We paused.

> So…in essence, when I meet a teacher who really *really* enjoys the whole idea of spending so many hours in the company of children and young people, I can feel it in the classroom, because the children know that they are liked and the relationships seem supremely wonderful. And that is when I see the very best teaching. It is a sacred moment. It starts with love.

Reflection from James Biddulph's Journal | 2020

The use of the word and concept of love in educational discourse remains relatively uncommon in the UK, "the word seems out of place in a world of outcomes, accountability and standardised tests" (Miller, 2000, p. 31). Similarly conflicting is framing the aims of education in relation to the soul and its enactment through life (Miller, 2000; Schweig and Gor, 2021). Yet, critical scholarship has begun to open space for such perspectives and scholars throughout history, in various contexts, have been pointing to the value of spirituality in education. Education, as an act of love and imagination (Schweig and Gor, 2021), has the potential to form compassionate democratic citizens who might contribute to a more just and hopeful world (Biddulph and Baldacchino, 2023).

As Alison Peacock writes in her forward to this book, too often education is framed by politicians as a costly problem to be fixed, tinkered with, or reformed in piecemeal ways. Rarely is it recognised as the powerful means of spiritual empowerment and liberation it can and must be. Have we arrived at the time of human existence when, "...we can reclaim our souls. Instead of denying and oppressing the soul, we can learn to let the soul manifest itself in the world. Instead of confining the soul, we can learn to celebrate the soul. By reclaiming the soul, we find that the classroom, or any educational encounter, takes on new vitality and purpose" (Miller, 2000, p. 4)?

Harmonising the relationship between the soul and it's yearning to make sense is a leitmotif in this book and why education for the soul is needed. Rabindranath Tagore, the great Bengal polymath (poet, writer, playwright, composer, philosopher, social reformer and painter) saw education as a means of awakening the soul through harmony with nature, creativity and the divine, writing that "the highest education is that which does not merely give us information but makes our life in harmony with all existence" (Tagore, 1929, p. 120). Similarly, the educational experiments at Yasnaya Polyana (a school that Leo Tolstoy established providing an innovative exploration of his educational philosophy and deep convictions about the transformative power of schooling) gave him the opportunity to examine how learning manifested for peasant children; he emphasised moral and spiritual freedom, insisting that "the essence of education lies in the freedom and development of the individual soul" (Tolstoy, 1967, p. 45).

Another of our inspirations is Bede Griffiths, a 20th century monk and philosopher, whose eclectic sojourn into the mystery of soul, spirit and the divine sojourned both West and East traditions. In *The Golden Thread,* he challenges one-sided scientific interpretations of lived experiences; instead, his message is to deepen our knowledge of the mystery which lies beyond materialism or scientific interpretation:

> For science as such is only concerned with phenomena, that is, with things as they appear to the senses: its function is, in the Greek phrase, to "save the phenomena", to account for the appearance of things. But of the reality which underlies the appearance of the real nature of things, science can give us no knowledge at all. We only begin to awake to reality when we realise that the material world, the

> world of space and time, as it appears to our senses, is nothing but a sign and a symbol of a mystery which infinitely transcends it. That is why the images in the palaeolithic cave were painted in the dark; it is only when we have passed beyond the world of images that we can enter into communion with the mystery which lies beyond.
>
> (Griffiths, 2003, p. 179)

We do not deny that science offers significant and often profound insights into the nature of the world. Yet to reduce learning solely to the empirical is to truncate human understanding (see Briggs and Reiss, 2021). This reduction is presented in *Auguries of Innocence,* another poem by William Blake (1863), in which he explores the infinite in the finite and (in the last stanza) the wide-awakeness that arises when we move beyond seeing through our eyes to instead exploring the world and the self through spiritual eyes – through the eyes of love.

> To see a world in a grain of sand
> And a heaven in a wild flower,
> Hold infinity in the palm of your hand
> And eternity in an hour.
> …
> We are led to believe a lie
> When we see not thro' the eye
> Which was born in a night to perish in a night,
> When the Soul slept in beams of light.
> God appears and God is light
> To those poor souls who dwell in night,
> But does a human form display
> To those who dwell in realms of day.
>
> William Blake (1863), "Auguries of Innocence"
> from *Poems, ed. Dante Gabriel Rossetti*

The exclusion of the spiritual – those emotive, intuitive, affective, embodied, loving and experiential dimensions of knowing – risks narrowing education to the measurable and the visible alone. Such a denial diminishes the possibility of a more comprehensive awareness of the world as it appears to us, of our purpose within it, and of that which ultimately transcends it. Indeed, "science and spirituality mediated by philosophy could enable young people to address foundational questions of life with greater openness and alacrity" (Das, 2026, p. 171). Jiddhu Krishnamurthi, scholar and thought leader, wrote beautifully about the wider purposes of education and of living, balancing science, conventional purposes of education, with something deeper and life-giving-meaning-creating:

> Education is not just to pass examinations, take a degree and enjoy, get married and settle down...but also to be able to listen to the birds, to see the sky, to see the extraordinary beauty of a tree, and the shape of the hills, and to feel with them, to be really, directly in touch with them
>
> (Krishnamurthi, 1974, p. 8)

He is talking about love in education and education as loving encounter with the world, the self, community and the beyond (Krishnamurthi, 1974). Referencing the *Śrīmad Bhāgavatam*,[4] Nitesh Gor explains different forms of love which, if translated into the context of education, might point toward opportunities to advance a pedagogy and educational experience that achieves what Krishnamurthi is suggesting: (1) appreciation as a sense of wonder and awe, (2) service described at attitude of supporting and helping others, (3) friendship as a well-wisher where competitive qualities are reduced, (4) guardianship as protection and guidance (Gor, 2025, pp. 240–241). In such classrooms, worth is not reducible to exam results; rather, learners encounter themselves as inherently valuable and capable of acting with courage, integrity and compassion. There becomes a sense of agency. One of the learners at Avanti Schools Trust emphasises the value of relationship-making so inherent in his educational experience:

> ...it [Avanti] is ripe with opportunity. In every door, every window of Avanti, every time you cross, like through the threshold into that classroom you know you will be fulfilled...I feel that the teachers at this school, you bond to them instantly. They feel like real people, they bond with you, they share stories that are related to the learning. They don't just teach for the job, they teach with a passion, and I think that is so incredibly important, and that's why I love the teachers at Avanti.
>
> Jake[5] | aged 13 | recorded in 2025

Although not the only themes explored in this book, equality, diversity and love stand as vital considerations, qualities that remain profoundly human in an age when artificial intelligence is beginning to make life or death decisions and permeate almost every aspect of our lives. Entering the second quarter of the 21st century, such things are not only timeless ideals but urgent necessities for shaping education, leadership and society itself.

Questions for the journey

We have presented many interconnecting questions. In sum: if every classroom and school is a kind of Kurukshetra, a field of dilemmas, decisions and possibilities, then perhaps educators today, like Arjuna, could pause and ask:

- What is education for?
- What is the point?
- What else might be?
- Where and how can we be bold and respond positively, hopefully and imaginatively?
- How shall we act?

Ancient philosophy will not necessarily answer these questions for us. But it may help us to dwell in them more deeply and differently, and to see that education depends not only on policy and metrics, but on the wisdom with which we choose to act. In this way, the field of education becomes more than a site of instruction or reform; it becomes a field of becoming, where questions of meaning, purpose and ultimately soul, must be faced.

Notes

1 The *Bhagavad Gītā* – A dialogue on the battlefield of Kurukṣetra between Arjuna and Krishna, offering a timeless synthesis of philosophy, ethics and spirituality.

2 *Arjuna* a warrior prince of the Pandava dynasty, is the central disciple of Krishna in the *Bhagavad Gītā*. On the battlefield of Kurukshetra, his moral crisis prompts Krishna's teachings on duty, selflessness and spiritual wisdom. Arjuna embodies the human struggle between doubt, conscience and the pursuit of righteous action.

3 *Krishna*, revered as the Supreme Personality of Godhead in Vaishnava tradition, is the divine charioteer and guide of Arjuna in the *Bhagavad Gītā*. He reveals timeless truths on dharma (purpose), devotion and liberation, teaching surrender to the Divine as the path to eternal peace and loving union with God. He is also a teacher and good friend of Arjuna.
4 *The Śrīmad Bhāgavatam has four 'seed' verses that were spoken by Krishna (the Supreme Lord) as inspirational knowledge to Brahma (the secondary universal creator and engineer). These seed verses were expanded over time and reached their complete form soon after the Mahabharata war, close to 5,000 years ago. It is a compilation – made by Vyasa, the same compiler of the four Vedas – of narratives that convey and explain the essential philosophical and theological teachings of Hinduism in significant depth.*
5 Pseudonym.

4 Viewing the battlefields in life

An age of quarrel and hypocrisy

There is another battlefield within which the soul of education sits. There is growing recognition that prevailing models of social, economic and ecological organisation are unsustainable. Humanity is consuming natural resources at rates that exceed planetary limits, accelerating biodiversity loss and contributing to a human-induced mass extinction of species (Biddulph, Shuckburgh and Pearse, 2026). Environmental degradation now poses direct risks to human wellbeing, while extreme global inequalities compound these pressures, leaving already marginalised communities disproportionately exposed to harm. Social cohesion is increasingly strained, and climate-related disruptions threaten access to basic provisions such as food, water and shelter. Alongside these material challenges, many societies are experiencing a crisis of meaning, characterised by declining sense of purpose, belonging and hope, particularly among young people.

In the Vedas, there is a concept called *Kali Yuga*, often translated as "the Age of Quarrel and Hypocrisy," which provides a useful interpretive lens for reflecting on these conditions; it is a period characterised by social and moral decline, in which wisdom, truth, and integrity are progressively eclipsed by materialism, fragmentation and short-term interests. Texts such as the *Śrīmad Bhāgavatam* (Bhaktivedanta Swami Prabhupāda, 2013, pp. 12.2.1–12.2.20) describe a paradoxical era of external advancement accompanied by inner deterioration.

For contemporary education, this perspective has important implications. If young people are growing up in a world marked by ecological precarity and social fragmentation, education cannot be limited to instrumental or economic aims alone. It must also engage with questions of meaning, values, and inner (trans)formation. In this sense, attending to the soul in education is not a peripheral concern, but a necessary response to the conditions

DOI: 10.4324/9781003487654-5

shaping human life in the present era. As we write, we are aware of the criticism that some might levy towards what might be considered a 'progressive' notion of education. The question remains: is what we are delivering children and young people meeting their needs in a world that is fraught with fast paced challenges and fractured kaleidoscopic difficulties?

As we have noted throughout in other aspects of the Vedic philosophy, the metaphysical framing of *Kali Yuga* may not resonate with you; yet, many of the qualities that *Kali Yuga* seeks to describe are nevertheless keenly felt in contemporary life, even if they are not named in the way the Vedas suggest. To situate education and its purpose more coherently, and to show why we think bringing soul and spirituality back into education with more concerted effort, we identified twelve manifestations of this so-called age of quarrel and hypocrisy – an age of dualities:

- Information overload versus Wisdom decline
- Connectivity versus alienation
- Material prosperity versus spiritual poverty
- Longevity versus vitality
- Freedom of choice versus paralysis of too much choice
- Global interconnectedness versus social fragmentation
- Education expansion versus decline of character education
- Environmental awareness versus environmental destruction
- Technological empowerment versus human disempowerment
- Abundance of food versus increased malnutrition and poverty
- Rights and freedoms versus inequality and oppression
- Expression versus censorship

In examining each one, we invite you to reflect on how these dynamics may surface in your own lives, communities, or workplaces and to consider both the challenges they pose and the possibilities they open for more conscious, values-driven responses. Taking each in turn, we offer a brief overview to relate the dilemmas to our lived experiences and in the context of our school classrooms.

1. Let us begin with the overload of information and the reduction in wisdom. The volume of information available to humanity today is unprecedented: a smartphone can open repositories of knowledge that once required years of travel or specialised access. Yet, this extraordinary

abundance coincides with a decline in discernment. Neil Postman's classic warning that modern society suffers from "a glut of information and a scarcity of wisdom" (Postman, 1985) seems prophetic in the age of generative AI, search engines, and social media feeds. The challenge is not how to access knowledge but how to interpret it. Young people are able to summon answers instantly, but too often without the capacity to judge their trustworthiness. Influencer-driven half-truths appear as persuasive as painstakingly verified scholarship. Here, schools face a profound task: not merely producing efficient processors of data but cultivating what Aristotle once called *phronesis* – practical wisdom, the ability to discern what is good, just, and appropriate. If education reduces itself to information delivery, it risks abandoning the very qualities that make knowledge humane and purposeful. We are not suggesting that teaching children knowledge is no longer relevant – that would play into the polarised discourse which we challenge in our discussions herein.

2. The paradox of information without wisdom is mirrored by another: connectivity without community. Billions of people are digitally linked, yet loneliness is now recognised as a public health crisis, severe enough for the UK to appointed a Minister for Loneliness. Sherry Turkle (2011) has described this paradox poignantly as being 'alone together' – perpetually connected, yet profoundly isolated. Social media platforms that promise belonging often transform the human self into a metric. Young people growing up in this environment may experience their worth as contingent on likes or how many followers, even while lacking deep relationships of trust. Schools stand at a crucial threshold. The pressing question is whether we will educate young people to be known as commodities in an algorithmic market or known as persons within human community. How schools foster community and belonging is vital.
3. Material prosperity adds to the contradictions of our age. For some, life has never been richer in terms of material goods, instantaneous entertainment, or consumer choice. Yet psychological distress, anxiety, and depression are rising rapidly, particularly among adolescents (Twenge, 2017). Amartya Sen's (1999) capability approach helps to illuminate the tension: prosperity measured by material resources is insufficient if it does not expand what people are truly able to be and do. Schools encounter this paradox daily. Some children arrive overstimulated from screens, others arrive hungry due to economic precarity, and all are

increasingly aware of the existential threat of climate change. Prosperity without inner awareness produces not flourishing people but fragility and insecurities. Education is therefore about reframing material abundance as gratitude. How can we enable children to encounter prosperity not as a hollow promise but as a resource to be redirected towards generosity and meaning? And also to look beyond materialism to identify what might make them truly whole?

4. Most of the world's population is living much longer than ever before. The tension between longevity and vitality sharpens the picture about the value constructs young people make in their lives. Medical advances now extend life expectancy across much of the globe. Yet vitality, the zest and energy of living well, appears to be in decline. Adolescents report unprecedented levels of burnout and anxiety (WHO, 2021), while adults often live extended lives accompanied by chronic illness. Zygmunt Bauman (2005) observes that late modern life is increasingly "liquid" – longer but more fragmented, insecure and fragile. Schools witness this in learners arriving hyper-stimulated, under-rested, and physically inactive. Extending life without deepening vitality risks producing 'long calendars with thin days.' What if education were restructured not only to prepare for future employment but to sustain a life worth living? Practices such as breathwork, outdoor learning, artistic engagement and digital hygiene are crucial acts of recalibration.
5. Choice through a powerful consumer culture is very much part of contemporary life. Choice, however, also reveals a paradox. Barry Schwartz (2004) described the "paradox of choice," in which abundance of options produces not liberation but paralysis. Modern societies celebrate choice as the very essence of freedom, yet for many young people, excess choice generates anxiety rather than empowerment. Learners are counselled to keep every door open, but the result is often indecision and exhaustion. Consumer culture reinforces this paralysis, with endless scrolling on streaming platforms or online shopping sites leading to dissatisfaction rather than fulfilment. Freedom without orientation becomes a new bondage. Education therefore has a formative responsibility: to cultivate discernment. Mentoring, reflective pedagogy, and encounters with exemplars can help young people to commit – to say a larger "yes" that allows other doors to close. In the words of Sen (1999), development is not merely expanding choice but fostering the capabilities to choose well.

6. The contradictions intensify when we consider globalisation. Ulrich Beck (2006) portrays ours as a world where crises such as pandemics and climate change tie humanity together in shared vulnerability. Yet, the very conditions that demand unity are accompanied by increasing polarisation, populism and mistrust. Young people are taught the ideals of global citizenship (Nussbaum, 1997) but simultaneously encounter culture wars and polarised media that reward contempt over dialogue. The deeper task is to form young people capable of holding difference within bonds of respect, developing civic courage that resists both bland relativism and aggressive dogmatism. The provocation is simple but urgent: what does it mean to educate for global knowledge?
7. The paradox of expansion without depth appears most acutely in education itself. Opportunities for formal schooling and higher education have expanded enormously across the globe, yet this expansion has not always been matched by the cultivation of character. Martha Nussbaum (2010) warns that when education becomes primarily instrumental – valued for its economic utility rather than its humanistic role – societies risk producing "useful machines rather than complete citizens." Credentials multiply, but humility, integrity, and empathy often wither. This imbalance is felt from early childhood, where play and moral formation are sidelined by relentless test preparation, to higher education, where universities pursue rankings more than wisdom. The question: if education is reduced to credentialing, what remains of its formative power? In relation to the rise of AI, what will we expect humans to do in the future and how will technology make us redundant? Surely, we now need to reimagine the purpose of education.
8. A further paradox lies in the realm of ecology. Never before have human beings been so aware of environmental limits, yet ecological destruction accelerates (Biddulph, Shuckburgh and Pearse, 2026). Bruno Latour (2017) has argued that modernity has failed to reconcile human progress with ecological boundaries. Governments pledge net zero while subsidising fossil fuel industries; schools teach children about recycling while corporations expand single-use plastics. Knowledge does not automatically produce transformation. The gap between awareness and action reveals a deficit of moral courage. For schools, the task is not simply imparting ecological facts but cultivating

habits that will change ways of living now and for the futures when our learners become adults and leaders in their own right. What if education were structured around stewardship rather than consumption? What might that look like in classrooms across the globe? Could we imagine learning environments where reverence for the earth is as central as numeracy and literacy?

9. Technology embodies perhaps the starkest paradox of all. Shoshana Zuboff (2019) describes our era as one of "surveillance capitalism," in which human experience is mined for behavioural prediction and control. Devices and algorithms extend human capacities but simultaneously constrain human agency. From classrooms shaped by personalised learning dashboards to workplaces governed by algorithmic surveillance, the paradox is empowerment without autonomy. The danger is invisible authority: systems we cannot see or question, but which nonetheless shape our choices. Consider, for example, 'drone armies' with AI selected targets outside human control. Schools must therefore equip young people to interrogate technology, to understand not only how to use tools but how to preserve human dignity within their use. The critical question is: will future citizens be passive users of opaque systems, or active shapers of technologies aligned with human flourishing?
10. Another symptom is food systems which offer another sobering contradiction. Humanity produces sufficient food for all, yet hunger persists alongside obesity and diet-related diseases. Sen (1981) demonstrated decades ago that famines often arise not from scarcity but from failures in distribution and entitlement. Today, this insight remains tragically relevant. Urban 'food deserts' coexist with overstocked supermarkets; agricultural subsidies favour monocultures that exhaust the soil while small farmers' struggle. Crises of climate change and war only magnify these inequities. Schools can make a decisive difference by embedding food literacy: school gardens, cooking lessons, and teaching that connects biology, ethics and geography. How might young people learn to see food not merely as commodity but as shared trust, an ecological and moral act? There was also the disturbing experience of watching supermarkets rapidly empty of food supplies during COVID. It was a stark indication of how utterly dependent we all are on supply chains outside our locale. Few grew their own food and even fewer would know how to source food in the wild.

11. The paradox of rights without justice emerges in political life. Formal frameworks increasingly enshrine human rights, yet structural inequities persist. Iris Marion Young (1990) reminds us that injustice is not merely the violation of formal rights but the perpetuation of structures that exclude and marginalise. Despite legislative progress, gender pay gaps, racial discrimination, and inequities in accessibility persist. Education must therefore go beyond recounting injustices to equipping young people to act against them. Paulo Freire's (1970) critical pedagogy insists that education must be a practice of freedom, enabling learners to read the world and act to transform it. The provocation is unavoidable: will education reproduce superficial freedoms or form citizens courageous enough to pursue deeper justice? To that question are the issues that Dewey (1916, 1934, 1938), Greene (1973, 1978, 1988, 1995, 2000) and Biddulph and Baldacchino (2023) refer as democratic education.
12. Finally, expression itself is caught in contradiction. Jürgen Habermas (1984) envisioned the public sphere as a space of rational-critical debate. Today, governments and corporations alike proclaim commitment to free speech while curtailing it when what is said proves inconvenient. In this crowded yet fragile public square, schools carry an urgent responsibility. Classrooms must become laboratories of dialogue, spaces where disagreement is practised with civility and truth is pursued collaboratively. The question here is twofold: what conditions allow speech to be both free and responsible, and how can education foster a public ethic of dialogue rather than an economy of outrage?

Summary

This all feels very overwhelming and, taken together, the paradoxes reveal not isolated dilemmas but a shared pattern: the erosion of wisdom, community, character, and justice in the face of abundance, power, and technological capacity. Each contradiction – information without wisdom, connection without communion, prosperity without depth, longevity without vitality, choice without orientation, unity without trust, education without character, awareness without action, technology without autonomy, food without justice, rights without equality and expression without dialogue – points to the same crisis within the education landscape: the loss of education's soul or core purpose.

What, then, does learning from *Kali Yuga* mean for modern education? Firstly, it calls us to recover purpose. In an age of paradoxes and confused priorities, schools must cultivate character, discernment and hope, grounded in the recognition of every learner as a bearer of irreducible worth. Knowledge becomes preparation for ethical judgement and action; dialogue, a discipline of truth-seeking. Secondly, *Kali Yuga* demands new professional practices: spaces for reflection, stillness and *phronesis*, integrating contemplative disciplines, critical pedagogy and service-learning. In this way, education moves beyond credentialing towards wisdom, community and courageous action.

The following questions invite all of us, whether or not we are familiar with this philosophy, to reflect on how the conditions of our time might echo what has been called the age of *Kali Yuga*:

- If you were writing a school report for our political leaders, what grade would you give for their integrity, consistency and sincerity or do you notice hypocrisy and contradictions?
- How is it that societies are advancing in wealth and technology, yet rates of loneliness, anxiety and suicide are rising especially among the young?
- In your own life, do digital connections make you feel closer to others, or strangely more isolated?
- Are you content with the state of the natural world – its forests, rivers, air and climate – or do you sense decline?
- Does your community feel hopeful and joyful, or does it carry a heaviness and confusion, even without clear reason?
- Do you sense that truth and lies are more tangled than ever, making it harder to discern what is real?

5 Exploring the lost soul of education

In this chapter, we start by tracing how the history of schooling from a largely Western and UK stance seems to have often overlooked the deeper needs of the soul. We then take a look at the ideas of key relevant historical thinkers. The purpose of the chapter is an embarkation point for our ongoing journey, to situate our position and manifesto that education without consideration of the soul is insufficient for human flourishing and indeed society's flourishing.

A (very) brief overview of the history of mass education: losing the soul?

Children born today will retire in or around the turn of the century, the year 2100. That is a sobering thought. What will their world be like? What knowledge and skills must they develop to navigate a complex life journey – one that seems more precarious, uncertain and fraught with risks than ever before (see Chapter 4)? Moreover, how can such questions be asked in a context where there are also undeniable advances in health, life expectancy, literacy and technology? The paradox of progress alongside growing disadvantage, inequality and social injustice remains unresolved. Today, even the very principles of diversity and inclusion are challenged by protectionist, nationalistic and myopic visions of society's future.

Perhaps every generation worries about what the future will hold for its young people. In 2010, the *Cambridge Primary Review* (Alexander, 2010) – one of the largest national reviews on primary education in the

 DOI: 10.4324/9781003487654-6

UK – asked precisely this question. Its recommendations were broad and hopeful, calling for a rich curriculum and a renewed vision of the purposes of schooling. Yet, its voice was quickly lost amid political change, rejected in favour of a narrower, knowledge-based and technocratic view of learning, one that privileged measurable outcomes over deeper human development. This rejection was not new. It was part of a long trajectory in which education, repeatedly, has been framed less as a pathway to human flourishing and more as a tool for economic productivity. In our sojourn of the history of education, we focus on four areas: economic aims, the tension between rhetoric and reality, inequality and the global spread of a UK model of education.

Andreas Schleicher, Director for Education and Skills at the OECD, writes that,

> We are facing unprecedented challenges – social, economic and environmental – driven by accelerating globalisation and a faster rate of technological developments. At the same time, those forces are providing us with myriad new opportunities for human advancement. The future is uncertain and we cannot predict it; but we need to be open and ready for it. The children entering education in 2018 will be young adults in 2030. Schools can prepare them for jobs that have not yet been created, for technologies that have not yet been invented, to solve problems that have not yet been anticipated. It will be a shared responsibility to seize opportunities and find solutions. To navigate through such uncertainty, students will need to develop curiosity, imagination, resilience and self-regulation; they will need to respect and appreciate the ideas, perspectives and values of others; and they will need to cope with failure and rejection, and to move forward in the face of adversity. Their motivation will be more than getting a good job and a high income; they will also need to care about the well-being of their friends and families, their communities and the planet.
>
> (Schleicher, 2018, p. 2)

There is also an irony in Schleicher's words given that it is also the OECD which collates, develops and promotes the PISA tests which have arguably narrowed the concept of a good education to core subjects and reduced understanding of educational success. There is something missing in the way we educate children and young people that seems to be rooted in the history of state education.

The development of state education in the UK: education as a means to wealth

Before the state assumed responsibility for schooling, education in England was local and diverse. Churches, charities, and private organisations provided instruction, often guided by religious and philanthropic motivations. The Industrial Revolution (c.1760–1870) transformed this landscape. Rapid advances in technology and mass production required a new workforce: disciplined, punctual, literate and numerate. Factories needed workers who could follow instructions, operate machinery, and accept hierarchical authority. The Elementary Education Act of 1870 (the Forster Act) marked a significant moment as the state formally assumed responsibility for education. Its intent was not primarily to nurture creativity or civic responsibility, but to secure the economic base of an industrialising nation. Schooling was to produce "useful" citizens – productive workers whose basic skills aligned with the needs of industrial capitalism. Industrial growth required industrial workers, and so an industrial education system was born.

This economic framing of education has proved remarkably resilient. Despite shifting political climates and educational philosophies, successive governments have continued to treat education as a means of economic growth. The assumption has been that investment in schooling would yield a proportionate increase in national prosperity. While education has many benefits, this narrow economistic view has come to dominate policy discourse, obscuring alternative purposes such as personal flourishing, democratic participation, or moral and spiritual development. The Christian ethos of schools did encourage good Christian behaviours from learners, but overwhelmingly the system's aim was to develop the economy. The parallel with today's technological revolution is striking. Just as the Industrial Revolution displaced agricultural workers, current debates about artificial intelligence raise existential questions about the future of work. Will AI become the threshing machine of our age, stripping us and our children of work and purpose? Or will it serve as a tool to extend human creativity and wellbeing? Such questions echo those first raised in the 19th century and remind us that education's purpose has always been entangled with shifting economic horizons.

Mid-20th century attempts to reframe education: rhetoric versus reality

The early 20th century witnessed a gradual broadening of educational purposes. Callahan (1962) describes the drive to scientific efficiency in managing schools in America as a pernicious force that left the system bereft of humanity. The tragedy as he analyses it is in the wholesale application of business models to the education system in the attempt to find efficiencies. In so doing, non-education qualified administrators made huge demands on teachers without awareness of what we suggest are the sacred interactions between teacher and learner that required more than finding cost saving efficiencies but instead needed life affirming, relational and multilayered competencies.

Alongside economic utility, policymakers began to emphasise social cohesion and civic responsibility. The 1944 Education Act in England was a landmark moment. It not only extended free secondary education to all but also articulated a vision of schooling that embraced the "spiritual, moral, mental and physical development" (SMSC) of children. Education was framed as a public good, vital to the reconstruction of society after the devastation of war.

The inclusion of spiritual, moral, mental and physical development in the 1944 Education Act established, in statutory form, a long-standing understanding of education in the UK as concerned with the formation of the whole person. Although later legislation refined this focus into what became known as SMSC, most notably through the 1988 Education Act and the inspection responsibilities of Ofsted from 1992 onwards, the underlying principle has remained consistent: schooling exists to nurture young people's personal and social development alongside academic achievement. However, it has often lacked a coherent overarching definition in practice. While inspection frameworks describe its individual components, they rarely articulate a unifying vision of human development. Focusing on the soul offers a way to strengthen the spiritual dimension of SMSC by naming the inner life of the learner: their sense of meaning, purpose, conscience and connectedness. Framed in this way, spiritual development is not an optional or "soft" addition, but the integrative core that gives coherence to moral, social and cultural learning.

The decades that followed saw attempts to embed this broader vision. The 1950s and 1960s highlighted child-centred education, social responsibility and personal growth. Progressive pedagogies emphasised creativity, play and holistic development, contrasting sharply with traditional models focused narrowly on discipline and rote learning. The debate between "progressive" and "traditional" education became polarised, yet it at least kept alive the notion that schooling could be about more than economic preparation.

However, rhetoric did not match reality. While legislation promised equality of opportunity, in practice the system remained stratified. Grammar schools, elite private schools and comprehensive schools coexisted, arguably reproducing class divisions. Within schools, children were differentiated through tracking, streaming and selective examinations. Structures of gender inequality persisted, and racial segregation – whether explicit, as in the US, or implicit, as in Britain – limited opportunities for many. Historians have shown that these inequalities were often justified by discourses of meritocracy and cultural superiority, masking the structural barriers that ensured privilege was reproduced (Kafka, 2019). While families and communities sometimes resisted, establishing alternative movements such as Waldorf Steiner schools, Free Schools or homeschooling, these options were most accessible to middle-income families. Far from resolving inequality, the education system often reinforced it, despite the rhetoric of reform. By the late 20th century, Britain's education system appeared progressive on paper but remained unequal in practice.

Inequality and the education-economy link: evidence from the UK, US and beyond

The persistent inequalities of schooling reveal the limits of treating education primarily as an economic instrument. The idea that education causes national wealth has been widely assumed but is increasingly questioned. Economists such as Pritchett (1996/2001) demonstrated that expanding schooling across developing countries did not automatically lead to economic growth. Instead, education's benefits depended heavily on wider institutional and social contexts. Bils and Klenow (2000) argued that causality often runs in the opposite direction: prosperity enables educational expansion rather than education creating prosperity. Easterlin's (1981) historical work reinforced this point, showing that economic growth frequently preceded mass education. It is also important to acknowledge here that technological innovation is leading to significant changes in the types of skills and knowledges that are required for economic growth.

Taken together, this evidence unsettles the comforting narrative that education is a straightforward engine of prosperity. While higher education may increase individual earnings, this effect does not aggregate neatly to the national level. Credential inflation means that as more people earn degrees, their relative value declines. Underemployment and "overqualification" have become common, particularly for younger graduates. In the UK, many recent graduates work in non-graduate jobs, a pattern echoed in the US, where nearly 40% of college graduates are underemployed according to the Federal Reserve Bank of New York.

This mismatch between educational attainment and economic opportunity reveals the fragility of the education-economy link. If raising education standards does not guarantee economic development, then the fundamental question remains: what is education really for?

Beyond the UK: the global spread of a soul-less model

The British model of industrial education was not confined to the UK. Exported through empire, it reshaped schooling across the globe. The National Society for Promoting the Education of the Poor, founded in 1811, promoted Anglican teachings and a vision of social order designed to reinforce hierarchy both domestically and across the empire.

India provides a striking case. By the time the British consolidated their control, centuries of invasion and internal decline had already weakened the subcontinent's rich and diverse educational traditions. The imposition of Victorian-style schooling, however, delivered the final and most enduring rupture. India's one million government schools today still bear traces of this colonial legacy: curricula and pedagogies remain tethered to rote learning, memorisation and examination. This industrial model of education displaced older, more holistic traditions rooted in dialogue, reflection, and spiritual cultivation. Nineteenth-century British administrators, driven by the dual imperatives of evangelism and empire, saw education as both moral mission and political instrument, a means to legitimise their 'right to govern' and to 'civilise' those under imperial rule. The result was a proselytising, industrial-style schooling system that effectively severed the link between education and the cultivation of the soul. Ironically, even as it claimed to nurture the Christian spirit, it replaced inner awakening with conformity, reflection with obedience and wisdom with efficiency.

This pattern is not unique to India. Across the world, colonial and postcolonial education systems mirrored Britain's emphasis on discipline, hierarchy and economic utility. While they brought undeniable benefits in terms of literacy and basic skills, they also embedded a vision of schooling that is narrow, instrumental and detached from the deeper purposes of human flourishing. In this sense, Britain exported not only mass education but also an education stripped of its soul. Today, as nations grapple with technological upheaval, ecological crisis and social fragmentation, the need to recover that soul is more urgent than ever.

(Re)searching for the soul of education

In preparing this book, we looked for the insights of relevant thinkers who through their life experiences wrote about their search for the meaning of life. Three themes arise: experience, virtues and simplicity.

In *Man's Search for Meaning,* Viktor Frankl affirms the soul's deepest yearning for meaning, and that love lies at the heart of this quest. How can love be part of the educational experience, not sentimental but essential, because "the salvation of man is through love and in love" (Frankl, 2004, p. 57)? Henry David Thoreau followed the yearning of his inner self: "I went to the woods because I wished to live deliberately," he wrote, longing to encounter only "the essential facts of life" and to "see if I could not learn what it had to teach" (Thoreau, 1995, p. 67). Thoreau's call to simplicity is more than aesthetic preference; it is a spiritual practice, an uncluttering of life so that the soul may encounter the Real without distraction. In a world that is increasingly complicated and fast paced, with many existential uncertainties, is there a way for educators to slow the pace of thinking and learning to allow for time to make sense of it all? Tolstoy suggested that it is not enough to rely on rational systems alone for life to gain meaning. Instead, he suggests that it is derived from listening, responding and grappling with the enduring call of conscience, love and responsibility to self and other (Tolstoy, 1967). Similarly, the pioneering Indian reformer Savitribai Phule (1831–1897), writing and acting in the mid-19th century, opened schools for girls and Dalit[1] children, framing education as a sacred duty to uplift the oppressed, insisting that ignorance was a form of spiritual bondage and that learning could liberate both soul and society.

Drawing from Rousseau's (1979) insistence that to exist is to feel, a soul-full education begins with the conviction that consciousness is not merely a rational faculty but an awakening to our deepest, most natural feelings. For Rousseau, conscience is a divine instinct, a primordial moral sense that arises before thought and guides us toward what is good by resonating within the heart. Such a view reframes education as an invitation to return to the inner sources of wisdom that modern noise, distraction and external judgment often silence.

Taking a next step back in history, our exploration took us to the 17th-century philosopher John Locke. In his treatise *Some Thoughts Concerning Education* (1693/1989), Locke argued that education was not simply about intellectual training but about shaping the moral and rational capacities of the soul through habit, discipline, and the cultivation of virtue. As he famously declared, "'Tis virtue then, direct virtue, which is the hard and valuable part to be aimed at in education" (Locke, 1693/1989, p. 92). For Locke, intellectual progress without moral formation was insufficient; education must attend to both character and understanding.

Locke's vision situates the soul as educable and responsive to environment, framing pedagogy as the means by which human beings become moral agents. He stressed that the child's development depended less on innate ideas than on experience, habit, and example: "Of all the men we meet with, nine parts of ten are what they are, good or evil, useful or not, by their education" (Locke, 1693/1989, p. 1). In this sense, Locke rejects predetermination and emphasises the transformative potential of education to cultivate freedom, reason, and virtue. His philosophy resonates strongly with contemporary discourses around character education and holistic learning, reminding us that education is not reducible to technical knowledge but is concerned with the formation of persons. In contrast, the Vedic philosophy explains that the individual soul does have its own unique qualities and purpose; as unique individual spiritual selves, the role of the educator is to nurture these innate qualities (one's true calling or purpose) in their learners, so that there is movement into greater self-awareness, realisation and full potential.

A few centuries before Locke was rethinking education in Europe, scholars in India were exploring a philosophy that resonates powerfully in a post-human post-truth contemporary world. It is called *acintya–bhedābheda*, or "inconceivable oneness and difference." Developed by *Śrī Caitanya Mahāprabhu*[2] (1486–1534) and his followers, this *Vedāntic* teaching addresses one of life's central questions: how does the individual, the universe and the Divine relate to each other? How are we interrelated and interconnected and also unique and separate?

A Vedic philosophical point: Inconceivable oneness and difference

The principle of *Acintya-bhedābheda* or 'oneness and difference' is simple to state but profound to grasp. In essence, all beings and all phenomena are simultaneously one with, and different from, the Divine (or Ultimate Truth). Before we expand on this complicated philosophical point, we invite you to consider these questions to explore the paradox of oneness and difference in a way that feels relevant to your everyday life, education and society:

- In a world that emphasises individual identity and self-expression, how do we also honour our deep interconnectedness with others and with the natural world?
- How might holding together both oneness and difference help us navigate tensions around diversity and unity in schools, communities, or nations?
- In relationships, what does it mean to see the other as both distinct and yet inseparably connected to ourselves?
- How might recognising our shared essence with all beings change the way we respond to issues such as climate change, inequality, to our choices of food or conflict?
- On a personal level, when have you experienced a moment of "one-ness" with nature, another person, or a community and how did that coexist with your own sense of individuality?

Acintya-bhedābheda is not just abstract metaphysics – it has real-world relevance. It finds expression in many aspects of life. For example, parents and children are distinct individuals, yet each sees themselves reflected in the other, with the child carrying forward something of the parent while being wholly new. Communities exist only through individuals, but shared values and rituals create a collective identity greater than its parts. As humans, we are one with nature in dependence and sustenance yet also experience ourselves as unique and imaginative beings.

This philosophical position is important for our concerns about equality, diversity and love. *Śrī Caitanya Mahāprabhu* was essentially saying that there can be individuality and connectedness at once, at the same time; holding both positions equally. For example, that there is one God, but many names. Or that there is one Truth, but many perceptions, experiences, understandings. The fact that there are such diversities does not negate or diminish the view that there remains an Ultimate force (or Supreme/Divinity/Truth/God) that is beyond the differing views. This is one of the reasons why he also said that God Consciousness is non-sectarian, that it is a Truth that is relevant for all people, no matter which country they come from, what languages they speak, their colour, creed, gender, sex, sexuality, age, etc. (though he did not specifically refer to such categories the message is inherent).

This complex philosophy is part of the ongoing dialogue in classrooms, staffrooms, offices and in the case of Meera and Sahil, in their car, as they drove to Avanti, where they work as Head of Philosophy Religion and Ethics and Head of Operations respectably.

A morning conversation on the way to work | Sahil and Meera Agrawal

Sahil: You know, Meera, I've been thinking about something you said the other day, that Krishna Consciousness is non-sectarian. What does that actually mean? I mean, it's rooted in a specific tradition, right? It's Hindu, no?

Meera: Well, "Sectarian" simply means something that's limited to a particular group, something exclusive by nature. It's like saying, "Only if you belong to this faith, or follow these rituals, can you reach God." Non-sectarian, on the other hand, is open. It recognises that there can be many paths toward the same goal.

Sahil: So, you're saying Krishna Consciousness isn't bound to one religion, even though it comes from the Vedic tradition?

Meera: Exactly. It's not about labels, it's about purpose. The Vedic view asks a simple question: What are we all trying to achieve? The answer is connection with the Divine. That is the essence of every spiritual pursuit. Whether someone calls that Divinity Krishna, Allah, Christ, or simply the Universe, it's the same search. The practices may differ, but the goal is identical.

Sahil: That makes sense. So, the Vedic perspective is that there are many routes to the divine?

Meera: Precisely. The sectarian approach says, "Only my route is valid." Krishna Consciousness says, "Here is one beautiful route, but take any that helps you realise your divine nature." That is why it is universal, not exclusive.

Sahil: You know, that reminds me of something I heard from Srila Prabhupada [the founder of the International Society for Krishna Consciousness ISKCON, also known as the Hare Krishna Movement], that he explained it's the same as science, which is non-sectarian when it seeks truth openly. Since anyone can practise the scientific process.

Meera: That's a lovely connection. Science, when practiced purely, doesn't belong to any sect. It's a process: you form a hypothesis, you experiment, you observe. The goal is truth. But when a scientist says, "There is no truth beyond what science can prove," then it becomes the sect of science.

Sahil: So, Krishna Consciousness is like a spiritual science. The hypothesis is that there's something beyond matter, the experiment is through connecting to divinity maybe through chanting, service, and meditation, the result is transformation, joy, and detachment for material longings.

Meera: Exactly. It invites everyone to try, to test, and to experience. No boundaries, no conversions, only a sincere journey toward the divine. That is what makes it truly non-sectarian.

Sahil works in Business Services at Avanti Schools Trust and Meera is Head of Philosophy, Religion and Ethics at Avanti House Secondary

In educational terms, Meera and Sahil's conversation about *Acintya-bhedābheda* and Krishna (God) Consciousness as non-sectarian invites a view of learning that is inclusive, dialogic and truth-seeking. Their morning chat models an approach to education where difference is not erased but embraced as part of a shared pursuit of understanding. Just as Meera describes many routes leading to the same goal, classrooms become spaces where multiple perspectives, cultures and worldviews coexist and are honoured. The teacher's role, like the spiritual guide she describes, is to facilitate enquiry rather than impose belief, to create conditions in which each learner can explore their own route to meaning while remaining connected to others through a common search for truth and goodness.

Sahil's link between spirituality and scientific enquiry adds another educational layer: both rely on curiosity, testing, reflection and openness to discovery. Education, then, becomes a 'spiritual science' in which learners are encouraged to experiment with ideas, to question, and to experience transformation through learning. In this light, *Acintya-bhedābheda* points toward an education that is universal yet personal, where the coexistence of individuality and unity mirrors both the diversity of learners and the shared human longing to know, to connect and to become.

In a world of polarised discourses, especially within education (the 'either/or,' the 'standards or creativity,' the 'high stakes accountability or professional autonomy,' etc) the philosophy promoted by *Śrī Caitanya Mahāprabhu*, allows for both and all to co-exist. We can have high standards and promote creativity. We can have high expectations of accountability and valued professional wisdom and autonomy. We can have individual progress and community flourishing together. In short, *Acintya-bhedābheda* offers a framework for our paradoxical age, made more relevant given that human identity is increasingly unstable because technology, AI and biotechnology blur the boundaries of what it means to be human.

Questions

- In preparing children for jobs that may not yet exist, are we neglecting the deeper task of helping them discover who they are and why their lives matter?
- When schools move faster each year (more content, more assessment, more pressure) where in a child's education is the space to pause, reflect and listen to the quiet voice of their own conscience and purpose?
- Where have you been successful in the education system and because of that success are you repeating systems and approaches with children in your schools because they worked for you?
- What must we let go of? What must we adapt? What must we create?

Notes

1 In the traditional Indian caste system, a member of the caste that is considered the lowest and that has the fewest advantages (Oxford Dictionary).

2 *Śrī Caitanya Mahāprabhu* (1486–1534) – Social and spiritual reformer whose life exemplifies the Vedic model of education. A brilliant scholar who taught grammar, logic and rhetoric before turning to a life of *bhakti* (devotion), showing that intellectual mastery reaches fulfilment in love of God and service to humanity.

Interlude

Summarising the concept of soul for the soul in education

In the first five chapters, we set out to ask a simple, unsettling question: what is education for if it loses its soul?

We began with the *Bhagavad Gītā,* a conversation between student and teacher in which Arjuna's education is a search into the nature of the Self, the purpose of life and the art of right action. In bringing diverse perspectives together, we see that the soul, whether conceived through psychology, philosophy or Vedic theology, represents the deepest dimension of human identity, the site of meaning, connection and becoming.

To make sense of the soul educationally is to recognise learning as both inward and outward movement: a process of awakening awareness, refining consciousness and aligning action with purpose. The emerging pedagogy of the soul therefore calls educators to integrate relational work, virtues and self-awareness into practice.

Before we focus in on particular beliefs, virtues and values of a Vedic-inspired inclusive education for the soul (a new terrain), let us take stock of the principles we have explored concerning the nature of the soul and its relationship with the material world.

We start with the concept that, "I have a body, but I am not my body… I have emotions, but I am not my emotions… I have thoughts, but I am not my thoughts" (Mahaffey, 2019, p. 182). To reiterate the difference between soul and body, Bhakti Charu Swami helpfully explains,

> When the soul leaves the body, the body ceases to function. Thus, death is the soul's departure from the body. At the outset, we should consider that the body is already dead. The body is made up of the elements of earth, water, fire, air and ether – all of which are inert and

DOI: 10.4324/9781003487654-7

> lifeless by nature. The body is thus composed of inert or dead matter. Therefore, it is logical to conclude that this gross [material] body in its physical form is dead. What then makes the body alive? The body is alive due to the presence of the soul. Based on this, consider who we really are…when we say "I", to whom are we truly referring? When I, the spirit soul, am in this body, the body is alive. When I, the spirit soul, leaves this body, the body dies but the soul remains…
>
> (Swami, 2025, pp. 21–22)

For the purpose of the thesis in relation to education, we understand the soul as:

> the conscious, spiritual self – distinct from the body and mind – whose essential nature is enduring existence, deep awareness, and inner joy.

It is the part of us that feels strong, joyful, hopeful and interrelated. The part that gets us through difficulties and helps us appreciate through awe, beauty and wonder, the awesomeness of self, others, the world and beyond all we can see, hear, feel and conceive. From a Vedic perspective, several key assumptions emerge:

> The first: that, in essence, we are spiritual beings (souls) and that the body we inhabit is temporary, evolving and ultimately ends with death. The soul, however, is ever existing; it is unique and also connected to something much bigger (some calling it the Divine). It is the sunshine but not the sun. It is the drop but not the ocean. It is same and different.
>
> The second: that the ultimate purpose of life is for the soul to become aware of its true nature and conscious of its relationships with something bigger than itself; something beyond self; which could be defined as Truth, Nature, Connection, Transcendence or the Divine (in whichever name is preferred).
>
> The third: that the soul can be educated through creating an environment, or a landscape of loving relationships, with opportunities to talk about spirituality that in turn spark new ideas, new awareness and a virtues-laden imaginative possibilities thinking.

If these concepts do not immediately resonate, perhaps because your personal understanding of spiritual identity is framed differently, or because you take a more humanistic perspective, the same principles might be expressed through the lenses of social justice, social responsibility or a recognition that, while we are each distinct individuals, our lives are profoundly interconnected (for readers who are interested in the psychology of spirituality we recommend Domash (2021), Miller (2015) Beauregard and O'Leary, (2007), Newberg and Waldman (2009) and Sheldrake (2017)). In this framing, the ideas might be understood as follows:

Uniqueness and agency: Each person possesses a distinctive identity and the capacity to exercise agency in shaping the course of their life.

Interconnection and responsibility: Our individuality is lived within a network of relationships and communities, calling us to make choices that contribute to collective wellbeing – locally, nationally, and globally.

Cultivating virtues: The virtues that sustain personal and communal flourishing can be nurtured in children and young people both explicitly, through intentional teaching, and implicitly, through the example set in everyday interactions and relationships.

PART B

Setting out on the Journey

Exploring six beliefs of the soul of education

6 Introducing six beliefs for human flourishing

This is a short chapter to introduce you to the six beliefs that we say contribute to human flourishing. Before we begin our presentation of the six beliefs identified in the Vedic tradition, we would like to introduce you to Katre[1] who was once a learner attending an Avanti Hindu faith School. Not a Hindu himself, in a short 'stories video' created as part of the Avanti social media, he articulated his own soul searching, guided by a set of beliefs about people, learning and the nature of relationships and connections. His opening words show the Avanti Way (the philosophical guide for Avanti Schools Trust) as both a guiding framework and a lived experience.

> "Hello, my name is Katre. I was originally born in Lithuania. Came to Avanti three years ago, joined in year 9. I am currently in Year 12.
>
> In Year 7, the school I initially went to I was surrounded by a very very bad crowd of people, drugs, knife, knife crime, gangs, all of that and just in general that reflected on my academics, on my personal life, my family was always concerned. I was caught coming back from school at 3am, 2am every single day.
>
> A big thing that was present at the time was post code wars and, as in like school v school violence, and I was around drugs, drug dealing, selling drugs, taking drugs, all of that, which was, you could imagine at the age of where I was between Year 7 and Year 8, and even a little bit further than Year 8, I was so young, yet my mind was cluttered with drugs, violence, knife crime, all of that, all of this gang family whatever business and that shouldn't be where such a young person's mind should be at.

DOI: 10.4324/9781003487654-9

> When I came here [Avanti school], it really put everything into perspective and showed me the bigger picture and showed me that I should not, not even be doing anything like that in my free time, let alone before or after school. I've been able to turn around my academics, be polite, respectful, composed and one of the main things Avanti has actually taught me was self–discipline and maturity, as now I can happily say that I'm who I want to be and growing closer to all that I want to achieve."
>
> Recorded as part of an Avanti voices project.

Katre's reflection shows how the beliefs and virtues extend beyond school, shaping discipline, maturity, and academic focus while strengthening his sense of identity.

What we hope to emphasise is that a Vedic approach is always situated in hope because the understanding of the soul is defined as non-born and non-dying, ever living and therefore with the opportunity for growth to realise true spiritual potential. Whilst this concept may not resonate completely with your world view, take for one moment the notion that our potential is inexhaustible because we are more than the physical body and more than the labels we associate with our identity (which we argue are limiting). Take for one moment that if we remove some of the initial labels (ability, SEND, gender, role, career etcetera) there is greater possibility to arrive at a philosophical position that sees the true essence of a person or any living thing; with that view, inclusion, interconnection and interrelatedness are even more likely. Richard Moran argues that hope is not naïve optimism but the courage to affirm possibilities in the face of uncertainty (2022). In another book referencing hope, Lars Svendsen makes a helpful distinction that: "hope is not the same as optimism; it is possible to hope without believing that the odds are in your favour" (2023, p. 17). He further suggests that "hope involves the refusal to accept the present as final" (Svendsen, 2023, p. 42), a stance that strongly aligns with the Vedic invitation; hope, therefore, lies not in denying the darker realities of our age but in cultivating the spiritual and moral capacities of the young, who are seen both in the Vedas and in contemporary philosophy as bearers of renewal and as those capable of imagining what is not yet, but might be and always in the process of becoming (Greene, 2000).

'The Avanti Way', a living philosophical framework which guides thinking at Avanti Schools Trust, and which is hopeful, expresses a spiritual philosophy of education inspired by the teachings of an Indian Hindu Saint named, *Śrī Caitanya Mahaprabhu*.[2] These six beliefs are a consolidation of what we believe are the essential principles that underly the soul's quest.

They provide a basis for the virtues and practices that Avanti seeks to nurture and promote, which we argue are important for the whole of society. Although these beliefs are not arranged in a hierarchy, they do follow a natural progression that helps to make sense from an educational perspective. We will explore each in turn but for now, briefly:

- Realising potential is a universal aspiration: nurturing each learner so their gifts unfold in service of the whole. Potential is not confined to material or social circumstances; it involves recognising capacities beyond immediate limitations.
- Yet, potential can only truly be realised if learners are empowered to make choices, acting with discernment and integrity amid life's complexities. To be human is to face choices, and to grow is to learn how to choose well. Education therefore cultivates reflective judgement, discernment and moral literacy so learners act responsibly for both their selves and society.
- Choice leads to interconnection. Our decisions are never made in isolation but within webs of relationship. Recognising interconnection means seeing beyond material difference to a deeper shared reality. *Śrī Caitanya Mahaprabhu* envisioned radical interconnectedness: all beings are linked to one another and the Divine (however conceived as God, nature, energy or consciousness). Strengthening this awareness invites gratitude, stewardship and care, countering the isolating tendencies of contemporary culture.
- Interconnection opens to diversity. When we honour diversity, we see truth refracted through many perspectives. *Śrī Caitanya Mahaprabhu* dissolved caste and social boundaries through communal singing of God's various names, anticipating modern calls for pluralism. In education today, diversity is more than tolerance: it is celebration, affirming gender, age, sexuality, race, culture and spirituality as lenses to a fuller reality. Classrooms that welcome varied contributions build bridges across differences and affirm our shared humanity.
- From this grows purpose: living with meaning, serving others, and contributing to the wellbeing of the world. For *Śrī Caitanya Mahaprabhu*, life's ultimate aim was *seva* (loving service).

- Finally, love binds all together. *Śrī Caitanya Mahaprabhu* placed divine love at the centre: not sentiment, but the highest form of knowledge. In education, this means cultivating relationships of trust, compassion and belonging, where teachers and learners flourish together.

What does this mean when considered altogether? In this framing, a learner shaped by these beliefs grows into a person who recognises their unique potential and seeks to use it for the good of others. They develop the capacity to make thoughtful choices, guided by discernment, integrity and moral awareness. Understanding that every decision affects others, they see themselves as part of an interconnected world and act with care for people, communities and the planet. They value diversity as a source of insight and creativity, welcoming different perspectives as pathways to deeper understanding. Such a person lives with purpose, motivated by service and contribution rather than self-interest alone. Grounded in compassion and belonging, they build relationships rooted in trust and respect, embodying a love that expresses itself through responsibility, gratitude, and a commitment to the flourishing of all.

Although these ideas come from the Hindu *Vaiṣṇava* tradition of *Acintya-bhedābheda* – the paradox of being both one and different – at their heart is a vision of human flourishing that goes beyond boundaries of religion or culture, echoing *Śrī Caitanya Mahaprabhu's* message of inclusive devotion, shared love, and the beauty of diversity. In this, the Avanti Way offers a framework not only for the Trust's schools but for contemporary education more broadly, placing soul, community, and service at the centre of learning.

What follows is a more in-depth exploration of each belief, taking each in turn. Each chapter begins with a short statement to summarise how each belief builds on the previous one. Each chapter ends with a narrative, drawing from James' professional experiences but not referring to any one particular child, teacher or context – they are a conglomerate of true vignettes and stories narrated to illustrate the six beliefs in practice.

Notes

1 Pseudonym.
2 Born in 1486 CE in Navadvīpa (present-day West Bengal, India) and passed away in 1534 CE in Purī, Odisha, India.

7 Realising potential

> We begin with a single, grounding belief: that every person has unlimited potential.

The word potential has often been used to cap the progress or to suggest that everyone has a potential that is limited, predefined or predetermined (Peacock, 2015). To illustrate this, in a rewritten conversation (drawn from the same conversation James has had over many years with various parents and educators), the system's emphasis on diagnosis and labelling, illustrates how 'potential' has the potential to limit learning.

I am always curious about how we make children feel valued, welcomed with a sense of belonging. I am also conscious how the system encourages labelling of children and young people that could limit the realisation of their true potential. This is a remembered narrative of conversations I have had with a number of educators.

I was visiting a school and saw a child who was dysregulated. I sat and observed how he was engaging and how the Teaching Assistant (TA) was working well with him. She came to sit next to me when the young man was beginning to engage with his friends.

James: Hi, lovely to see you. So, tell me about this young man.
Teaching Assistant: He is SEND.
James: I mean, tell me his story.

DOI: 10.4324/9781003487654-10

Teaching Assistant: He is Autistic.

James: Yes, but what is his story? Does he have a sibling? What about his family life?

Teaching Assistant: No child protection issues and he has a younger sister. He cannot work independently and does not work well in groups. His speech and language isn't good or his handwriting so we have to scribe for him mostly.

James: And what does he like to do? What is he good at?

Teaching Assistant: Ah. He has many things.

What followed was a stream of consciousness, telling me about all the qualities of the child, who was excellent at maths and technology, who liked being with a few friends, although he did not speak much with them, and who liked to run but didn't like to catch balls, who needed clear boundaries and instructions and very few changes in the school day, who felt sad at any transition and didn't like to eat peas.

But what I noticed is how we typically start with what children cannot do; their limitations, labels and deficits occupy the space; the positives, strengths and skills feature as secondary – if remembered at all.

James' reflections | Personal Journal, August 2025

As we have suggested, in our modern educational landscape, the relentless pursuit of achievement, success, and performance often overshadows a more profound understanding of human potential. This focus on outcomes – on scores, accolades, and the visible markers of 'success' – whilst the process to achieve economic, social and cultural capital is limiting and can even become a detraction from the deeper, essential qualities that everyone possesses. Beneath these external measures, there lies within each of us – children, parents and teachers alike – an incredible potential that is boundless and multidimensional, waiting to be nurtured on intellectual, emotional, physical and spiritual levels. To tap into this latent potential requires a transformative approach to education, one that not only imparts knowledge but awakens the self.

Layered identities: uncovering the concentric circles of self

We use the word potential differently. The Vedas teach that human beings are inherently complex, multi-layered and constantly evolving. Our lives are woven from many threads, each expressing a different facet of who we are. As we grow, some of these threads, our identities, shift, deepen or transform. Yet, within Vedic philosophy, there is an understanding that at the centre of every person lies an essential being: a core self, untouched by external labels or expectations. These external labels may include our family background, language, cultural traditions, gender, sexuality, race, friendship groups and, more recently, the identities we construct within the two-dimensional realms of technology and artificial intelligence. Despite their influence, these labels do not fully define us.

This inner core represents our purest essence, unfiltered by the roles society asks us to play. Surrounding it, we gather a constellation of identities that express different dimensions of our lived experience. Some identities are inherited, some consciously chosen, and others emerge gradually through time and circumstance. A helpful way to picture this is to imagine the self as a series of concentric circles. At the centre is the unchanging core, while each surrounding ring represents a distinct layer of identity, together forming the richness and dynamism of who we are.

This understanding of layered identity aligns closely with Erik Erikson's theory of psychosocial development, which emphasises that identity formation is an ongoing, dynamic process shaped by life experiences and the social roles we inhabit. Erikson argued that at each stage of life, individuals confront particular developmental challenges that influence their sense of self, gradually guiding them towards a more integrated and coherent identity.

For instance, during adolescence, young people navigate what Erikson termed the stage of *identity versus role confusion*. This is a period marked by exploration: experimenting with different roles, responding to social expectations, and discerning which aspects of self to feel authentic. It is also a time when external influences, peers, culture, social media and emerging digital identities can heavily shape one's self-perception. Here, the metaphor of concentric circles can be particularly helpful, enabling young people to recognise which roles or labels are central to who they are and which represent more temporary or situational layers.

In everyday life, this layered structure might appear in many ways. At the centre lie deeply rooted identities – personal values, spiritual beliefs and intrinsic qualities such as empathy, curiosity or courage. Surrounding this core are identities shaped by cultural, ethnic or national contexts, which offer belonging and orientation but remain dependent on circumstance. Further outward sit socially ascribed identities, such as "student," "young person," or "athlete." These roles provide structure and purpose yet do not capture the fullness of the individual's essence.

By seeing identity as layered rather than fixed, young people can appreciate that each dimension contributes to how they understand themselves, while also recognising that no external label or role has the power to define them entirely. Instead, identity becomes something to explore, refine, and inhabit with increasing self-awareness.

Education can play a profound role in helping learners discern between their authentic self and the roles they play. Imagine a young person struggling with the identity of being 'the quiet young person.' They may internalise this label, seeing it as an unchangeable part of who they are. However, when they are supported in seeing this as merely one outer layer, they gain the freedom to redefine themselves. This process aligns with psychologist Carl Rogers' concept of the 'fully functioning person' – someone who is open to new experiences, authentic in self-expression, and guided by an inner locus of control rather than external pressures. By fostering this inner journey, education can help individuals step beyond labels and social expectations to live more fully.

Spirituality: the journey from superficial to essential

If we envision ourselves through these concentric circles, spirituality emerges as the journey inward – a peeling away of the outer layers to reveal the essence of self. This journey involves introspection and the recognition that many of the roles and labels we cling to are temporary garments that do not define our true nature. In spiritual terms, this journey is often described as a process of 'letting go' of the ego – the part of us that is entangled in external validations and social constructs.

This inward journey is a theme in many philosophical and spiritual traditions. In Vedic terms, the practice of self-enquiry is an introspective method aimed at peeling away the layers of the self. By questioning the origins of thoughts, emotions and identities, practitioners gradually separate themselves from transient identities, realising a deeper, unchanging essence. According to this philosophy, our core self – the *Ātman*[1] – is beyond all social and material identifiers; it is eternal and indivisible, and reaching this understanding is the pinnacle of spiritual growth.

Similarly, Buddhist philosophy speaks to this journey of moving beyond the constructed self. In Buddhism, the concept of 'anatta,' or non-self, teaches that the self is not a fixed, permanent entity but a collection of experiences, thoughts and memories. The path to enlightenment involves understanding the illusory nature of the ego and detaching from it. For learners, recognising the non-permanent, constructed nature of identity can free them from rigid self-definitions, allowing for personal growth and the realisation of a more fluid, adaptable sense of self.

In an educational setting, guiding learners and educators on this journey towards the core self can help them recognise the limitations of identity-based labels. We begin to see that beneath the roles of 'young person,' 'teacher' or 'leader' lies a deeper self not defined by race, gender, or occupation but by an intrinsic humanity shared across all people. Spirituality, then, invites us to identify less with the transient and more with the timeless, moving beyond the outer layers to align with our essential nature.

Spiritual practices, whether theistic or non-theistic, serve as tools on this journey. Mindfulness practices, for instance, help individuals observe their thoughts and emotions without attachment, creating space between the self and fleeting experiences. Meditation offers a similar pathway, inviting practitioners to turn inward, beyond social identities, towards a place of stillness. Reflective practices, such as journaling, can also serve as a mirror, revealing to us the layers of our identity and helping us to discern what feels true. Creative expression, like art or music, similarly opens a channel to the soul, giving form to our inner lives and connecting us with something greater.

For learners, such practices can be integrated into the school day through brief mindfulness exercises, creative sessions or quiet reflection times. These activities allow learners to step away from the demands of external achievement and reconnect with their own sense of inner value. Over time, this inward journey builds a resilience and self-assurance that is not tied to academic or social validation, fostering a sense of purpose that sustains through life's inevitable ups and downs.

Reducing dependence on superficial identities

The Vedic philosophy reminds that the significant outcome of the journey towards the essential self is that we reduce our dependence on superficial identities, thus liberating ourselves from the constraints these labels often impose. Many of our outer identities come with societal expectations and norms that create artificial boundaries, limiting our understanding of self-worth and potential. In education, where learners are often defined by grades, behaviours and roles within the classroom, these boundaries can be particularly constrictive. Consider the example of a young person labelled as 'gifted.' This identity can bring pride but also anxiety, as it raises expectations and pressures. The fear of failure can become overwhelming, leading the young person to feel that any struggle diminishes their core worth. Conversely, a child labelled as 'underperforming' may internalise this label, feeling as though their potential is capped by the academic metrics assigned to them. These labels are ultimately restrictive because they reduce complex human beings to simplified roles. Anthony Seldon has spoken about the need to reflect on our assumptions about children and young people to check that we are not knowingly or inadvertently projecting the adults' desires and expectations onto the young person's emerging sense of self. For some families, the answer to the question "what do you want to do when you are grown up?" is limited to doctor, engineer, lawyer and dentist.

Jean-Paul Sartre's existentialist philosophy argues that existence precedes essence. According to Sartre, human beings are not defined by pre-existing roles or identities but are free to create and recreate themselves. For Sartre, identifying solely with societal roles is akin to living in bad faith, where one denies their inherent freedom by conforming to external labels. In an educational setting, supporting learners in reducing their reliance on superficial identities can liberate them to explore their potential without fear or constraint.

Additionally, Erich Fromm's (1976) concept of 'being' versus 'having' offers insight into the drawbacks of clinging to roles and labels. Fromm argued that modern society encourages a mode of existence based on possession – we define ourselves by what we have, including our titles, achievements, and possessions, rather than who we inherently are. By teaching learners to value 'being' over 'having,' educators can help them cultivate an identity that is resilient, rooted in intrinsic worth, and not reliant on external markers of success.

Spiritual growth, however, offers an alternative path, say the scriptural texts. Rooted in a spiritual identity, learners and educators alike can navigate life with resilience, free from the limitations of external achievements and perceived shortcomings. This aligns with Carl Jung's notion of individuation – a process through which individuals integrate the many facets of their psyche to achieve wholeness. In this context, education encourages individuals to seek coherence and integrity, fostering an inward journey that provides clarity, strength and an understanding of their place in the world.

Consciousness: deep questions to spark reflection

At the heart of spiritual enquiry is the exploration of consciousness – the awareness that gives rise to experience and understanding. Introducing learners to deep, existential questions offer a powerful tool for self-discovery, prompting them to explore the nature of reality and their place within it. For instance, teachers might ask: What comes first, consciousness or the brain? Is the brain merely a channel for consciousness, or is consciousness an emergent property of the brain's complex functions? Such questions encourage learners to consider the boundaries between mind, body and spirit, expanding their understanding beyond conventional subject boundaries.

Further questions can probe the nature of life and death: What differentiates a living being from a dead one? If we can pinpoint this transition, why can't we reverse it? What does this tell us about the forces that animate life? Engaging with such questions invites learners to ponder the mystery of existence and consider the non-physical dimensions of reality. Theoretical physicists like David Bohm (1980) suggests that consciousness may not be a byproduct of the brain but a fundamental aspect of reality. This perspective aligns with ancient spiritual traditions that view consciousness as the substratum of existence, inviting learners to explore their role within a conscious universe.

In educational settings, these questions challenge learners to consider the broader implications of their existence, enabling them to understand themselves as more than biological organisms. This enquiry aligns with Socratic pedagogy, where education is less about imparting knowledge and more about guiding learners in exploring fundamental questions. By adopting a Socratic approach, teachers encourage learners to think deeply, question their assumptions, and reflect on their place in the world. In this way, education transforms from a mere transmission of facts into the cultivation of wonder, where science and spirituality intersect to offer a richer understanding of self and reality.

To nurture a connection with the inner self, it's essential to engage in practices that uplift consciousness. A practical approach is to identify activities that bring both joy and spiritual upliftment. These activities vary from person to person, and might include spending time in nature, painting, meditating, journaling, dancing, or simple acts of kindness. By curating a list of 10–20 activities and committing to practise one each day, we create daily opportunities for spiritual growth and self-alignment.

These practices serve as intentional acts of self-nurturing, grounding us in our essential identity. The philosopher Søren Kierkegaard (1849) spoke of the necessity of 'being oneself,' which he saw as embracing one's core identity amidst the distractions of society. Uplifting activities help individuals to centre themselves, building a foundation that fosters resilience, peace, and purpose. Over time, these moments accumulate, creating a rootedness that allows individuals to navigate life with authenticity and grace.

Moreover, engaging in uplifting activities can create a ripple effect on one's environment. Positive psychology suggests that people who engage in activities that bring them joy and fulfilment also tend to foster positive interactions with others, contributing to a supportive, nurturing environment. In schools, learners who regularly participate in activities that uplift them not only benefit individually but also positively influence the classroom atmosphere, promoting a culture of kindness, respect and openness.

In this context, education requires a profound shift. To truly support human development, it must reach beyond academic achievement or career preparation and become a journey of self-awareness, where intellectual, emotional, physical and spiritual growth are nurtured together. Parents and teachers play a vital role in creating environments that help learners look within and recognise their inner potential.

This holistic approach empowers young people to cultivate resilience, empathy and purpose, qualities that transcend conventional measures of success. Classrooms become spaces where self-discovery and enquiry work in harmony, supported by practices such as reflective journaling, meaningful dialogue and contemplative exercises that strengthen learners' connection to their core selves. Redefining education in this way positions it as a journey towards realising the soul: uncovering and nurturing the deepest layers of self. Here, success is not defined by external outcomes but by the depth of understanding, integrity and compassion each learner develops as they grow into life.

A narrated example of realising potential

We are in a busy London secondary school, where Maya, a Year 9 student, continues to be known by teachers as "quiet, capable, but disengaged." Her grades are average, and she rarely speaks in class. She is one of those 'ghost' children who don't cause any challenge in a class and who we can quickly forget are there, sitting quietly at the back of the class.

One afternoon, during a new weekly philosophy for children (https://p4c.com/) session, the teacher invites the group to reflect on the layers of identity that they carry, labels from home, school, friendships and online life, and then to write about what sits beneath them.

Maya hesitates, then begins sketching concentric circles in her notebook. In the centre, she writes a single word: *curiosity*. It surprises her. No report card has ever mentioned it, yet she recognises it as something alive within her. Over the next weeks, she starts exploring this inner quality – asking questions in science, staying behind to help in art and journaling during morning reflection. She starts to realise that by engaging more proactively, she gets more out of the learning and becomes more seen by others.

Her teacher notices the shift. Instead of praising her for performance, he asks, "What part of your core self felt awake today?" This simple question becomes a turning point.

By the end of the term, Maya volunteers to lead a small project on local air quality – something she once would have avoided for fear of being seen. The project succeeds, but more importantly, Maya discovers a grounded confidence not tied to achievement, but to a growing alignment with her essential self.

In this classroom, education becomes less about labels and more about awakening. Potential is exponential beneath the limiting 'first impression' labels.

Note

1 *Ātman, Brahman, Paramātmā, Bhagavān*

- *Ātman*: your inner self or soul, beyond body and mind.
- *Brahman*: the spiritual energy that connects all things.
- *Paramātmā*: the divine presence within everyone.
- *Bhagavān*: the personal form of the Divine – like Krishna – who can be loved and related to.

8 Empowering choice

Accepting that we have unlimited potential, the second step is to believe that we have freewill and choice; and the educational act is to empower those choices.

From a better understanding of the inner self and its limitless potential, we now move to how this worldview enables and empowers greater choice. In a world where many aspects of our lives feel beyond our control, the capacity to choose how we respond to our circumstances remains an essential, empowering force. This idea, long debated by philosophers and examined by psychologists, underscores the belief that while external events may shape the conditions of our lives, they do not ultimately determine our character. Instead, our choices reflect and cultivate our inner resilience, fostering a strength of character rooted in virtues such as courage, self-discipline, and integrity.

Empowering choice is, therefore, not merely about navigating individual decisions but about nurturing the underlying framework from which we make those decisions. From philosophical discussions on free will to modern scientific insights on the brain's dopamine system, and from ethical frameworks to understanding the influence of societal pressures, this chapter delves into the psychology, science, and spirituality of empowering choice.

The capacity to choose: psychological and philosophical foundations

One of the most enduring questions in philosophy concerns the nature of free will: do we truly have the capacity to choose, or are our actions determined by factors beyond our control? For centuries, thinkers have

DOI: 10.4324/9781003487654-11

weighed in on this debate. Jean-Paul Sartre, for instance, famously argued that humans are "condemned to be free," (1946) insisting that individuals are always responsible for their choices, even under conditions of immense pressure or hardship. For Sartre, even choosing to yield to external forces is itself a choice and reflects a decision to relinquish one's own agency.

In psychological terms, the belief in one's capacity to choose has been shown to have significant effects on mental health and well-being. Julian Rotter's (1966) concept of *locus of control* highlights how individuals who believe they have control over their lives, or an *internal locus of control*, tend to be more resilient and proactive in the face of challenges, compared to those who feel controlled by external forces. Psychologists have also demonstrated through studies that individuals with a strong sense of agency exhibit greater motivation, well-being and success in achieving their goals. Carol Dweck's research on growth mindset suggests that people who believe in their ability to change and develop – essentially, in their capacity to make choices that shape their character – demonstrate greater perseverance, adaptability, and resilience. These findings underscore the importance of cultivating a belief in the capacity to choose as a foundation for personal growth.

The power of "no": building character through self-control and integrity

A fundamental aspect of free will lies in the capacity to say "no." This ability to resist impulses, social pressures or unproductive habits represents a critical exercise of agency. Neuroscientific studies have shown that self-control is associated with activity in the prefrontal cortex, the part of the brain involved in complex decision making, planning and moderating social behaviour. Individuals who demonstrate higher self-control tend to have better health, greater life satisfaction and stronger relationships. The famous Stanford marshmallow experiment conducted by Mischel, Ebbesen and Raskoff Zeiss (1972) illustrate how children who could delay gratification – resist the immediate temptation of a marshmallow for a promised reward of two marshmallows later – had better life outcomes years later, including higher academic achievement and lower rates of substance abuse. There are, of course, other potential factors for the delay ability, including how hungry the children were, whether they had had breakfast for example and these indicate the various social cultural factors at play – and the importance to remain curious and not settle on assumptions without some critique. However, self-regulation remains a key part of the discussion about empowering choice.

Character traits such as self-discipline, courage and integrity enable us to make choices aligned with our values rather than being swayed by fleeting desires. For instance, self-discipline allows us to pursue long-term goals over immediate gratification, while courage enables us to confront challenges that might otherwise deter us from acting in line with our principles. Integrity, meanwhile, keeps us aligned with our true values, even in the face of external pressures to compromise. Philosophers like Immanuel Kant emphasised the role of autonomy and moral law in guiding ethical behaviour. Kant argued that autonomy, or self-governance, was a defining quality of moral agency, and that true freedom involves adhering to principles of respect and universal justice. This view implies that a virtuous character is essential to make choices that are not merely reactions to external stimuli but expressions of one's inner convictions.

Furthermore, the exercise of free will depends on recognising when we are being influenced by automatic thoughts or unconscious biases. Our minds are constantly proposing actions or judgments based on past experiences, and unless we have the strength of character to critically evaluate these automatic responses, we risk becoming passive participants in our own lives. Studies in cognitive–behavioural psychology have shown that we can learn to identify and challenge unhelpful thought patterns, replacing them with more constructive ones. By practicing mindfulness and reflection, we develop the capacity to observe our thoughts without automatically acting on them, thereby cultivating a conscious approach to decision-making.

The danger of a reductive view: recognising the limits of materialism

Free will and the capacity to choose are ultimately compromised by a reductive view of life that limits human identity to material or biological processes. As neuroscience and psychology have developed over the past century, some thinkers have argued that free will is an illusion, merely a byproduct of physical processes in the brain. This deterministic view, while supported by certain studies of brain activity preceding conscious decisions, is also challenged by other research that suggests a more complex interplay between consciousness and choice.

In her book *Mind & Body*, philosopher Mary Midgley (1980) criticises the reduction of human beings to mere physical entities, arguing that while biology provides insights into behaviour, it does not capture the richness of human experience, autonomy and moral responsibility. She asserts that human consciousness, with its capacity for reflection, empathy and self-awareness, transcends mere physical existence. Midgley's views echo the philosophical perspective that an overemphasis on reductive materialism risks undermining our sense of agency and responsibility. If we believe that our choices are purely determined by biology, we might feel less inclined to strive for personal growth, social responsibility or spiritual development.

A more holistic view of identity integrates both the physical and the spiritual dimensions, recognising that while biological factors influence our experiences, they do not define our capacity for choice. By understanding ourselves as beings with spiritual depth, we empower ourselves to make decisions that reflect our highest ideals, rather than merely responding to physical impulses or social conditioning. Such an understanding aligns with the dharmic perspective, which emphasises the importance of recognising and nurturing the inner self as a source of strength, wisdom and moral clarity.

Contentment versus superficial pleasures: the role of dopamine and the pursuit of lasting happiness

In today's society, the pursuit of pleasure often takes precedence over the pursuit of genuine contentment, leading many individuals to chase superficial rewards that provide only temporary satisfaction. Neuropsychology has shed light on this phenomenon, revealing that dopamine, a neurotransmitter associated with pleasure and reward, plays a central role in motivating behaviour. When we engage in activities that stimulate dopamine release – such as consuming sugar, social media scrolling, or shopping – we experience a temporary "hit" of pleasure. However, as neuroscientist Dr. Anna Lembke explains in her book *Dopamine Nation*, the constant pursuit of these dopamine-driven rewards can actually reduce our baseline level of happiness, leading to dependency, dissatisfaction and even addiction.

The dopamine cycle highlights the limitations of seeking happiness in external stimuli. While dopamine rewards can motivate action, they often create a cycle of craving that leaves individuals perpetually seeking the next pleasure without achieving lasting satisfaction. In contrast, the pursuit of contentment, which encompasses emotional fulfilment, purpose and a sense of belonging, tends to produce a more stable and enduring form of happiness. This distinction aligns with the philosophical idea of hedonic versus eudaimonic well-being, as outlined by Aristotle. Hedonic well-being involves the pursuit of pleasure and the avoidance of pain, while eudaimonic well-being entails living in accordance with one's values, cultivating virtues and striving for a life of meaning.

A shift from the pursuit of superficial pleasure to the pursuit of contentment reflects a deeper understanding of happiness, one that values long-term fulfilment over short-term gratification. Psychological research supports this view: studies on gratitude and mindfulness practices have shown that individuals who cultivate appreciation for what they have tend to report higher levels of life satisfaction and lower levels of stress and anxiety. By focusing on contentment rather than constant pleasure-seeking, we develop a more resilient and sustainable form of happiness, one that empowers us to make choices that reflect our true values and priorities.

The Lucifer Effect: recognising the power of situational influence

One of the most sobering insights into human behaviour is the degree to which individuals can be influenced by external factors to act in ways that contradict their values and moral beliefs. Psychologist Philip Zimbardo's Stanford Prison Experiment (2007) is one of the most well-known demonstrations of this phenomenon, which he later termed the "Lucifer Effect." In the experiment, college learners were assigned roles as "guards" or "prisoners" in a simulated prison environment. Within days, many participants began to display abusive and authoritarian behaviour, leading Zimbardo to conclude that almost anyone, given the right circumstances, could be led to act in ways that defy their personal ethics.

The Lucifer Effect suggests that situational influences can have a powerful impact on our choices, often overriding our internal moral compass. While the Stanford prison experiment represents an extreme example, similar dynamics occur in everyday situations, where individuals may conform to social norms or adopt behaviours that align with group expectations rather than their personal beliefs. For instance, research on conformity by Solomon Asch found that people are often willing to agree with a group's opinion, even when it contradicts their own observations. This tendency to "follow the crowd" can lead individuals to make choices that align with the status quo rather than their own ethical standards.

Recognising the influence of situational factors on behaviour is essential for empowering choice, as it enables individuals to be more mindful of external pressures and consciously resist them when they conflict with their values. Cultivating a strong sense of character, rooted in virtues such as courage and integrity, enables individuals to maintain their principles even in challenging environments. By developing an awareness of the Lucifer Effect, individuals can learn to recognise when they are being influenced by situational factors and make deliberate choices that reflect their true beliefs.

Modes of goodness, passion and ignorance: a framework for conscious decision–making

The framework of the Modes of Goodness, Passion, and Ignorance, derived from the ancient Indian text the *Bhagavad Gītā*, offers a valuable tool for understanding and categorising the motivations behind our choices. These three modes, like primary colours, combine in various ways to produce an infinite variety of mental states, emotions and behaviours. Each mode represents a distinct set of motivations, attitudes, and values that shape our actions and influence our overall consciousness.

The mode of goodness

- Drawn towards constructive activities like reading, self-improvement and mindfulness
- Has a strong work ethic; has integrity, is committed and is dependable
- Seeks knowledge beyond textbooks, enjoys deep discussions
- Practices honesty and accountability
- Shows gratitude towards all colleagues
- Emotionally balanced and handles stress calmly

The Mode of Goodness is characterised by clarity, mindfulness and a commitment to the long-term welfare of oneself and others. In this mode, individuals are motivated by a sense of duty, compassion, and a desire to act ethically. Choices made in the Mode of Goodness reflect an awareness of consequences and a willingness to prioritise the well-being of all stakeholders. This mode is often associated with virtues such as honesty, empathy and responsibility. In the workplace, decisions in the Mode of Goodness might involve transparent communication, fair treatment of employees and a commitment to social responsibility.

One example occurred when Elena, a class teacher, walked into James Biddulph's (her Headteacher) office and declared that she had just taught the worst maths lesson of her career. The lesson had not gone as intended. Yet, instead of retreating into defensiveness, she chose dialogue and transparency. She stepped into uncertainty – *Will I be judged? Will this change how I'm seen?* By naming the failure herself, she removed fear from the room. The conversation became developmental rather than evaluative. Together, they analysed what had happened and what might improve next time.

Her openness strengthened trust. James saw a serious professional committed to her craft. Over time, such honesty builds psychological safety. It also ripples outward: Elena later shared her reflections with colleagues, modelling reflective practice and encouraging others to speak openly about their own learning.

What began as failure became a catalyst for growth. The poison was transformed into medicine because she met it with courage and clarity. In doing so, Elena demonstrated that in the mode of goodness, one takes responsibility for effort and learning – without clinging to ego or fear.

The Mode of Goodness aligns with Kantian ethics, which emphasises acting out of respect for moral principles rather than personal gain. Kant argued that ethical actions are those taken with a universal respect for all people, treating individuals as ends in themselves rather than means to an end. This perspective resonates with the Mode of Goodness, as it encourages individuals to consider the broader impact of their actions and to act in ways that reflect integrity and care.

The mode of passion

- Highly competitive, desires to be the top and seen as the best
- Motivated by approval and recognition from colleagues and peers
- Gets frustrated easily when facing challenges

- Engages in socialising excessively, sometimes neglecting workload
- Tends to multitask excessively, leading to lack of focus
- Swings between high motivation and burnout

The mode of passion is driven by desire, ambition and a focus on short-term gratification. In this mode, individuals are motivated by the pursuit of pleasure, recognition and personal gain. While the mode of passion can fuel creativity, innovation and determination, it can also lead to selfishness, competition, and burnout if left unchecked. Decisions in this mode are often characterised by impulsive actions, pride and a lack of consideration for long-term consequences.

James Biddulph's early career offers a vivid illustration of the mode of passion. When he first began teaching, he quickly became an Advanced Skills Teacher for Music and Creativity, winning the London Award for Outstanding New Teacher of the Year. He immersed himself in the arts: children wrote poetry, danced, composed music and performed. He even made a teaching video with Michael Rosen, the famous children's poet and author. The work was vibrant and life-giving. Classrooms pulsed with imagination, and children flourished through rich performance opportunities. This was the nectar of passion. Energy was high. Recognition followed. Creativity felt expansive and purposeful.

Yet, with time and reflection, James could see another layer. Alongside the genuine desire to create transformative experiences for children, there was a quiet pleasure in being admired – in knowing that his Headteacher and colleagues valued his work. The ego was gently stroked. The mode of passion often carries this duality: noble intention intertwined with personal validation.

The poison was not in the creativity itself but in its unsustainable intensity. Such outward-driving energy eventually depleted him. There were periods when James was exhausted, rushing from one initiative to the next, with little time for friends or family. The same force that generated opportunity also generated strain. In the mode of passion, action is purposeful and impactful, but it can become tethered to recognition and momentum. The work bears fruit, yet without balance it can quietly consume the one who carries it.

The mode of passion can be likened to the hedonic treadmill in psychology, where individuals constantly seek new sources of pleasure or success, only to find that the satisfaction quickly fades. This pursuit can become a cycle of craving, where the initial reward is followed by a desire for even greater rewards, leading to a sense of dissatisfaction. In contrast to the Mode of Goodness, the mode of passion often prioritises personal desires over ethical considerations, resulting in decisions that may bring immediate satisfaction but lack depth and purpose.

The mode of ignorance

- Procrastination and no real management of time or priorities
- Has a pessimistic attitude towards life and work
- Patterns of dishonesty about responsibilities
- Disengaged from work and unresponsive to colleagues
- Easily addicted to distractions like social media scrolling
- Poor personal hygiene and disorderly habits

The mode of ignorance is associated with apathy, confusion and a disregard for consequences. In this mode, individuals may act out of habit, ignorance or a desire to escape responsibility. Choices made in the mode of ignorance are often impulsive, careless and driven by a desire for short-term relief rather than meaningful fulfilment. This mode is linked to behaviours such as procrastination, substance abuse and denial of reality.

James Biddulph recalls a moment from his own schooling that illustrates the mode of ignorance: reactive, careless and wounding.

When he was struggling to understand a trigonometry equation, his maths tutor, Mrs Kay, turned to him and said, "Come on James, you can't be this stupid, it really is not that difficult." It was a short sentence, spoken perhaps in frustration, perhaps in haste. Yet, its impact was lasting. Thirty years on, he still remembers the moment vividly, and his relationship with maths has never fully recovered.

The mode of ignorance often operates in this way. It is not always dramatic or intentionally cruel. It can arise from impatience, stress or unconscious bias. But it reduces the learner to a fixed judgement. In that instant, curiosity narrows, confidence contracts and identity absorbs the label.

The poison here is subtle but enduring: a lingering narrative of inadequacy that shapes future engagement. What might have been a temporary difficulty became part of a longer story about capability.

A soul-led education does not pretend such moments do not occur. It acknowledges their reality and their power. It insists that we notice them, repair them where possible and cultivate the inner awareness that makes them less likely. The first step is not shame, but honesty and awareness, recognising how easily ignorance can surface and choosing a different way of being.

The mode of ignorance resonates with the concept of learned helplessness in psychology, where individuals who feel unable to change their circumstances become passive and disengaged. Studies by psychologist Martin Seligman demonstrated that animals and humans exposed to uncontrollable stressors often fail to take action even when opportunities for change arise. In a similar way, the mode of ignorance reflects a state of inertia, where individuals become disengaged from their responsibilities and ignore the potential impact of their actions.

By recognising these modes within ourselves, we can assess the motivations behind our choices and consciously strive to make decisions in alignment with the mode of goodness. This framework offers a practical tool for cultivating awareness and promoting ethical decision making, empowering individuals to act with intention and integrity. We will explore this further in Chapter 8.

Cultivating a dharmic perspective: moving beyond self-interest

The concept of *dharma* provides a profound lens for understanding the purpose of choice beyond individual self-interest. Rooted in Indian philosophy, *dharma* refers to the inherent duty, purpose, or moral responsibility of an individual. Unlike moral frameworks that prescribe specific behaviours, dharma encourages individuals to evaluate each decision based on its alignment with their true nature, values, and contributions to society. This perspective suggests that choices are not solely about personal benefit but also involve a commitment to the well-being of others and the world.

Dharma transcends religious dogma and instead provides a guiding philosophy that encourages conscious living. In modern contexts, adopting a dharmic approach means evaluating decisions based on their alignment with long-term goals, ethical principles and a broader purpose. For example, a business leader guided by dharma would consider the impact of their actions on employees, customers and the environment, rather than focusing solely on profit. Such an approach promotes a sustainable and compassionate view of success that prioritises holistic well-being over individual gain.

Cultivating a dharmic perspective begins with regular reflection on our motivations and an honest questioning of whether our choices align with our deepest values. When we consider both personal and collective outcomes, we develop a sense of responsibility that reaches beyond momentary desires. In this way, empowerment is not found in limitless freedom but in choosing actions rooted in our highest principles.

Empowered choice, then, is not merely the ability to decide; it is the ongoing cultivation of character, resilience and integrity. By understanding the forces that shape our behaviour, free will, dopamine-driven impulses, situational pressures and the modes of goodness, passion and Ignorance, we become better equipped to act with clarity and purpose. Ultimately, choosing with integrity requires continual self-awareness and a commitment to growth. When our choices reflect our inner truth and serve the greater good, we move beyond impulse towards lasting fulfilment, creating lives grounded in meaning, responsibility and positive impact.

A narrated example of empowering choice

At a bustling urban sixth form college, Sam was known for always saying "yes." Yes, to extra coursework, yes to group expectations, yes to the unspoken pressure to perform. Beneath his polite compliance, however, lived a quiet exhaustion. One morning, during a tutorial on conscious choice, his teacher introduced the modes of goodness, passion and ignorance, inviting students to reflect on the motivations behind their daily decisions.

That afternoon, Sam faced a familiar crossroads. His friends urged him to skip a study session to join them at a new gaming café. Normally he would go along, driven by the mode of passion – seeking approval, fearing exclusion. But this time he paused, recalling the conversation about agency and alignment. He took a slow breath and asked himself a simple question: *Which choice reflects how I want to be and who I want to become?*

For the first time, he said "no" not out of avoidance, but because of a keener sense of integrity. He spent the hour revising calmly, feeling an unfamiliar steadiness grow inside him.

Later, when he explained his decision to his friends, something shifted. They nodded, surprisingly respectful. Sam realised that choosing with intention didn't isolate him; it liberated him.

From that day, "no" became a doorway, away from limitation and towards authorship of his own life.

9 Strengthening interconnection

With unlimited potential, we learn that there is freewill of choice. In seeing the world through this lens, we begin to understand that all others have unlimited potential and freewill of choice. There is now a potential to interconnect as equal souls in the endeavour to enact the freewill of choice to realise our unlimited potential.

The belief in interconnection lies at the heart of many philosophical and spiritual traditions, reflecting a commitment to respecting and caring for all forms of life – human, animal and plant. Saint Francis believed it through his vegetarianism and Sri Caitanya Mahaprabhu spoke about a deep sense of equality. This principle, central to both ancient and modern ethical systems, emphasises our role as responsible custodians of a shared planet. By understanding that all life is interconnected and interdependent, we are called to act with mindfulness, empathy, and humility, living in ways that minimise harm to other beings and to the environment.

In this chapter, we will explore the scientific, philosophical, and ethical dimensions of interconnection, beginning with the ancient principle of *ahimsa* (non-harm), moving through ecological perspectives, and considering the practical implications of our choices – particularly in diet, social ethics, and our treatment of animals and the planet. Through these perspectives, we can come to appreciate how interconnectedness shapes our identity, responsibilities and role within a broader ecological and cosmic framework.

DOI: 10.4324/9781003487654-12

Ahimsa: the principle of non-harm

The concept of *ahimsa*, originating in ancient India, is a foundational idea in Hinduism, Buddhism and Jainism, and serves as a moral compass for those who strive to live a life that minimises harm. Rooted in Sanskrit, *ahimsa* means "non-violence" or "non-harm," but it extends beyond the absence of physical violence. It encompasses a broader commitment to compassion, empathy, and respect for all life, urging individuals to make decisions that reduce suffering for all beings.

Gandhi, a prominent advocate of *ahimsa*, described it as "the highest duty," arguing that non-violence is an active force that goes beyond passivity. Gandhi's interpretation of *ahimsa* involved both refraining from harmful actions and actively promoting kindness and compassion, an idea that continues to influence contemporary discussions on ethical living. However, *ahimsa* is not a rigid concept; it allows for personal interpretation. Different individuals may practice *ahimsa* in diverse ways, reflecting their unique circumstances, cultural beliefs and resources. For some, it may mean adopting a vegetarian or vegan diet, while for others, it may involve sustainable living practices or reducing their carbon footprint.

From an ethical perspective, *ahimsa* challenges the anthropocentric view that humans are superior to other beings. By acknowledging that all life holds intrinsic value, *ahimsa* calls for an ethics of care, encouraging people to consider the welfare of all beings in their daily choices. Without this guiding principle, societies risk slipping into exploitation, objectification and insensitivity. The absence of *ahimsa* can be seen in practices that cause unnecessary harm to animals, degrade ecosystems, and contribute to social injustices.

Historical misunderstandings: Descartes and McGraw on animal and infant sensitivity

Throughout history, there have been several misunderstandings about the capacity of animals and infants to feel pain. In the 17th century, the philosopher René Descartes famously argued that animals are mere "machines" without consciousness or the ability to feel pain (1637). Descartes' mechanistic view led to centuries of scientific experiments on animals without anaesthesia, rationalised by the belief that animals lacked subjective experiences. This perception of animals as insentient beings justified practices that caused great suffering, establishing a cultural norm that animals could be used as resources without moral consideration.

In the same vein, in 1941, Myrtle McGraw promoted the idea that infants do not experience pain in the same way adults do. This belief, coupled with limited scientific understanding of infant neurology, led to the practice of performing surgeries on infants without anaesthesia until well into the 1980s. Only in recent decades has medical research confirmed that infants not only feel pain but may experience it more intensely due to their developing nervous systems. The historical oversight reflects a broader issue: when we fail to recognise the subjective experiences of others – whether animals, infants or different cultures – we risk treating them as objects rather than beings worthy of respect.

These misunderstandings highlight the dangers of a disconnected view that overlooks the intrinsic value and sensitivity of other beings. By challenging these outdated notions, we can move towards an ethical framework that recognises the sentience of both animals and humans, affirming their capacity for suffering and their right to humane treatment. This shift underscores the importance of practising *ahimsa* not only in how we relate to other humans but in how we interact with all forms of life.

Personalising nature: from objectification to respectful engagement

A critical step towards embracing interconnection involves shifting from an objectified view of nature to a more personalised, relational perspective. In modern society, the natural world is often treated as a collection of resources to be exploited rather than as a living ecosystem deserving of care and respect. By referring to nature as "Mother Nature" or personifying the earth as a nurturing entity, we shift our perception from seeing the environment as a passive object to viewing it as a living, interconnected, interdependent system that sustains us and the whole web of life.

This shift aligns with the biophilia hypothesis, proposed by the biologist E.O. Wilson (1984), which suggests that humans have an innate affinity for nature and other living beings. Wilson's theory posits that human health and well-being are deeply connected to our relationship with the natural world. Research supporting this hypothesis has shown that time spent in nature is associated with lower stress levels, improved mental health and a greater sense of purpose. By cultivating a personal connection with nature, individuals are more likely to develop a sense of responsibility towards its preservation, an outcome that aligns with the principles of *ahimsa*.

Moreover, the philosophy of deep ecology, championed by thinkers like Arne Naess (1973), advocates for recognising the intrinsic value of all living beings, irrespective of their utility to humans. Deep ecology encourages individuals to engage with nature as equals, not as conquerors or exploiters. This perspective invites us to appreciate the natural world in its own right, cultivating a sense of awe, humility and gratitude. By personifying nature, we foster empathy and reduce our tendency to objectify, exploit or harm other beings.

The ecological benefits of a plant-based diet

A practical application of the principle of interconnection is reflected in dietary choices, particularly the shift towards vegetarianism or veganism. The impact of diet on the environment is a growing area of research, with numerous studies indicating that plant-based diets are more sustainable and less harmful to ecosystems than diets heavy in animal products. According to a comprehensive study published in Science by Poore and Nemecek (2018), adopting a plant-based diet could reduce an individual's food-related greenhouse gas emissions by up to 73%. The researchers found that plant-based diets require less land and water than meat-based diets and contribute significantly less to deforestation, habitat destruction and biodiversity loss.

In addition to its environmental benefits, a plant-based diet is associated with health advantages. Research indicates that vegetarian and vegan diets can reduce the risk of chronic diseases such as heart disease, hypertension and diabetes. The American Dietetic Association has affirmed that appropriately planned plant–based diets are healthful and nutritionally adequate, supporting health and preventing disease across all stages of life.

The documentary *Game Changers* (2018) further popularised the benefits of a plant-based diet, particularly highlighting its positive impact on athletic performance and overall health. By adopting dietary habits that align with the principles of *ahimsa*, individuals can make choices that benefit both their well-being and the environment, reducing harm to animals and conserving resources for future generations.

Consciousness and quantum field theory: a scientific perspective on interconnection

The principle of interconnection finds support not only in ethical and ecological considerations but also in scientific theories, particularly in the field of quantum physics. Quantum field theory (QFT), a foundational framework in modern physics, suggests that all particles and forces are interconnected within a vast field of energy. In this view, particles are not isolated entities but are manifestations of an underlying field that connects them. Quantum entanglement, a phenomenon in which particles remain interconnected regardless of distance, further illustrates the deep interconnectedness within the fabric of reality.

Physicists such as David Bohm (1980) have extended this notion of interconnectedness to consciousness, proposing that all aspects of existence are part of a holistic system. Bohm's *implicate order* theory suggests that the apparent separateness of objects and beings is an illusion, and that underlying this perception is a unified, interconnected reality. This perspective aligns with philosophical ideas of interconnection, supporting the view that all beings are linked within a greater whole.

Philosophical interpretations of quantum physics resonate with the concept of *ahimsa* by underscoring the interconnectedness of life. If all beings are interconnected at a fundamental level, then causing harm to others may also disrupt the balance of the whole. This view promotes a sense of responsibility and empathy, as individuals recognise that their actions have ripple effects across the interconnected web of life. By understanding ourselves as part of a larger, interconnected cosmos, we are encouraged to make choices that reflect respect, compassion and harmony. Alongside critiques of industrial agriculture, it is important to acknowledge farmers whose practices are rooted in compassion, ecological responsibility and deep connection to the land. Through the work with Harmony Education, Patrick Holden of the Sustainable Food Trust, sees ethical husbandry as integral to sustaining healthy ecosystems. Recognising these perspectives offers a more balanced, nuanced account of the wider field. It is a complex matter.

The social dimension of interconnection: from individualism to community

Interconnection challenges the dominant individualistic worldview by positioning human beings as embedded within social, cultural, and ecological networks. Ubuntu, a foundational concept in African philosophy, captures this reality through the principle, *"I am because we are."* It suggests that identity, dignity and well-being emerge through relationships, not in isolation. In this view, the self is shaped and sustained by the communities to which one belongs.

Psychological literature reinforces this relational perspective. Research consistently shows that a strong sense of belonging, meaningful social bonds and reciprocal support correlate with increased life satisfaction, resilience and emotional stability. Positive psychology further highlights that empathy, cooperation and prosocial behaviour deepen one's sense of purpose and broaden perspectives, helping individuals transcend self-centred patterns and engage more fully with others.

Living with an awareness of interconnection therefore involves recognising our participation in the lives of others and acting with a sense of shared responsibility. This orientation can motivate civic engagement, environmental activism and ethical leadership – practices that strengthen the social fabric and cultivate more compassionate, equitable communities.

The ethical implications of interconnection: moving from exploitation to custodianship

Understanding interconnection also carries ethical consequences. When the world is perceived primarily as a resource to be used, human actions tend towards exploitation, of land, species and even other people. A relational view, however, calls for custodianship: a commitment to protect, sustain and regenerate the ecosystems and communities upon which life depends.

The ethic of stewardship expresses this shift. Ecological thinkers such as Aldo Leopold (1949) argue that humans are members of a broader "land community," with responsibilities to all its constituents. His land ethic invites individuals to act in ways that maintain the integrity, stability, and beauty of the biotic community, an approach that resonates with both ecological science and spiritual traditions that emphasise harmony with nature.

Modern frameworks such as the United Nations' Sustainable Development Goals echo this custodial mindset. By integrating environmental sustainability with social justice and economic well-being, the SDGs articulate a global commitment to safeguarding planetary health while enabling human flourishing. This orientation underscores a key implication of interconnection: ethical action is never merely personal, it is inherently collective, shaping the conditions for life now and for generations to come.

Practical steps to strengthen interconnection in daily life

Strengthening interconnection is not merely a philosophical ideal; it requires practical actions that reflect our commitment to living harmoniously with the environment and other beings. Below are some tangible steps individuals can take to integrate interconnection into their daily lives:

1. *Adopting a Sustainable Diet*: Choosing a plant-based or environmentally conscious diet reduces harm to animals and lowers one's carbon footprint. By making mindful food choices, individuals can align their dietary habits with principles of *ahimsa* and environmental sustainability.
2. *Practising Mindfulness*: Developing mindfulness through meditation or reflection helps individuals become more aware of their thoughts, emotions and actions, promoting empathy and compassion. Mindfulness fosters an appreciation of the interconnectedness of all beings, encouraging individuals to act with kindness and understanding.
3. *Engaging in Community Service*: Volunteering and community involvement strengthen social bonds and promote a sense of shared purpose. By contributing to the welfare of others, individuals reinforce the interdependent nature of human society and support the well-being of their communities.
4. *Reducing Waste and Consumption*: Minimising waste, recycling and making sustainable purchasing choices contribute to environmental preservation. By reducing consumption, individuals demonstrate respect for natural resources and help protect ecosystems from degradation.

The principle of interconnection invites us to re-examine how we live and relate, shifting from an extractive mindset to one grounded in respect, empathy and custodianship. Whether expressed through *ahimsa*, sustainable living or the insights of contemporary science, recognising our interdependence reshapes the choices we make.

As members of a shared planet, we carry a responsibility to protect and nourish the web of life that sustains us. When we act in ways that reflect this truth, we deepen our sense of purpose, strengthen our compassion, and contribute to a more balanced and humane world. This requires more than philosophical understanding; it asks for practical commitment, daily choices that honour the intrinsic worth of all beings. In embracing interconnection, we affirm our place within a larger whole and cultivate a life that nurtures both personal fulfilment and collective well-being.

A narrated example of strengthening interconnection

I was visiting Open-heart Primary, on a grey Tuesday afternoon. I had been asked to work with Year 6 (11-year-old children). We sat in a circle around a low table covered with food: burgers, lentil stew, crisps, apples. Their teacher, Ms Patel, had written one question on the board: *"Who is affected by what we eat?"*

At first, the answers were small. "Me." "My family." "The shop where we buy it."

We watched a film about farming, the history of it and the now globalised interrelatedness of it. Then Ayaan, who loved animals but had never thought much about farming, recalled a short film the class had seen about soil, rivers and the lives of farmers and animals across the world. As the credits rolled, the room felt unusually quiet.

In the discussion that followed, Ms Patel asked, "what kind of world would we have if we changed our choices – for people, animals, and the planet?" Ayaan thought about animals and his choice in his packed lunch.

That evening, Ayaan asked his parents if they could try one vegetarian day each week. He designed a poster for school: *"Kindness on Our Plates"* and invited classmates to join a "planet-friendly lunch club," where they shared recipes, stories from their families' food traditions, and gratitude for those who grew their food.

10 Enriching diversities

When interconnection deepens, difference becomes more visible. Because we already understand one another as equal in potential and agency, diversity no longer divides us. Instead, it enriches us. Inclusion becomes a natural expression of this understanding.

With interconnection in our minds, it becomes possible to see diversities as opportunity. The diversity of human perspectives is an enduring and enriching feature of our world, shaping not only individual lives but also the collective knowledge, values and social structures of societies. While we all experience the same reality, each of us observes it from a unique perspective, formed by our backgrounds, beliefs, and personal experiences. Recognising and embracing these diversities, particularly within education, opens pathways to enriched understanding and empathy. Through open-hearted dialogue, we move beyond surface-level interpretations to achieve a deeper, collective insight into complex issues. This chapter explores the role of dialogue in fostering diversity, developing empathy and enhancing decision-making, with insights from philosophy, psychology and educational theory.

Embracing diverse perspectives: the unity of truth

The idea that multiple perspectives can offer different but complementary insights into a shared truth is an ancient one, deeply embedded in many philosophical and cultural traditions. Remembering the phrase *Ekam sat*

DOI: 10.4324/9781003487654-13

vipra bahudha vadanti – Truth is one; the wise speak of it in different ways, suggests that although we may articulate our understanding in various ways, we are ultimately referring to the same underlying reality. This idea encourages us to view different perspectives not as competing truths but as unique approaches to understanding a complex and multifaceted world.

The ancient Indian story of the blind men and the elephant illustrates this concept vividly. In the story, a group of blind men each touches a different part of an elephant – one feels the trunk, another the tail, another a leg – and each concludes that the elephant is like the part they have touched. The one who feels the trunk says, "An elephant is like a snake," while the one who touches the leg says, "No, it's like a tree trunk." This story highlights how partial perspectives can lead to seemingly contradictory conclusions when they are viewed in isolation. Only through pooling their insights could the men come to a more accurate understanding of the elephant. This narrative serves as a reminder that our individual perspectives are inherently limited and that engaging in dialogue allows us to integrate diverse viewpoints into a more complete picture of reality (Biddulph, 2017).

The role of dialogue in education: philosophy and oracy

Dialogue plays a central role in bridging diverse perspectives and is foundational to education's mission of fostering critical and empathetic thinkers. Oracy, the ability to express oneself fluently and to participate effectively in spoken communication, is as crucial to learning as literacy and numeracy. According to education researchers Robin Alexander and Neil Mercer, oracy not only improves cognitive development but also fosters social cohesion, as it enables individuals to articulate their thoughts clearly while listening and responding to others respectfully. Oracy involves more than just speaking; it encompasses the skills of reasoning, articulating ideas, and engaging in productive dialogue with others.

Engaging in dialogue with others not only enhances our understanding of diverse perspectives but also develops our capacity for empathy. Empathy, as psychologist Carl Rogers described it, is the ability to "enter the private perceptual world of the other and become thoroughly at home in it" (1957). Empathy enables individuals to move beyond their own perspective and appreciate the thoughts, feelings, and experiences of others. Dialogue serves as a conduit for empathy by exposing individuals to ideas and experiences that differ from their own, thus broadening their understanding and deepening their capacity to relate to others.

In his *Theory of Moral Development*, psychologist Lawrence Kohlberg (1981) posited that dialogue plays a crucial role in developing moral reasoning. According to Kohlberg, individuals progress through stages of moral understanding, each characterised by increasingly complex ethical considerations. Engaging in dialogue allows individuals to encounter a range of moral perspectives, fostering the development of a more nuanced and principled understanding of right and wrong. Dialogue, therefore, not only builds empathy but also strengthens our capacity to deal with complex issues by helping us move beyond simple, black-and-white thinking.

Dialogue can prevent us from rushing to assumptions, a tendency that psychologist Daniel Kahneman (2011) explores in his book *Thinking, Fast and Slow*. Kahneman explains that our brains are wired for efficiency, often leading us to make quick judgements based on limited information. While these cognitive shortcuts can be helpful, they can also lead to stereotyping, misunderstanding, and conflict. Dialogue encourages individuals to slow down and consider a broader range of information, reducing the likelihood of cognitive biases and promoting a more accurate, inclusive understanding.

Dialogue and the acceptance of diversity: conflict resolution and social harmony

Dialogue and the acceptance of diversity are essential not only for individual development but also for conflict resolution and social harmony. In the educational context, fostering an environment where dialogue is encouraged can significantly reduce conflicts on the playground and within classrooms. Studies have shown that schools that prioritise dialogue-based conflict resolution experience fewer incidences of bullying, higher levels of mutual respect among learners, and more effective communication skills overall. The importance of dialogue extends beyond the schoolyard, serving as a critical tool for promoting peace and understanding in diverse societies.

The political philosopher John Stuart Mill (1859), in *On Liberty*, argued that open dialogue and the acceptance of diverse viewpoints are essential for a healthy society. Mill contended that even if a particular viewpoint appears incorrect, allowing it to be expressed and debated provides an opportunity for society to strengthen its understanding of truth. By challenging one another's assumptions, individuals refine their beliefs and develop a more robust conception of the truth. This concept is particularly relevant in democratic societies, where the clash of diverse perspectives is essential for informed decision-making and the protection of individual freedoms.

Knowledge, truth and the Gettier Problem: recognising the complexity of knowledge

Dialogue invites us to acknowledge the complexity of knowledge and the limitations of certainty, a point illustrated by the Gettier Problem in epistemology. The Gettier Problem, presented by philosopher Edmund Gettier in 1963, challenged the classical definition of knowledge as "justified true belief." Gettier's thought experiments demonstrated that it is possible to have justified beliefs that are true by coincidence rather than because of sound reasoning. This realisation complicates the concept of knowledge and suggests that truth is not always as easily defined or grasped as we might assume.

The Gettier Problem highlights the value of keeping our minds open to multiple perspectives and the limitations of rigid assumptions. In a world where knowledge is often complex and context–dependent, dialogue provides a means of exploring ideas from different angles, allowing individuals to refine their understanding and appreciate the diversity of possible truths. Embracing this complexity does not imply that there is no truth; rather, it recognises that truth is multifaceted and that our understanding of it can be enriched by considering multiple viewpoints.

Diversity without compromise: balancing conviction and open-mindedness

An important consideration in embracing diversity is the misconception that openness to other perspectives requires individuals to compromise their own beliefs, values or convictions. In fact, engaging with diverse perspectives through dialogue does not necessitate abandoning one's core principles. Philosopher Alasdair MacIntyre (1981) emphasised that holding firm to one's values is not incompatible with engaging in open dialogue. In his view, moral integrity involves standing by one's beliefs while remaining open to dialogue that can deepen and refine those beliefs. This approach encourages individuals to approach dialogue with humility, acknowledging that while their beliefs are valuable, they are always open to further development.

Educational settings provide a unique opportunity to foster this balance between conviction and open-mindedness. By teaching learners that they can remain true to their beliefs while respecting and engaging with others, educators equip young people with the skills to navigate a pluralistic world. Research in intercultural education has shown that learners who are exposed to diverse perspectives from an early age develop a greater capacity for tolerance and respect. This balanced approach to diversity allows learners to appreciate the value of their own culture and values while recognising the richness of alternative viewpoints.

Dialogue and decision-making: avoiding groupthink and echo chambers

Diversity through dialogue has significant benefits for decision-making, particularly in preventing groupthink and the formation of echo chambers. Groupthink, a concept developed by psychologist Irving Janis, occurs when a group prioritises harmony and consensus over critical thinking, leading to poor decisions. Groupthink often arises in homogenous groups where members share similar backgrounds and perspectives, resulting in a limited range of ideas. In contrast, diverse groups that engage in open dialogue are more likely to consider a wider range of options, critically evaluate different perspectives, and reach more effective decisions.

Echo chambers, a related phenomenon, occur when individuals are exposed primarily to viewpoints that reinforce their existing beliefs. Social media platforms, for example, often use algorithms that show users content aligned with their preferences, creating echo chambers where alternative viewpoints are rarely encountered. This can lead to polarisation, as individuals become more entrenched in their views and less willing to engage with opposing perspectives. Dialogue provides an antidote to echo chambers by facilitating genuine engagement with diverse viewpoints, broadening individuals' understanding and fostering more balanced, well-informed perspectives.

The benefits of diversity in decision-making are evident in various domains, from business to governance. Studies have shown that diverse teams outperform homogenous ones in problem-solving and innovation, as they draw on a broader range of experiences and perspectives. A McKinsey report on diversity in the workplace found that companies with diverse teams are more likely to outperform their competitors, highlighting the practical value of inclusivity. By fostering dialogue that respects diversity, organisations can tap into a wealth of insights, avoid cognitive biases and make more informed decisions.

In educational settings, fostering dialogue and diversity equips learners with the tools to navigate an increasingly interconnected world. By teaching young people to engage with diverse perspectives respectfully, educators lay the foundation for a more inclusive, compassionate, and resilient society. As we continue to promote open-hearted dialogue, we not only broaden our understanding of truth but also cultivate a sense of shared humanity that transcends borders, beliefs, and backgrounds. Ultimately, the commitment to enriching diversities through dialogue reflects a recognition of our shared human experience. It affirms the importance of empathy, respect, and collaboration in addressing the challenges of our time, reminding us that the journey to understanding is an ongoing process, one that is best undertaken together.

A narrated example of enriching diversities

Ms Andrews' Year 10 class sat in a circle for their weekly dialogue session, an hour designed to explore identity and interconnection. On this particular afternoon, the prompt on the board read: *"What parts of who you are shape the way you see the world?"*

There was a long silence before Leila spoke. She shared, carefully, what it felt like to navigate school as a Black young woman – how teachers sometimes misread her confidence as attitude, how she carried stories her grandmother had given her about resilience and dignity.

Across the circle sat Noah, who had only recently come out as gay to one close friend. He had never said the words of his truth aloud in a classroom. But hearing Leila's honesty steadied something inside him. When it was his turn, he said quietly, "I'm learning what it means to be myself... and how scary and freeing that is. I am nervous about how you will respond to me and whether you will continue to like and include me. I fear that something of me will be damaged in the ways you perceive me."

The room shifted. Learners listened – I mean, really listened. No debate, no discomfort projected, just presence. No one laughed. There seemed an understanding of the heaviness of Noah not feeling he could be true about himself (in the past). A new realisation that there was difference but also a similarity – that we all want to feel our full-wholesome-flourishing selves and do not want judgement or exclusion or abandonment – we want acceptance.

Ms Andrews didn't praise their courage or turn their stories into lessons. Instead, she asked, "How does hearing these truths help us understand one another differently?"

Hands lifted.

"We see more than labels."
"We realise everyone's carrying something."
"We're not as different as we thought."

Over the term, the circle became a place where identities were not defended or compared, but explored: race, sexuality, faith, neurodiversity, culture, all held with equal dignity. The class created a mural titled *"Many Stories, One Human Family,"* each learner painting a symbol representing part of their identity and a thread linking it to others.

By the end of the year, something profound had taken root: the class no longer approached diversity as a set of categories to tolerate, but as an invitation to deepen connection. They began to understand that every person, regardless of race, sexuality or background, is a soul unfolding, choosing, learning, and reaching towards their potential. The diversity in the room was no longer a challenge to navigate. It had become the very source of their collective wisdom.

11 Expanding purpose

We are each of us individual souls. We each have unlimited potential, when seen with a spiritual lens and when seen from the soul perspective. We have choice to act. We see our interconnections and similarities in the pursuit to realise our potential. We see diversities within the unifying similarities. Now, we see beyond the differences and look beyond the individualism and temporality of the material (I am not the body…I am the soul and therefore my purpose is much bigger). The educational act for the soul's education is in expanding our sense of purpose.

In a world characterised by rapid change, individualism and complex challenges, the question of purpose has emerged as a vital component of education, personal growth and societal well-being. Expanding purpose extends beyond personal achievement or financial success; it encompasses a commitment to something greater than oneself. When individuals feel connected to a broader purpose, they experience enhanced well-being, a stronger sense of identity and greater resilience. This chapter explores how purpose – especially in the context of contributing to the welfare of others – leads to a more meaningful and fulfilling life. Using philosophical insights, psychological models and empirical studies, we will examine the transformative potential of expanding purpose, exploring the benefits it brings to individuals and society alike.

The concept of purpose: beyond the individual self

Philosophers, psychologists and spiritual traditions across the world have long debated the significance of purpose in human life. Friedrich Nietzsche, the German philosopher, succinctly captured this sentiment when he said,

DOI: 10.4324/9781003487654-14

"He who has a why to live for can bear with almost any how" (1889). Nietzsche emphasises that having a reason or purpose in life provides the strength and resilience needed to overcome challenges and endure hardship. Without purpose, individuals are left adrift, lacking direction and susceptible to existential despair.

Nietzsche's assertion aligns with findings in positive psychology, a branch of psychology that studies human flourishing and well-being. According to psychologists like Martin Seligman, purpose is a crucial component of a fulfilling life. Seligman's PERMA model of well-being – comprising Positive Emotion, Engagement, Relationships, Meaning and Achievement – places meaning as a foundational element of psychological health. Purpose, or a sense of meaning, is not only an antidote to existential crises but also a pathway to joy and satisfaction. For young people, cultivating purpose early in life can provide a sense of direction and resilience, equipping them to navigate life's challenges with greater confidence.

Maslow's hierarchy of needs and the kosha model: a holistic perspective

One of the most widely recognised psychological models that addresses purpose is Maslow's hierarchy of needs. Developed by Abraham Maslow in the 1940s, this model suggests that human motivation is organised into a pyramid of needs, with each level representing a fundamental human requirement. At the base of the hierarchy are physiological needs, such as food, water and shelter. Above these are safety needs, followed by love and belonging, esteem and, finally, self-actualisation. Self-actualisation, the pinnacle of Maslow's hierarchy, represents the fulfilment of one's potential and purpose, often through creativity, personal growth and a commitment to ideals beyond personal gain.

The *Upanishads*, a collection of ancient Indian texts, present a similar concept through the kosha model, which describes the layers of human existence as concentric sheaths. According to the kosha model, the self is composed of five layers or "sheaths": *annamaya kosha* (the physical body), *pranamaya kosha* (the energy body), *manomaya kosha* (the mental body), *vijnanamaya kosha* (the wisdom or intellectual body) and *anandamaya kosha* (the bliss or spiritual body). Moving from the physical to the spiritual, the kosha model aligns with Maslow's hierarchy by suggesting that as individuals meet their basic needs, they progress towards more abstract and self-transcendent goals, ultimately reaching a state of bliss or unity with a greater purpose. Self-transcendence in spiritual philosophy, particularly within traditions like the *Bhagavad Gītā*, doesn't deny the existence of an eternal spiritual self. Rather, it refers moving beyond the identification with the material aspects of self, like the body, mind and ego-driven desires, to align with the deeper, unchanging nature of the Self.

Both Maslow's and the kosha models highlight the importance of self-transcendence. While Maslow initially placed self-actualisation at the top of his hierarchy, he later revised his model to include self-transcendence as the highest human aspiration. Self-transcendence, according to Maslow, involves connecting with something beyond oneself, whether through service to others, spiritual pursuits or dedication to a cause. This alignment between Western and Eastern models underscores a universal human inclination toward finding purpose, a pursuit that not only fulfils individual needs but also benefits society as a whole.

Purpose and well-being: psychological and physical benefits

Research in psychology has established a strong link between a sense of purpose and psychological well-being. Victor Frankl, a psychiatrist and Holocaust survivor, argued in his book *Man's Search for Meaning* that purpose is essential for survival and resilience. Frankl's logotherapy posits that the primary human drive is not pleasure, as Freud suggested, but rather the search for meaning. Purpose, according to Frankl, enables individuals to endure suffering and find value in life's experiences, even under the harshest conditions. His insights, drawn from personal experience, emphasise that purpose is a powerful psychological resource, providing hope, motivation and a sense of fulfilment.

Empirical studies support Frankl's assertions, showing that individuals with a strong sense of purpose experience lower levels of stress, depression and anxiety. A study published in *The Journal of Positive Psychology* found that people with a sense of purpose reported greater life satisfaction and resilience, particularly during times of adversity. Another study, conducted by Patricia Boyle (2010) at the Rush Alzheimer's Disease Center, found that individuals with a higher sense of purpose were less likely to develop cognitive decline and dementia, suggesting that purpose not only benefits mental health but also promotes cognitive longevity.

Purpose has been linked to physical health benefits as well. Research has shown that individuals with a strong sense of purpose have a lower risk of cardiovascular disease, better immune function, and even increased life expectancy. A study conducted by Celeste Leigh Pearce (2013), published in *Psychosomatic Medicine*, found that people with a high sense of purpose were more likely to engage in health promoting behaviours, such as exercising regularly and maintaining a balanced diet. These findings suggest that purpose acts as a protective factor, influencing lifestyle choices and promoting overall well-being.

Contribution and belonging: the role of purpose in identity formation

Beyond the psychological and physical benefits, purpose plays a vital role in shaping identity and fostering a sense of belonging. In adolescence and early adulthood, individuals undergo a period of identity exploration, as described by Erik Erikson (1950) in his theory of psychosocial development. Erikson identified identity versus role confusion as a central conflict during adolescence, a stage where individuals seek to understand who they are and what they stand for. A sense of purpose provides a foundation for identity, guiding individuals in making choices that align with their values and aspirations.

Finding a sense of purpose often involves contributing to something greater than oneself, whether through community service, social activism or creative pursuits. This commitment fosters a sense of belonging, as individuals connect with others who share their values and goals. Self-determination theory (SDT), developed by psychologists Edward Deci and Richard Ryan, highlights the importance of relatedness, one of the three core needs identified in SDT (the others being autonomy and competence). Relatedness refers to the human need to feel connected to others, and purpose provides a pathway for fulfilling this need, as individuals engage in activities that foster social bonds and contribute to collective well-being.

Purpose also mitigates the effects of social isolation, a growing concern in modern societies where individualism often takes precedence over communal values. Research has shown that loneliness and social isolation are linked to increased risks of mental health issues, cardiovascular disease and premature mortality. By fostering a sense of purpose, individuals are encouraged to engage with their communities, build meaningful relationships and contribute to the well-being of others, thereby reducing the risk of isolation and its associated health consequences.

Spiritual activism is an approach to social change that integrates personal growth with collective action, encouraging individuals to pursue purpose through service to others and the planet. This approach aligns with the principle of *karma yoga*,[1] which advocates for selfless action as a path to spiritual growth.

Spiritual activists view their work as an expression of compassion, empathy and interconnectedness, grounded in a belief that personal transformation is inseparable from social transformation. In recent years, spiritual activism has gained traction as a response to global issues such as climate change, social inequality and racial injustice. Participants in such movements often describe a profound sense of purpose, as they work collectively to address systemic issues and promote positive change. Studies on civic engagement and activism have shown that individuals who participate in social movements experience higher levels of psychological well-being, as they feel part of a meaningful endeavour that transcends personal interests.

Spiritual activism not only fosters purpose but also enhances resilience. By aligning their actions with values, individuals develop a stronger sense of integrity and self-worth. This alignment provides a source of strength during challenging times, as individuals draw on their commitment to a greater cause to navigate obstacles and maintain motivation. Spiritual activism thus serves as a powerful tool for expanding purpose, connecting individuals to a broader vision of justice, compassion, and solidarity.

Expanding purpose in education: preparing learners for a meaningful life

Incorporating purpose into educational curricula offers a pathway for preparing learners for a life of meaning and contribution. Education has traditionally focused on developing cognitive skills and preparing learners for the workforce, but an increasing number of educators and scholars argue that education should also foster personal growth and ethical development. By nurturing a sense of purpose, schools can empower learners to engage with the world in meaningful ways, equipping them with the skills and values needed to address complex global challenges.

Service learning is an educational approach that combines academic instruction with community service, providing learners with opportunities to apply their knowledge to real-world issues. Through service learning, learners develop a sense of purpose as they work to address social and environmental problems, gaining a deeper understanding of their role in society. Research on service learning has shown that learners who participate in these programmes demonstrate increased empathy, civic engagement and critical thinking skills. By connecting academic content with purposeful action, service learning fosters a holistic approach to education that emphasises both intellectual and moral development.

Philosophy and ethics courses can also contribute to expanding purpose in education. By encouraging learners to explore questions of meaning, morality and justice, these courses provide a framework for understanding one's place in the world and the responsibilities that come with it. As discussed in the last chapter, Socratic questioning and dialogue-based learning foster open-mindedness and critical thinking, enabling learners to reflect on their values and consider the broader impact of their actions. In this way, education becomes a vehicle for cultivating purpose, as learners are encouraged to explore their passions, engage with diverse perspectives, and envision a life of contribution.

Identity, wholeness and worth: how purpose makes us whole

Purpose has a transformative effect on identity, fostering a sense of wholeness and intrinsic worth. By dedicating oneself to a cause or purpose, individuals move beyond self-centred concerns and cultivate a sense of integrity and alignment. Purpose provides a framework for understanding oneself in relation to the world, offering a foundation for identity that is grounded in values rather than external validation. This process of becoming "whole" through purpose resonates with Carl Jung's concept of individuation. According to Jung, individuation is the process of integrating the conscious and unconscious aspects of the self, leading to a sense of wholeness and authenticity. Purpose, in this context, serves as a guiding force that helps individuals navigate the complexities of identity, as they reconcile their inner values with their actions in the world. By aligning their lives with a greater purpose, individuals achieve a sense of coherence and unity, as their identity becomes an expression of their deepest convictions.

Purpose also enhances self-worth, providing individuals with a sense of intrinsic value that is independent of external achievements or approval. Psychologist Nathaniel Branden argued that self-esteem is rooted in the alignment between one's values and actions. Purpose offers a pathway for achieving this alignment, as individuals dedicate themselves to causes that reflect their values. This alignment fosters a sense of worth that is resilient to external pressures, as individuals derive their self-esteem from their commitment to a meaningful life rather than from superficial measures of success.

Contributing to something greater than oneself enhances well-being and offers a pathway to lasting fulfilment. Research in positive psychology shows that people engaged in purpose-driven activities report higher life satisfaction, resilience and overall happiness. Purpose provides a depth of meaning that material pursuits cannot replicate. It also supports psychological growth: by taking on meaningful challenges, individuals develop skills, strengthen competence and experience a sense of accomplishment, needs emphasised by self-determination theory.

Purpose-driven contribution also strengthens communities. Higher levels of civic engagement and volunteerism correlate with better mental health, stronger social bonds and greater collective resilience. When societies encourage purposeful action, they foster shared responsibility and communal well-being, echoing communitarian perspectives on the importance of social contribution. Expanding one's purpose is therefore both a personal and collective journey. It connects individuals to a larger whole, nurtures belonging and inspires compassionate action. In recognising our capacity to serve others, we cultivate a life that is both personally meaningful and socially transformative.

A narrated example of expanding purpose

At Open-heart High School, the Year 12 enrichment programme included a new session called *Purpose Lab*, an hour each week dedicated not to careers or grades, but to exploring what it means to live for something larger than oneself. Most learners arrived unsure of what to expect. Among them was Priya, academically strong but quietly anxious about the future, and Callum, who often joked that nothing really mattered anyway.

Priya wrote about her grandmother, who never rushed her work, believing that listening was as important as medicine. "She made people feel seen and heard," Priya reflected, "and I think my life might be for noticing others in the same way." Callum paused for a long time before writing simply: "If I'm more than what I do, then maybe my life is for being someone others can talk to when things feel heavy."

In small groups, the students began sharing. No one compared ambitions or mocked vulnerability. Instead, they listened with a reverence that surprised them. They discovered that beneath different personalities, cultures and aspirations, each was searching for connection, contribution and meaning. They began to see their lives not as private projects to optimise, but as offerings.

Note

1 *Yoga* – Means "union" or "connection." Different paths to connect with the Divine:

- *Karma Yoga*: through selfless action, like serving others without expecting reward.
- *Jñāna Yoga*: through study and insight.
- *Aṣṭāṅga Yoga*: through disciplined meditation, physical discipline and mindfulness.
- *Bhakti Yoga*: through love and devotion, like singing, mantra chanting or prayer.

12 Nourishing loving relationships

At the fullest expression of a soul-led education, all of these beliefs come together in relationship. We are individual souls with unlimited potential, exercising freewill, living in connection, embracing diversity, and seeking purpose. Education becomes an act of care, grounded in deep attention, respect, and love. Through these relationships, lives are transformed. Potential is realised, purpose is lived, and education becomes a sacred responsibility.

Let us meet Annie, a member of the support team at one of the Avanti Schools who writes honestly and emotionally about the impact of working in a place that gave her the feeling of connectedness, spiritualism and fulfilment (even though she does not use this language). There will be countless schools across the globe that create cultures in which people like Annie have a voice, in places they are happy to share their stories and be open about the joys and challenges of life.

> My name is Ann but I like to be called Annie, this all goes back to a traumatic child hood where someone would call me Ann who was not very nice, yes I know my name is Ann, but Annie feels a little more softer to me and I did like to be connected with Annie the film as she was adopted the same as me, I was adopted by my half-brother at the age of 7, him and his wife showed me what a normal life could be, I was taken away from my mum and her boyfriend, my dad was my everything but he was much older than my mum and Social services would not let me live with him so I went to live with my big brother, so much has happened in my life and then into adulthood.

DOI: 10.4324/9781003487654-15

I have three children Fiona 23, Frankie 18 from my first marriage and Owain who is 13, from my marriage now he is a student here at Avanti, when we came to look around Avanti we knew straight away it was the school for our boy, the nurture and Avanti beliefs were just what we wanted for our caring little man it was then. It was then I also realised that I wanted to also be part of the Avanti Family. Just over 12 years ago I was diagnosed with stage 3 breast cancer I went through chemo, it showed be that no matter how high or tough that mountain is I can I will get there does not matter how but with courage, respect and Gratitude for a second chance, then four years ago it came back and I went through a mastectomy again I got there in the end. And I am here working at Avanti now part of our family…Avanti have shown Owain strength, love and embedded in him the true qualities to him and me, It is supporting our son to be a leader who has done many things supporting Charity such as the homeless appeal last Christmas food bank appeal and walking just over ten miles for a Charity in the community we live.

Just want to say thank you Avanti. I had a chat with our new CEO, James, and we talked about doing the inner work to make the outer life easier to manage or to get through. I told him I have my network of friends who understand and also Church and so it is working because it's been hard for me in many ways. This is what education could be – when we really do find ways for our learners – it is helping them for living now and in future and to understand the past.

Written narrative by Annie | Avanti Schools Trust

Annie's reflection embodies the essence of soul work, an ongoing journey of healing, belonging, and becoming. Her story reminds us that education, when rooted in compassion and authenticity, creates spaces where souls can grow together. Through vulnerability, Annie invites us into a community that listens deeply and honours the whole person. Her experience of finding connection and purpose within the Avanti family reveals how the soul's search for meaning is not a solitary act but a shared endeavour. In speaking openly about pain, gratitude and resilience, Annie shows how the inner work of the soul intertwines with the collective work of nurturing empathy, courage and love within a community that truly sees and supports one another.

Human relationships play a foundational role in our well-being, development, and capacity to live fulfilling lives. In every context – educational, professional, familial – the quality of our relationships shapes how we perceive ourselves and others, and it informs our ability to flourish. This chapter explores the significance of nourishing relationships in various spheres of life, including the workplace and education. Drawing on insights from psychology, education, philosophy and spirituality, we will examine how relationships affect well-being, learning and personal growth, and discuss how we can cultivate them to benefit ourselves and others.

The power of relationships: an essential human need

The significance of relationships to human well-being has long been acknowledged in philosophy, psychology and spiritual traditions. According to the Vedic tradition, two fundamental needs of the Self are to love and to be loved. Love in this sense transcends mere affection; it is a profound sense of connection that enables individuals to feel valued, safe and understood. This perspective resonates with attachment theory in psychology, which suggests that secure attachments provide a foundation for personal growth, resilience and emotional stability.

The Harvard Study of Adult Development, one of the longest-running studies on adult happiness, provides empirical evidence that close relationships, not wealth or fame, are the greatest predictors of long-term happiness and health. The study concluded that individuals with strong relationships experienced lower levels of stress, better health outcomes and increased life satisfaction. These findings underscore the transformative potential of relationships in shaping a fulfilling life. Relationships, when characterised by love and trust, allow individuals to thrive, as they offer a stable foundation upon which to confront life's challenges and pursue personal and professional goals.

Relationships sit at the heart of meaningful education. In every classroom, the quality of human connection shapes how young people learn, feel, and grow.

Relational education begins with a simple yet profound truth: learners flourish when they feel seen, safe and valued. Maslow's hierarchy reminds us that belonging and emotional security are prerequisites for learning; a young person who feels anxious, isolated, or misunderstood cannot fully absorb knowledge or take intellectual risks (Maslow, 1943). When teachers build trust and connection, they create the psychological conditions that make curiosity, engagement and resilience possible.

Research consistently affirms the importance of these bonds. Hattie's (2009) meta-analyses highlight teacher–pupil relationships as one of the most powerful influences on achievement. Similarly, Bergin and Bergin (2009) show that warm, supportive classroom relationships enhance emotional regulation, social competence and academic progress, especially for younger children who rely deeply on relational reassurance. A teacher's presence, attitude, and attentiveness can therefore become catalysts for a young person's confidence and long-term motivation.

Despite this, modern life often makes genuine connection difficult. Time, perhaps our most precious resource, has become one of the greatest barriers to nurturing relationships. A Harvard Business Review study found that many adults feel they lack the time to build meaningful relationships at work (Cross, Rebele and Grant, 2016). In education, teachers frequently describe feeling overwhelmed by administrative responsibilities, high workloads and performance pressures. These demands can crowd out the relational moments that truly matter listening to a learner who is struggling, supporting a colleague or investing in shared reflection.

Addressing this challenge requires both individual intention and systemic support. Teachers can carve out small but consistent spaces for relationship-building, greeting learners at the door, creating rituals of connection or prioritising one-to-one conversations when they matter most. Yet schools and wider systems also have a responsibility to enable this work. When leaders reduce unnecessary bureaucracy, protect time for collaboration and value relational practice alongside academic outcomes, they create cultures where connections can thrive. Leadership, therefore, is not merely an administrative function but a relational one.

At the core of strong relationships lies relational ethics, the commitment to act with integrity, care, and respect. Gilligan's (1982) ethic of care emphasises that ethical behaviour is rooted not in abstract rules but in how we treat one another. Relational ethics invites us to listen deeply, respond compassionately, and honour the dignity of others. Integrity is essential here: when individuals align their actions with their values, they establish trustworthiness and consistency. This steadiness gives relationships substance, enabling genuine openness and dialogue.

Kant's (1785) insistence that every person should be treated as an "end in themselves" echoes this relational stance. It reminds us that relationships are not transactional; they are encounters with beings who hold intrinsic worth. When respect becomes a guiding principle, classrooms and workplaces transform into spaces where people feel recognised rather than used, appreciated rather than judged.

Beyond their social and ethical dimensions, relationships also hold spiritual significance. Many spiritual traditions, including Vedic philosophy, teach that connection, compassion and love are essential to human fulfilment (Easwaran, 2007). These perspectives suggest that relationships are not merely helpful for well-being, they are profound expressions of our shared humanity. Positive psychology aligns with this view, showing that loving, supportive relationships reliably predict increased meaning, joy, and life satisfaction (Seligman, 2011). When approached with openness and gratitude, relationships become sources of renewal, offering strength during difficulty and perspective during uncertainty.

Education grounded in relational principles intentionally cultivates these capacities. It teaches young people the skills of listening, empathy, collaboration and emotional literacy, skills increasingly vital in a world shaped by digital communication and fragmented attention. Relational education prioritises face-to-face connection, encourages cooperative learning and gives learners opportunities to navigate interpersonal challenges with guidance. Social and emotional learning research shows that such approaches enhance academic outcomes, emotional well-being, and social competence (Shonkoff and Phillips, 2000). When schools teach relational skills explicitly, they prepare young people not only for exams but for life.

Ultimately, loving and supportive relationships have transformative power. They shape our sense of self, strengthen our resilience, and inspire us to contribute positively to the world. In education, they create environments where learners can take risks, trust their abilities and feel held through difficulty. For teachers and leaders, they provide the emotional foundation that sustains the work of teaching, a profession rooted not in transactions but in human growth.

A narrated example of nourishing loving relationships

Each day, Jack arrived at the Assistant Headteacher's office straight from the football pitch – flushed, breathless, angry. The story was always the same: someone hadn't followed the rules. It wasn't fair. Voices had been raised. Swearing and insults had been used.

Mr Riley did not rush to fix it. He did not lecture. He did not dismiss. He observed and listened while Jack paced violently. Sometimes Jack threw things off Mr Riley's desk. He waited while the heat slowly left the room. Be present then find solutions later.

When Jack finally sat down his anger abating, Mr. Riley said quietly, "I can see how angry you are. I'm wondering if what really matters to you is fairness."

Jack looked up. "Yes."

More silence. More settling.

"It's not fair when they don't follow the rules," Jack added, this time without shouting.

"I agree," Mr Riley said. "Fairness matters. And you care about it deeply. That's a strength." Then he paused. "Have you thought that because you get what it means to be fair, you have a chance to teach your friends also?"

This was the challenge – not a rebuke, not a rescue, but an invitation.

Jack looked surprised and a small smile came to his face. Over a few days, they explored alternatives together: ways to speak before anger took over, ways to influence rather than explode, ways to hold to what mattered without losing himself in the heat of it. They drew the situation on paper, writing bubble text boxes to repeat the language spoken and what different words could do to change the situation. Lots of social story making.

Each time Jack came to his room (still angry sometimes because nothing changes over night – Rome wasn't built in a day!) and each time he left slightly calmer, Mr Riley said something he would repeat in different forms over the weeks that followed:

> My job isn't to save you from hard things. It's to walk with you through them. I won't step in every time it feels unfair. I believe

you can handle more than that. And because I believe in you,
I'm going to challenge you to find better ways to be heard.

This was not indulging a child with anger issues nor was it permissiveness. And it was not sentimental. It was love in its truest educational form:

to see a young person clearly,
to name the good within them,
to refuse to let them shrink to their worst moment,
and to hold them steady while they grow.

Over the following weeks, Mr Riley did exactly that. He redirected Jack back into learning. He held firm boundaries. He noticed small improvements and named them. He did not withdraw warmth when Jack faltered. Nor did he lower expectations when Jack pushed back.

Jack knew something important: Mr Riley liked him. But he also knew that liking did not mean giving in. It meant being taken seriously. It meant being expected to rise. And slowly, the football pitch changed – not because the rules were enforced more loudly, but because Jack was learning that strength without self-mastery is noise, and strength with awareness becomes leadership.

This is the quiet power of relationship grounded in truth and care:

to stay present in the storm,
to challenge without shaming,
to affirm without rescuing,
and to call someone forward into who they are capable of becoming.

This is nourishing loving relationships.

PART C

Walking the journey

Living by virtues and defining what is valued

13 Six virtues

Respect, self-discipline, integrity, courage, empathy and gratitude

In everyday language, the terms *virtues* and *values* are often used interchangeably. Yet, virtues carry a deeper sense: they are not simply what we hold dear (values), but the enduring qualities of character that enable human beings to flourish. Virtues shape who we are and how we live. This chapter introduces six composite virtues drawn from Vedic texts: qualities seen as essential for human flourishing. In the Vedic tradition, virtues are not abstract concepts but lived realities, expressed through story, poetry, dialogue and example. In Chapter 14, we explore what is valued in a soul-led education. In this chapter, we focus on six virtues.

For virtues to have meaning, they must be practised and experienced in the interactions between children and their friends, between colleagues, with parents and community members and between adults and children. When James Biddulph was the Headteacher of one of the Avanti Schools, he received an email that showed the impact that the Avanti approach to education was having on one child. Jahkai[1] joined the school having almost been excluded from a previous school. He was only six years old.

> Email received 14th February
>
> Dear Mr Biddulph,
>
> What has happened to my son? Each day he complains to me and is very demanding. And it is the school's fault!
>
> Jahkai is always eager to rush to school every morning often telling me I'm making him late for meditation which always makes me smile. This is just a short email to express my gratitude and thanks for

DOI: 10.4324/9781003487654-17

all of the hard and effort displayed by your staff in relation to Jahkai's behaviour and education at Avanti Court.

Although Jahkai is a charming, smart young boy, it is also fair to say that before he attended Avanti Court, he demonstrated some behavioural difficulties which stood in the way of his learning. Such behaviour lead (*sic.*) to me temporary stop employment (*sic*) to attend several meetings surrounding SEN processing as Jahkai's learning was on a fast decline. In the end, I took the very difficult decision as a parent with another child attending the same school to remove Jahkai from his old school.

If I am honest, I wasn't too keen on Avanti Court in the beginning, partly due to the lack of history. I felt I had no one to correspond with on a personal level, nowhere to really go to for a point of reference surrounding the school's ethics accept (*sic.*) the school's own website. My main concern was how Jahkai would fit in. In the end, I took a leap of faith and enrolled him in October with all my fingers and toes crossed.

Jahkai has been a pupil of Avanti Court for just over four months now and I can honestly say that he is a different child. In simple terms, descriptive words used for Jahkai prior might of (*sic*) been, Boisterous, Naughty, Uncontrollable. Now Jahkai is described by friends and family as Warm, Polite and Bright. I can see he enjoys playing with his peers and, more importantly, Jahkai's new *can-do* approach to learning has done a whole 360. He enjoys reading to me, he counts out all my money indicating where I am short, he listens to others when they talk and takes full accountability for his actions when he misbehaves, which is less often of late.

I could not be a prouder parent. Your school has taught my son ethics and values, to care for others and to want to do better as a young man himself.

I am forever grateful.

The educational challenge, then, is how to cultivate these qualities in young people within systems often dominated by performative pressures and when fitting in is more important than belonging in. This is what Jahkai's mother was writing about: how the virtues, values and beliefs at Avanti were nurturing in her child the qualities of being a 'better young man' rather than seeing his behaviours as problematic because they did not fit with the system. In this case, the system flexed because the virtues and beliefs were well articulated and lived out.

When the early-stage Avanti curriculum team set about exploring virtues, we first created a longlist, endorsed by Vedic texts such as the *Bhagavad Gītā* and the *Bhagavata Purana*. Table 13.1 collates the longlist, suggesting how the virtue may be seen in practice or in behaviours of children, young people and adults in schools.

As you might imagine, this longlist exceeded over 100 separate virtues. Our task was then to group and streamline without forcing or losing depth in the process. It emerged that there were six themes, or what we

Table 13.1 Collation of virtues from Vedic texts

Virtue	What we would see | Behaviours
Humility	Offers respect to all / Doesn't demand undue respect / Service attitude Aware of own shortcomings / Understands own talents as God-given / Admits mistakes Reflexive / Doesn't react with pride or anger / Accepts destiny
Empathy	Empathic / Kind and Caring / Loving / Considerate/ Compassionate / Forgiving / Sharing / Sympathetic /Amiable / Self-accepting /Builds rapport with others Concerned for animals and environment / Nonviolent / Sees the real self within
Self-discipline	Well-mannered / Self-controlled / Disciplined / Punctual / Patient / Grave Enjoys stillness, reflection, prayer and meditation / Introspective / Discerning Clean /Neat + tidy Conscientious /Has foresight /Avoids compulsive habits
Respect	Likes and respects self / Polite / Well-behaved /Courteous to all and elders Respects other faiths +cultures / Aptly treats private and public property Acknowledges other's needs, beliefs + boundaries / Sees the divine everywhere

(Continued)

Table 13.1 Collation of virtues from Vedic texts *(Continued)*

Virtue	What we would see | Behaviours
Integrity	Honest / Truthful / Keeps promises / Responsible / Reliable / Loyal / Reflexive Admits and rectifies mistakes / Content / Satisfied / Fulfilled / Magnanimous Authentic / Autonomous / Possesses self-worth / Keeps appropriate company
Courage	Self-assured / Self-reliant / Has esteem (in self, family and tradition) / Confident Meets own needs Creative / Innovative / Leadership in group / Optimistic / Motivated / Determined / Perseverant / Fearless Curious / Inquisitive
Gratitude	Says 'thank you' / Celebrates life/ Appreciates life; beauty; parents; teachers. Others' talents and contributions; gifts of God and nature/ Feels awe and wonder Reciprocates with others / Co-operative / Joyful / Playful / Humorous

might call 'meta virtues': respect, self-discipline, integrity, courage, gratitude and empathy. This was obviously not an exact science, and we were never going to arrive at a perfect solution, but we did feel that these six virtues captured the essence of much of what the Vedic texts endorsed as virtue.

What follows is a detailed exploration of each virtue. In each section, we follow the same structure: we start with the English word and include the Sanskrit translations; then we give an Oxford English Dictionary definition of the English word. After this, we include a story from the *Panchatantra* (the collection that some believe inspired Aesop's fables). The stories are drawn from India's philosophical and cultural oral traditions, and we share them to remain faithful to that heritage. They are retold by us here. As well as a story, we provide a lived example from one of the Avanti schools or staff members; the aim is to illustrate how the virtue is experienced in practice. Within these stylistic features, we include discussion about each virtue.

Six virtues for a soul-led education

Respect (ādara, vinamrata, śraddhā, ācāryopāsanam) is a foundational virtue

Definition (Oxford English Dictionary): *Respect (n.) – a feeling of deep admiration for someone or something elicited by their abilities, qualities, or achievements; due regard for the feelings, wishes, or rights of others.*

***The Brahmin and the Mongoose**, tells us about the respect... Once upon a time, in a quiet village, there lived a kind Brahmin (wise holy man), his wife, their baby, and a faithful mongoose. The Brahmin had raised the mongoose like his own child, and the creature grew loyal and gentle. One day, the Brahmin went out to the fields. His wife needed to fetch water, so she left the baby asleep in his cradle, telling herself she would return quickly. The mongoose lay near the baby, watchful. As the wife walked away, a snake slithered into the house, its eyes fixed on the cradle. The mongoose leapt up; teeth bared. After a fierce struggle, the mongoose bit the snake again and again until the snake lay lifeless. Proud of saving the baby, the mongoose waited at the door for the mistress to return. When the wife came back and saw the mongoose's mouth stained with blood, she gasped in horror. Certain the animal had attacked her baby, she shouted and, in anger, struck the mongoose with her pot of water. The poor creature fell dead at once. She rushed inside, only to find the baby fast asleep and unharmed, the dead snake beside him. Realizing what had truly happened, the Brahmin's wife wept bitterly, but her grief could not bring the faithful mongoose back.*

Respect is both a virtue and a practice. Philosophically, it rests on three foundations: recognising dignity, adopting humility, and sustaining that dignity through action, speech and fairness. In the story, the wife did not show dignity to the mongoose, believing instead in his evil action against her child, despite the fact that the mongoose had served the family with love and attention. In the Vedic tradition, respect is inseparable from pedagogy and devotion: humility and service (*seva*) form the ethical frame for learning and relationship. The seemingly simple tale shows how the mongoose lived with humility and service, respecting the humans through his attitude and actions towards them. The *Bhagavad Gītā* (4.34) encourages the learner to approach the teacher with humility, service and questioning, a recognition that true learning demands deference without submission. Respect thus shapes the disposition to listen, revise and integrate knowledge.

Affectively, respect regulates emotion: it tempers aggression, supports patience and nurtures trust. The wife did not show such regulation. Where respect is present, young people take risks, seek help, and persevere; where absent, shame or defensive pride dominate. Respect also conditions autonomy. Respect therefore becomes the social ground on which individuals and institutions flourish. In schools, respect takes form through attentive listening, disciplined conduct, and adults modelling humility. Teachers enact it by offering focused attention, explaining reasons for sanctions, avoiding shaming and admitting mistakes. Learners embody it when they listen carefully, accept feedback, treat peers fairly and care for shared spaces. At an institutional level, respect is cultivated through rituals, codes of conduct, restorative practices, and ongoing professional learning. Respect needs to be seen and enacted, as the young children in Tiva's class demonstrate.

The earth is not a rubbish bin: little voices of respect

At Avanti, we speak often of nurturing children to become spiritually compassionate changemakers but witnessing this in our youngest learners is something truly special. In our Early Years and Foundation Stage (EYFS) setting (class of four- and five-year-old children), a spark has been lit. Inspired by their learning about the natural world and driven by deep empathy for the environment, our children have become passionate eco-warriors. Moved by concerns about pollution and environmental care, the children decided to make their voices heard. With great care and creativity, they designed powerful posters filled with heartfelt messages and artwork. Their chants, loud, proud and joyfully composed, echoed with urgency and love for the Earth. The sunken lawn became their protest ground, where they marched with determination and delight, drawing attention from the whole school community. Our EYFS children have shown that when we educate the head, heart and hand together, transformation begins early. They are not just learning *about* the world; they are beginning to *change it*. We couldn't be prouder of our future changemakers.

By Tiva Corcoran, Early Years Senior
Leader at Avanti Gardens, Bristol

For a Western readership, this Vedic notion of respect resonates with contemporary educational theories that stress relationality and mutual recognition. Yet, it extends further by grounding respect not only in social contract but in metaphysical vision: every being is worthy of regard because every being participates in ultimate reality. Respect in education is not optional etiquette but a spiritual imperative. It creates conditions where learners feel safe to explore, where teachers remain humble in their guidance, and where the classroom mirrors the deeper truth of unity amidst diversity.

Self-discipline (tapas, ātma–vinirṇaya, sādhanā)

Definition (Oxford English Dictionary): *Self-discipline (n.) – the ability to control one's feelings and overcome one's weaknesses; the capacity to pursue what one thinks is right despite temptations to abandon it.*

*Our Panchatantra story for Self-discipline is called **The Wedge-pulling Monkey**. In a city where great temples were being built, carpenters worked from dawn till dusk. One day, a carpenter split a huge log of wood and drove a wedge into it, planning to return after lunch. Nearby, a troop of monkeys was playing. Curious about everything, they leapt from tree to scaffold. One monkey noticed the half-split log with the wedge stuck inside. He examined it, poked at it, and wondered what would happen if he pulled it out. The other monkeys shouted, "Leave it! Come eat mangoes with us!" But the monkey's curiosity grew stronger. Ignoring their calls, he sat on the log and tugged at the wedge. At first nothing happened. He tugged harder. With a crack, the wedge came free. But his tail, which had slipped into the gap, was caught as the log snapped shut. The poor monkey screamed in pain, trapped and helpless. By the time the carpenters returned, they found him stuck fast, thrashing and bleeding. The other monkeys scattered, frightened. The curious monkey, who could not resist meddling with what was not his, paid dearly for his impatience.*

Self-discipline may be understood as the ordered governance of appetite, attention and action. The monkey demonstrated a lack of self-discipline and was literally caught in the painful act! In the Vedic tradition, discipline is not suppression but the constructive shaping of the will into practice. The *Bhagavad Gītā* (6.16–17) highlights self-discipline in relation to moderation in food, recreation, work and rest as essential to sustained practice.

Contemporary psychology offers a parallel emphasis. Self-discipline supports executive function – planning, inhibitory control and sustained attention – and underpins resilience by fostering coping strategies and reducing impulsivity.

It also grounds moral agency: the regulation of desire enables action aligned with considered ends such as courage and integrity, rather than immediate appetite.

Within education, cultivating self-discipline should not take the form of moralising or punitive control but of autonomy-supportive structures that encourage intrinsic motivation. Clear routines, scaffolded practice, goal-setting and reflective feedback help to establish habits that build capacity over time. Self-discipline is thus both an individual disposition and a social achievement, dependent on supportive institutional culture. In schools, it is visible not as passive obedience but as habit: punctuality, sustained study, task completion, emotional regulation and persistence in difficulty. Teachers model self-discipline through careful preparation, calm responses, and consistent enforcement of norms. Institutional practices such as structured daily routines, incremental goals, deliberate practice and formative assessment further sustain its development. In our Avanti example, Dale explains how his own self-discipline brought him closer to a job that he realised he loved.

Living the Avanti Way: Self-discipline on a journey of growth

I first started volunteering at Avanti House Primary School in the summer of 2018, joining the estates team. From day one, I was blown away by how welcoming everyone was, especially the pupils. They didn't just say hello in passing, they genuinely made me feel like I belonged. There was something about the energy in the school that felt different genuine, uplifting, and full of purpose. I remember thinking, "Is this real?" As a father of two, I couldn't help but compare it to my own children's schools. The difference was huge. The atmosphere at Avanti wasn't just calm and respectful, it was full of life and meaning. You could feel the values being lived out, not just spoken about. The way staff and pupils treated each other with kindness and care really stayed with me.

As time went on, a full-time position came up and I didn't think twice about applying. By then, I already felt part of the Avanti family. The Avanti Way had started to shape me, both in and out of work. I found myself growing in confidence, not just in my role but in who I was as a person. It helped me become more mindful, more grounded and even a better dad.

One moment that really stands out for me was when I was promoted to Deputy Head of Estates. I didn't expect much of a reaction, but what followed truly touched me. Pupils I'd seen grow over the years came up to shake my hand, give me high fives or just say "well done" with the biggest smiles on their faces. A few even made little cards. One parent stopped me outside and said, "You really deserve this. You always go above and beyond, and the children see it." I was honestly speechless. It meant so much to be recognised, not with a big fuss, but with genuine appreciation from the very people we do this for.

What continues to amaze me is that, even now, when I return to Avanti House Primary School, pupils still remember me. They call out my name, stop to chat, and ask how I'm doing. There's something incredibly special about that. And it's even more rewarding when I see those same pupils later as they transition into Avanti House Secondary School. Watching their journey continue, seeing them carry the same values and kindness into the next stage of their lives, fills me with pride. It reminds me that the connections we make and the example we set really do last.

Now, seven years on, I'm still here. Still learning, still growing, and still proud to be part of something that goes beyond just education. I've seen children show incredible compassion, staff support each other through challenges and moments of real spiritual insight, sometimes from the youngest pupils. The Avanti Way isn't just a set of virtues on a wall. It's something we live and breathe every day. That needs Self-discipline for sure because life is not always so easy, is it?

Working at Avanti House Primary School has changed me. It's helped me realise the power of small actions, of consistency and of community. It's reminded me that whatever your role, whether you're teaching in the classroom or keeping the school running behind the scenes, we all have the chance to make a difference. And this requires Self-discipline which is one of our virtues: it is about working hard, focused on the mission to reimagine the purpose of education and trying, in whatever way we can in our role, to show the vision which is to inspire spiritually compassionate changemakers. None of that happens with chance it needs everyone to have Self-discipline and to do their part of the puzzle. I came to Avanti thinking I was just giving a bit of my time. But what I've received in return is far greater: a sense of belonging, purpose and the privilege of being part of something truly meaningful.

By Dale Craig, Deputy Head of Estates, Avanti Schools Trust

In Vedic thought, self-discipline is regarded as a foundational virtue, enabling the individual to direct energy purposefully rather than being scattered by desires or distractions. It is not repression but regulation – the conscious shaping of one's impulses to align with higher aims. In the *Bhagavad Gītā* (6.5), Krishna says, "One should uplift oneself by one's own mind and not degrade oneself. The mind is both the friend and the enemy of the self." Here, discipline is framed as mastery over the mind, such that it becomes an ally in the pursuit of truth and freedom rather than a tyrant dragging one into cycles of confusion. Therefore, from a Vedic perspective, self-discipline is the bedrock of genuine freedom.

Integrity (satyam, Trikāraṇa–śuddhi)

Definition (Oxford English Dictionary): *Integrity (n.) – the quality of being honest and having strong moral principles; the state of being whole and undivided.*

The Merchant's Honest Son *from Panchantantra tells of a wealthy merchant and his two sons. The elder was greedy, but the younger was honest and kind. When the merchant died, the elder brother seized most of the goods and sent the younger away with only a heavy iron balance. The younger son opened a small shop. He weighed every item with fairness, never cheating a customer. Soon people trusted him, and his shop prospered. One day the elder brother, now in debt, brought gold to sell. He asked his younger brother to weigh it. The honest son placed the gold on the scale, but secretly the elder had filled one side with wax so the balance would tilt unfairly. The sun's heat melted the wax, and the fraud was revealed. The crowd grew angry, shouting, "How dare you trick your own brother?" Ashamed, the elder hung his head. He realized that dishonesty had ruined his name, while his brother's fairness had won him respect and success.*

Integrity – understood as the consistency of thought, word and deed – lies at the heart of moral agency. The *Bhagavad Gītā* (16.1–3) identifies truthfulness and straightforwardness as divine qualities, framing integrity as both relational and metaphysical: it sustains social trust and orients the self towards a moral purpose. Philosophically, integrity extends beyond honesty to the integration of commitments into a coherent character, marked by alignment between what one thinks, says, and does. Such integrity enables trust, which is indispensable for teaching and learning; where it is absent, cynicism and disengagement quickly follow. Integrity also strengthens autonomy, since truthfulness to self and other grounds deliberation and accountability.

In educational practice, integrity appears in honesty in academic work, fidelity to promises, transparent marking and feedback, and consistency in applying policies. Teachers model it by explaining decisions, admitting mistakes and embodying the principles they teach. Schools can foster integrity through honour codes, calibrated assessment standards and restorative responses to breaches.

Keeping integrity to the Avanti Way

As a member of the central team at Avanti, we often do not get the opportunity to interact with pupils however we can be observers of their character formation and conduct at school. I have often observed children in the worship hall making space for children of other faiths, demonstrating the kind of respect that embodies the Avanti way. Our worship hall is also used for yoga classes with mindfulness practices.

These classes help to develop children's level of awareness of their state of mind and enables them to balance the pressures of a rigorous curriculum. As central staff members, we were required to visit one of our schools so we can gain insight into what happens on the ground. During our visit, we witnessed exemplary behaviour from children. They were made to do mindful colouring and their yoga class integrated complex Vedic concepts in an engaging manner. The pupils seemed to have really enjoyed this class and were more relaxed in the following classes. By encouraging pupils to engage with their internal states, it facilitates their journey of self-discovery, paving the way to become change makers in the real world. This is all about integrity in my view; it is about how we hold our values and virtues strongly and try and live them and create experiences for children and young people also. It is also about being true to the Avanti virtues and not going off alone and doing only what we think is right or correct.

Having integrity also means living the Avanti way with honesty in mind, body and soul – in the head, hand and heart.

By Dhara Suryakumar, Finance Department, Leicester

Integrity, in the Vedic vision, is not simply adherence to honesty but the alignment of thought, word, and deed in a manner that reflects both inner authenticity and outer responsibility. The Sanskrit concept of truth provides a foundation for this virtue: truth is not only factual correctness but fidelity to ultimate reality. To live with integrity is to bring one's life into harmony with that truth, cultivating coherence between the inner self and outward action. In the *Bhagavad Gītā* (16.1–3), integrity is implicit in the description of divine qualities such as fearlessness, purity of heart, truthfulness, and self-control, which together constitute the character of one fit for liberation. Integrity is therefore less about following external rules than embodying an inner consistency rooted in truth.

Integrity resonates with contemporary emphases on authenticity and transparency, particularly in educational and civic life. Yet, it also adds a profound dimension: integrity is not merely a pragmatic virtue that builds trust and social capital, but a spiritual necessity for self-realisation. In education, fostering integrity means encouraging learners to speak truthfully, act consistently and align their lives with values that transcend self-interest. In doing so, education not only builds trust in relationships but also cultivates a deeper sense of self-worth, as individuals experience the freedom of being undivided – whole in themselves and aligned with the truth that sustains the cosmos.

Courage (saurya/Dhṛti)

Definition (Oxford English Dictionary): *Courage (n.) – the ability to do something that frightens one; strength in the face of pain or grief.*

***The Lion and the Hare**: A fierce lion lived in a forest, preying on animals at will. Terrified, the animals begged him, "Great Lion, spare us the trouble of hiding daily. We will send one animal to you each day as food." The lion agreed. Each day an animal went to the lion. One day it was the hare's turn. The hare, small but clever, walked slowly. The sun began to set before he reached the lion's den. The lion roared in anger. "Why are you late?" The hare bowed. "Forgive me, mighty one. Another lion stopped me. He claimed he is master of this forest." The lion's eyes blazed. "Another lion? Show me at once!" The hare led him to a deep well. "He lives down there," he said. The lion peered into the water and saw his own reflection. Thinking it was his rival; he leapt in with a roar. The well swallowed him, and the forest was free. The animals cheered the hare's bravery and wit.*

Narratives from the *Rāmāyaṇa*[2] and the *Purāṇas*[3] – such as the heroism of Rāma or the devotion of exemplary figures – offer stories of courageous action in service of *dharma* (true purpose). In Vedic and classical ethics, courage is defined as the capacity to act rightly despite fear. The *Bhagavad Gītā* (2.31–37) frames courage within duty: rightful action must be pursued even when personal attachments render it painful. Philosophically, courage stabilises moral agency, enabling the pursuit of goodness such as justice, truth and service, even at personal cost. Distinct from recklessness, true courage is guided by prudence and concern for the common good.

In education, courage involves supporting young people to take intellectual risks, challenge injustice and persist in ethical action despite external pressures. It is visible when young people ask difficult questions, oppose bullying, or undertake demanding projects; when teachers address controversial material with integrity; and when leaders admit mistakes and correct course.

Courage (and empathy) in action

Two years ago, a student entered my Spanish class appearing completely disengaged. He rarely contributed, often switched off and seemed emotionally disconnected from the subject. His lack of confidence and motivation was evident, and at first it was difficult to see how he might progress. I began working with him one-to-one, tailoring interventions to his pace and interests, offering encouragement and building trust. The change was not immediate but gradual, nurtured through patience and consistency. Over time, something remarkable unfolded: he began to engage, to find his voice and to grow in confidence. Today, that same student is flourishing academically, working at a grade 9 level with near-native fluency, and has become one of the strongest Spanish linguists in his year group. His journey is nothing short of inspiring.

What has made his transformation so significant is how clearly it reflects the Avanti Way in action. He came to see that learning is not a race but a process of self-discovery, and that education is about nourishing body, mind and spirit. The classroom became a safe and supportive space where he could reflect, take risks and thrive. Through this experience, he has come to embody Avanti's virtues. His resilience enabled him to persevere when progress was slow; his positivity gave him courage to embrace challenges; his self-discipline allowed him to work independently towards excellence; and his respect for both peers and teachers shone through in every interaction.

Equally important has been the shift in his beliefs. He moved from the self-defeating mindset of "I can't do this" to an empowered conviction that "I am capable of growth." Spanish became more than a subject, it became a way of connecting with cultures, people, and opportunities beyond himself. Relationships were crucial to this transformation. Trust built through one-to-one sessions provided a foundation for confidence, while peer collaboration offered belonging and purpose. Overcoming his fear of mistakes was pivotal, as he learned to see errors as stepping stones rather than failures.

Now, he is emerging as a quiet leader, contributing with confidence, supporting classmates and aspiring to mentor younger young people as a language ambassador. His journey has deepened his sense of purpose, faith and community, and he now embodies unity, gratitude and respect, living proof of the power of education *with soul*.

Written by Neetu Sadhwani (Head of Modern Foreign Languages, Avanti House Secondary School)

Courage is not merely physical bravery but the inner fortitude to transcend fear, endure hardship and remain steadfast in the pursuit of truth. The Hare showed great courage in challenging the Lion's power and authority, and in so doing brought a better quality of life to the forest animals – they no longer needed to live in fear. It is a warrior attitude; in the mode of passion because it requires a certain energy. It is the quality that frees human beings from artificial boundaries that limit growth – whether those boundaries arise from social conventions, personal doubts or existential fears. The *Bhagavad Gītā* presents courage as indispensable for the spiritual warrior. Arjuna's crisis on the battlefield exemplifies the paralysis that comes when fear and confusion overwhelm conviction. Krishna reminds him that to retreat from his dharma is to succumb to cowardice, urging: "Yield not to weakness; it does not befit you. Cast off this petty faintheartedness and arise, O scorcher of foes!" (*Gītā* 2.3). Here, courage is framed as the capacity to act in alignment with duty (*svadharma*), even in the face of uncertainty and loss.

Gratitude (Kṛtajñatā/Anukampa)

Definition (Oxford English Dictionary): *Gratitude (n.) – the quality of being thankful; readiness to show appreciation for and to return kindness.*

Panchatantra's ***The Monkey and the Crocodile*** *tells of a monkey who befriends a crocodile. A monkey lived on a fruit tree by the river. He shared the sweet fruits with a crocodile who often visited. They became friends. The crocodile carried fruit home for his wife. But the wife grew greedy. "If the fruits are so sweet, imagine how sweet the monkey's heart must be! Bring it to me." The crocodile, torn between loyalty and desire, invited the monkey to his home. Midway across the river he confessed, "My wife wants your heart." The monkey was shocked, but calmly replied, "Friend, why didn't you say so earlier? I left my heart on the tree. Let us go back and fetch it." The crocodile turned toward the bank. As soon as they reached the tree, the monkey leapt to safety. "I gave you fruit, friendship, and trust," he said sadly, "but you betrayed me." The crocodile hung his head, ashamed. The monkey never crossed the river again.*

Gratitude can take many forms. The crocodile's wife did not show gratitude but rather envy and greed. Gratitude may be personal – thanking a parent, teacher or friend for the care and support they offer. It may be communal – recognising the contribution of colleagues, classmates or a whole school community. It may be historical or cultural – acknowledging the knowledge, traditions and institutions built by those who came before us. In many religious and philosophical traditions, gratitude also takes a spiritual form, directed towards the divine or to life itself.

Each type of gratitude shapes relationships in different ways. Personal gratitude strengthens bonds of trust and care; communal gratitude builds belonging and solidarity; historical gratitude connects learners to a wider story; and spiritual gratitude nurtures humility and reverence. In schools, gratitude can be encouraged in simple, practical ways: young people writing thankyou notes, keeping a gratitude journal or recognising one another's efforts in assemblies. Teachers and leaders can model gratitude by acknowledging the contributions of staff and pupils, and by naming the ways that collective effort supports learning. These practices help make gratitude a habit rather than a one-off gesture.

Yogesh is a long-standing member of staff at Avanti. Unfortunately, he was struck by a period of ill health that required him to take a long leave of absence. On his return, his comments about Avanti foreground the psychological benefits of spirituality, as experienced through relationships and a deep sense of communal care. His email to a colleague shares his thoughts:

Gratitude in a moment of crisis

I would like to express my deep gratitude to the entire Finance team for the exceptional care and support they extended to me during my period of illness. Every team member stepped in to take on my responsibilities, ensuring that I could focus fully on my recovery without any worries about work. It was truly heartwarming to witness such genuine compassion. The Head of Department was equally supportive, and to this day, everyone continues to show remarkable kindness, always mindful of my health and ready to help in any way. This, to me, is the true embodiment of the Avanti Way – demonstrating compassionate changemakers in every sense.

When I returned from my sick leave, many aspects of work, especially on the technological front, felt unfamiliar and new. My colleagues displayed incredible patience and genuine care in helping me learn and adapt to the new systems. Thanks to their strong sense of teamwork and our deep interpersonal bonds, I was able to overcome these challenges with ease. I feel truly fortunate to be part of such a wonderful team – people who are kind, caring and who live the Avanti Way and who bring spirituality in all we do, every day through their actions and relationships. It is this spirit that makes Avanti the best place to work.

By Yogesh Sharma, Area Finance Lead, Avanti Schools Trust, UK

In the Vedic tradition, gratitude is regarded as both a moral disposition and a spiritual discipline. It is not confined to polite acknowledgment but involves a deep awareness of one's interdependence with others and with the wider cosmos. To be grateful is to recognise that one's successes and even one's very existence are sustained by countless visible and invisible contributions.

For a Western readership, this Vedic conception of gratitude resonates with current interest in positive psychology, which recognises gratitude as a predictor of well-being and resilience. Yet, the Vedic framework goes further by rooting gratitude in ontology rather than psychology: to be grateful is not only to feel thankful but to live truthfully in recognition of dependence on others and the divine. In education, cultivating gratitude helps learners develop deeper connections with peers, teachers, and society at large, while also fostering ecological consciousness. Gratitude grounds the self in humility while expanding the self into joyful recognition of belonging to a greater whole.

Empathy (dayā/anukampa)

Definition (Oxford English Dictionary): *Empathy (n.) – the ability to understand and share the feelings of another.*

The Dove and the Hunter*: One cool morning, a hunter set his net under a banyan tree and scattered grains of rice as bait. Then he hid nearby. Soon a flock of doves, led by their king, flew down. Hungry and unsuspecting, they began pecking at the grains. Suddenly the net closed over them, and the hunter rushed forward, delighted with his catch. The doves fluttered in panic. "We are lost!" cried one. But the king spoke calmly: "Do not struggle alone. If we all flap our wings together, we can lift the net." Hearing this, the doves beat their wings at the same moment. The hunter gaped as the entire flock rose into the sky, carrying the net with them. His trap was empty! The doves flew to a nearby hill, where their friend the mouse lived. The king called out, "Brother, please help us. We are caught in this net." The mouse hurried out and began to gnaw at the ropes. Patiently, he freed each dove, starting with the king and ending with the smallest. At last, the flock was free.*

In Vedic and later devotional traditions, compassion is a central moral quality. The *Upaniṣads* emphasise ethical responsibility. Compassion is not simply an emotion but a moral disposition that binds communities together. Empathy, the ability to recognise and share in the feelings of others and gives practical form to this compassion. In the *Bhagavad Gītā* (12.13–14), Krishna describes non-hatred, friendliness and compassion as marks of the devoted person, qualities that expand one's circle of moral concern. Philosophically, empathy directs us beyond self-interest towards reciprocity and service.

Psychological research shows that empathy reduces aggression and strengthens cooperation, while in education it supports collaboration, restorative practice and intercultural understanding. In schools, empathy can be fostered through literature and history that open perspectives, service learning that encourages responsibility and structured practices such as circle time or perspective-taking exercises.

Adults model empathy when they notice young people's contexts, adapt expectations to need or resolve conflict by listening rather than blaming. Young people practise it when they listen attentively, include others or stand against unfairness. In this way, the Vedic vision of compassion as a binding force finds contemporary expression in the habits, relationships and cultures of schools.

Empathy and compassion lived each day

From my very first day at Avanti House Primary, I was struck by the school's gentle strength – a calm, caring environment where virtues aren't just displayed on walls but woven into the fabric of daily life. Each Monday begins with Collective Worship, a deeply grounding moment in the week. Children gather in a calm, reflective space, where messages of kindness, gratitude and self-discipline are shared through stories, song, and silence. It sets the tone – not just for the week ahead but for how we live and learn together. There's a quiet magic in seeing children so engaged in thinking deeply about compassion, responsibility and service.

Our virtue of empathy came to life in the most touching ways. One moment, in particular, stays with me: during breaktime, a six-year-old non-verbal child with additional needs began to wander across the playground. Without fuss, a classmate followed him closely, gently offering her hand. He pushed her away several times, but she didn't give up – her focus was entirely on keeping him safe. She sacrificed her own playtime without hesitation. Watching her persistence, empathy and calm was profoundly moving. It wasn't prompted or praised – it was instinctive, and it was Avanti.

By Pallavi Shingala, Class teacher, Avanti House Primary

In Vedic philosophy, empathy is not simply an emotional resonance but a disciplined capacity to perceive the self in others and others in the self. Rooted in the Sanskrit concepts of *dayā* (compassion) and *karuṇā* (sympathetic concern), empathy broadens human perspective beyond self-centred concerns and prevents hasty, narrow judgments. The *Bhagavad Gītā* (6.32) offers a striking articulation: "The yogi, by comparison with his own self, sees the true equality of all beings, whether in happiness or distress." Here, empathy is framed as an extension of self-understanding; one recognises one's own vulnerability and joy mirrored in others, and this recognition becomes the basis for ethical engagement.

For a Western readership, Vedic empathy resonates with contemporary interest in emotional intelligence, intercultural sensitivity, and restorative practices in education. Yet, the Vedic account deepens the conversation by rooting empathy not only in social or psychological benefits but in metaphysical reality: empathy arises from recognising the self's kinship with all life. Education that fosters this virtue equips learners not only to handle interpersonal complexity with patience and openness but also to resist the tendency to rush to assumptions in an age of polarisation. By broadening perspective in this way, empathy becomes both an intellectual and spiritual discipline, vital for navigating diversity and sustaining a shared human future.

Questions for the journey

Living virtues consistently and meaningfully takes effort and motivation. It is about seeing the world through a different lens – one of community mindedness and collaboration. Chapters 5–12 introduced our six beliefs. This chapter turned to the six virtues, how they were identified, why they matter, and how they might take shape in practice.

Before we begin the next chapter, which explores the literature on values in education, it may be helpful to pause and reflect. The questions are prompts to hold in mind as we read, teach, parent and live together:

- What virtues shape the way I relate to others?
- What do I hope to pass on, whether as a teacher, parent or role model, and how do I make them visible in practice?
- How do power, privilege or culture shape which virtues are considered "universal" in schools and society?
- What virtues do I inherit from tradition, family or faith and which do I need to question, reinterpret or let go of?

Notes

1 Jahkai is a pseudonym to protect his anonymity
2 The *Rāmāyaṇa* is one of India's major Sanskrit epics, traditionally attributed to Vālmīki and composed between approximately 500 BCE and 200 BCE. It narrates the life of Prince Rāma, exploring themes of duty (dharma), devotion, justice and moral integrity through epic storytelling.
3 The *Purāṇas* are a large body of ancient Indian texts composed roughly between 300 and 1500 CE. They convey cosmology, mythology, genealogy, and ethical teachings through stories of gods, sages and heroes, making philosophical and spiritual ideas accessible to wider audiences.

14 Three values

Educational excellence, character formation and spiritual insight

In the previous chapters, we introduced six beliefs and six virtues rooted in Vedic philosophy. Building on these, we now turn to the question of values – what we hold to be significant and worth pursuing in education. The term *value* refers to the principles, standards or priorities that guide our choices. According to the Oxford English Dictionary, values are "the principles or standards of behaviour; one's judgement of what is important in life." Similarly, the Cambridge Dictionary describes values as "the beliefs people have, especially about what is right and wrong and what is most important in life, that control their behaviour." Consider Yaafi[1]:

> Peace be upon you. My name is Yaafi. I am from Dubai in the Emirates. When I was leaving Dubai, I was very scared because I was leaving behind my sense of security, my friends, my family; everything that I had known and loved for 18 years since the day I was born. However, I was very pleasantly surprised. When I came here [Avanti House Secondary School], everyone was so welcome and opening to me and my culture.
>
> ...I was very materialistic. However, since I have come here, I have seen people from all sorts of socio-economic backgrounds coming together in worship and prayer, putting asides their differences and coming under one common cause, and this has really opened up my eyes to the community, being more receptive to other people's beliefs, and I am very thankful for this experience.

DOI: 10.4324/9781003487654-18

> Before I used to be closeted person with quite a low self–esteem. I was very overweight, but since I have come here, I've become more driven, more organised. I know where I want to be in the next five years.
>
> Recorded as part of Avanti Stories Social Media.

Yaafi is referring to his personal values, and what is valued in his school: learning to be with difference, to connect with diversity, to think beyond material gain, to develop self-esteem, self-discipline and purpose. His experiences refer to his education rooted in spiritual insight, forming character qualities that empower him to achieve (and to contribute the whole community), and being driven with purpose to 'know where he wants to be.' He describes the value of cultures of learning that are deliberately inclusive, celebrating diversity of faiths, worldviews, languages and abilities and essentially relational at their core. Knowing that there is compelling evidence about happiness and its impact on academic outcomes, the value given to belonging, through relationships strengthened with dialogue and mutual care create the conditions in which every child and adult can flourish and contribute.

From a Vedic standpoint, what is valued in education relates to the answer to the question, what is judged as important in life? We have mentioned the central view that the soul – the inner true self – is what gives life and is the aspect that when understood can bring joy and happiness. To begin with, the Vedas value the full complexity of being human and in living. Placing spirituality at the centre of school life is valued: for example, practices of reflection, stillness, gratitude and service that nurture inner freedom, resilience and purpose, alongside rigorous scholarship.

Put simply, values express what we care about most. Yet, values differ from virtues: values articulate *why* we act, while virtues show *how* we live them. A school may value inclusion, but it becomes real when a teacher patiently ensures every learner can participate. Values are vision; virtues are their lived expression. The *Bhagavad Gītā* illuminates this beautifully. Arjuna values compassion and duty, yet Krishna reminds him that these find true fulfilment through courage, discipline, and devotion to a higher good. His lesson is timeless: values without virtues remain abstract. Together, they nurture both inner character and outer educational excellence.

Values in education: exploring the literature

Education is never value neutral. To speak of values in education is to enter a field at once philosophical and practical, universal and contextually shaped. It traverses questions of ethics, moral formation, citizenship, democracy, wellbeing, spirituality and human development. It also speaks of the qualities we think are important for individual and collective thriving. It goes to the heart of what matters for people in communities (Flutter, 2025) and how what matters becomes manifest in realities, behaviours and ways of being (Biddulph and Gilbride, 2025; Bourdieu, 1977).

What society values is reflected in the policy directions of governments, the curriculum choices, inspection frameworks and attitudes about teachers and teaching. Every pedagogical encounter, whether a classroom dialogue, an assessment practice, or the structuring of a school day, carries within it implicit and explicit values. Schools are also places of ritual; across the year, within a term, a week and a day, young people and the adults who work with them engage in assemblies, roll calls, celebrations, movements and discourses that demarcate, through symbolic gestures, what it means to learn and work, to be at school. These rituals, symbols and movements bring forth the values that shape not only what is taught but also how it is taught, and to what ends. Values orient the culture of a school, the ethos of its community, i.e. 'what is valued,' and the lived experiences of children, young people and educators alike. In this sense, values in education are not an optional addition to the "real" work of teaching and learning; they are the soul of education, the animating force that gives coherence, direction and meaning to the enterprise of schooling.

Given that governments typically control education policy, let us briefly consider contemporary statements from governments about what is valued in education. The first is from the 2025 Republican Donald Trump administration, which emphasises families, communities, and opportunities, while advancing a political view that the state should play a reduced role in the control of education. As the Order states: "Our Nation's bright future relies on empowered families, engaged communities, and excellent educational opportunities for every child. Unfortunately, the experiment of controlling American education through Federal programs and dollars – and the unaccountable bureaucracy those programs and dollars support has plainly failed our children, our teachers, and our families" (Trump, 2025). There are various political interpretations of the explicit and implicit values at play here.

In the UK, more widely used is the term British Values which encompass having value in: Democracy, the rule of law, individual liberty, mutual respect and tolerance of different faiths and beliefs. As part of their safeguarding and child protection duties, schools in the UK are required to promote these values implicitly and explicitly. In 2024, the UK Labour Party manifesto outlined six areas of focus for education: "Deliver high and rising standards in early education. Support all our children to achieve and thrive. Create a better system for inspecting and improving our schools. Enable school staff to help our children to succeed. Prepare young people for their futures. Equip young people with experiences to get them ready for work and ready for life" (Labour Party, 2024). The values here situate education as valuable for the economic development of the country, developing accountability measures, early years education as important for a good start and the power of educators to help every child to succeed, recognising professional development for teachers as important.

In India, the 2024 election campaigns placed strong emphasis on the principle of free education for all and on widening access to educational opportunities (Indian National Congress, 2024). Meanwhile, a review of political party manifestos in South Africa suggested a mixed vision of the purposes of education and its advancement in uncertain times (TIMSS-SA, 2024). Whilst political statements about what is valued provide insight into the meta narratives of political agendas, to suggest what society values, it is within the intimacy of the classroom that children and young people experience and embody what is truly valued.

Over the past two decades, the scholarly field of values education has expanded considerably, drawing together research from philosophy, psychology, neuroscience and pedagogy. For example, the Australian *Values Education Good Practice Schools Project* (VEGPSP), a landmark national initiative between 2005 and 2008 invested nearly AUD$30 million in enabling schools to design and implement locally grounded approaches to values education. Its reach was vast: some 400 schools, thousands of teachers and many more learners were directly involved in cultivating and documenting "good practice" in values-based education.

The findings of VEGPSP were compelling. Schools that engaged intentionally in values-based practices became calmer, more trusting and more collaborative environments (Lovat et al., 2009; Lovat and Toomey, 2009). This is the same finding in the *Learning without Limits* research that demonstrated that cultures of trust, co-creation and with an ethic of everybody, evoked powerful learning and teaching communities (Peacock, 2015; Swann et al.,

2012). In the VEGPSP, teachers reported greater professional motivation and wellbeing; learners experienced stronger relationships, resilience and pro-social behaviours. The project demonstrated that values education was not simply about inculcating moral codes but about transforming the culture of schooling in ways that nourished both human flourishing and academic achievement. In short, values-based education (VbE) provided the soil in which the "soul" of education, its capacity to nurture relationality, meaning, and transcendence, could take root.

Historically, values in education were often framed within moral or religious instruction (Wright, 2000). Schools sought to cultivate civic duty, ethical conduct or denominational faith, usually through prescriptive or didactic approaches. By contrast, the VEGPSP, UCPS and Avanti Schools advance a new paradigm, one that understands values as co-constructed, dialogical, and deeply interwoven with pedagogical quality and relationships. Toomey and Lovat (2007) first articulated this as the "double helix" effect: the intertwining of explicit values teaching with quality teaching. Just as a double helix gives structure and life to DNA, the explicit articulation of a school's values combined with research-based pedagogy gives coherence and vitality to educational practice.

Values education is often linked with character education, "[it] has a long history in Britain and has been argued to have always been part of the aim of general education, even if it was not explicitly stated" (Arthur, 2003, p. 11; also Arthur et al. (2017)). More recently, it is reported that,

> Character development is not something that can be taught in isolation; it must be nurtured consistently across the whole school journey. From early years through to adolescence, children benefit from structured opportunities to practice leadership, problem-solving, and collaboration. Embedding character education across all stages of schooling helps build confidence, supports wellbeing, and prepares young people for both school and life beyond the classroom.
>
> (Schools Week, retrieved on 25th September 2025 https://schoolsweek.co.uk/building–character–increasing–engagement–and–growing–leaders–a–whole–school–approach/)

The Jubilee Centre (which researches and promotes character education) frames character in broadly Aristotelian terms, viewing it as the foundation of human flourishing and a central aim of education. Character is defined as a set of traits and dispositions that inform motivation, guide conduct and are both morally evaluable and educable (Arthur et al., 2017). The qualities that society desires in its young people shape expectations of education, since every civilisation has sought to pass on not only knowledge and skills, but also values, to the next generation.

This can also be seen in another example from the *Church of England's Vision of Education: deeply Christian, Serving the Common Good* (Church of England, 2016). Intentionally rooted in values and spirituality, inspired by a theological claim that education is about "life in its fullness" (John 10:10), their vision is structure around four key aims: (1) educating for wisdom, knowledge and skills, (2) educating for hope and aspiration, (3) educating for community and living well together and (4) educating for dignity and respect (Wolf et al., 2021). People carry with them beliefs that in turn define what they value, which translate into ways of living and in the qualities of living that we have called virtues. We now explore different aspects that we state are explicitly valuable in a soul-led education.

Valuing happiness in education: the statistical evidence

Research by Antonio Damasio (2003), Mary Helen Immordino-Yang (2007) and others (including Carol Dweck, 2006) underscored that cognition cannot be disentangled from emotion: memory, attention, and reasoning are all shaped by affective processes. Daniel Goleman's (1996) influential work on emotional intelligence further affirmed that qualities such as empathy, self-regulation, and social skills are central to human development. Ron Toomey (2010) and colleagues situated values education within this growing body of evidence, showing how explicitly teaching and embedding values produced the trusting relationships essential for higher-order learning. Subsequent neuroscience has only reinforced this picture. Research on brain hemisphericity (McGilchrist, 2009; Siegel et al., 2016) suggests that Western education has often privileged narrowly analytical, left-brain functions at the expense of more integrative, relational and creative right-brain capacities.

The consequence, as we continue to argue in this book, has been a kind of "soullessness"; a reduction of education to test scores, metrics, and fragmented knowledge, at the expense of empathy, imagination, and holistic wellbeing. It results, perhaps, in antisocial behaviours, disengagement, falling attendance data, a rise in exclusions from school, poor mental health – a general feeling of not fitting in. Contrary to the claim that education is solely about knowledge, particularly subject specific knowledge, there is compelling statistical evidence that prioritising well-being and cultivating happiness among learners, educators, and communities has a profound positive impact, both holistically and on the very academic outcomes that the system places at its centre.

Across global education systems, success continues to be measured primarily through examination outcomes, progression statistics, and international rankings such as PISA. These measures, while not without value, provide only a partial view of the true purpose of education. The evidence is increasingly clear: happy children learn better (Layard and Hagell, 2015). When wellbeing is prioritised, learning outcomes improve, teachers remain in the profession for longer, and societies flourish. Happiness and wellbeing are not "soft" or secondary concerns but statistically relevant and economically significant drivers of long-term flourishing (Clark et al., 2018). Schools that ignore these realities risk perpetuating cycles of stress, inequality, and diminished potential. If education is to recover its soul, it must embrace happiness not only as an ethical imperative but as a policy priority.

The link between wellbeing and academic performance is robust and consistent across contexts and has statistical relevance. Layard (2020) suggests that children's emotional health is statistically shown to be a far stronger predictor of their life satisfaction in adulthood than academic qualifications alone. This finding is reinforced by longitudinal studies in the UK, US, and other OECD countries, which reveal that wellbeing in childhood predicts employment, earnings, health, and relationship outcomes decades later (UNESCO, 2021; Clark et al., 2018). A large-scale meta-analysis by Durlak et al. (2011) showed that social and emotional learning programmes in schools improve academic performance by an average of 11 percentile points, in addition to reducing behavioural problems and improving mental health. Similarly, the PATHS programme (Promoting Alternative Thinking Strategies) has been shown to reduce aggression and improve both wellbeing and attainment (Greenberg et al., 2003). Likewise, the *Healthy Minds curriculum*, tested in a randomised control trial across 26 UK schools, led to significant improvements in life satisfaction, global health, and physical wellbeing (Challen et al., 2019).

These interventions prove a critical point: systematic attention to wellbeing does not detract from academic results but enhances them. Why then do governments, from whichever political persuasion, not develop policies around happiness, especially in education? Where are the bold leaders to enable this to happen? Our view is that rather than waiting for governments, our opportunity as school leaders and educators is to grapple with what is valued in communities, in collaboratives of school educators, for children, listening to what they value and to weave what is valued into the fabric of the school life, curriculum, culture and ways of being and working.

Interestingly, children's happiness is inseparable from the wellbeing of their teachers. Layard and Hagell (2015) argue that teacher mental health is one of the most powerful determinants of pupil outcomes and yet is consistently overlooked in policy frameworks. Mindfulness-based interventions, such as the Mindfulness-Based Stress Reduction (MBSR) programme, have been shown to reduce teacher burnout and improve classroom climate (Jennings et al., 2017). Contrary to common assumptions, reducing class sizes has relatively little effect on learning compared to investing in teacher training, pay and sabbaticals (Hattie, 2009). A radical yet pragmatic policy proposal, as Layard and O'Donnell (2015) note, is to prioritise teacher wellbeing as central to education reform. Teachers who feel supported and valued not only stay in the profession but also model resilience, compassion and joy – qualities which directly shape the ethos of the classroom. Yet, governments struggle to implement (or even notice) such evidence.

One could argue that part of the damage to teachers and support staff well-being is the overemphasis on accountability which breeds cultures of fear and panic and even, tragically, in suicide and work-related death. Equally, the narrow pursuit of grades risks leaving young people ill-prepared for life's broader challenges and leaves teachers despondent and uninspired. In Layard's (2011) framing, education must encompass the cultivation of "life skills" such as emotional regulation, empathy, healthy living, and resilience. These skills are empirically linked with better mental health, stronger relationships, and greater productivity. Spiritual literacy, too, should not be neglected.

Valuing the primacy of relationships: towards Human Flourishing

We found a consistent message that quality relationships are vital, that dialogue is necessary to deepen relationship-making and to form and transform ideas and beliefs, and that experiences which create shared memories contribute to an education that has lasting meaning. As Coe (2013, p. 8) reminds us, "learning is not a direct consequence of teaching" but emerges through the interplay of relationships, feedback and reflection. This highlights that relationships in education are not incidental; they are cultivated through trust, mutual respect, and opportunities for dialogue. In this sense, meaningful educational relationships are both the soil and the scaffolding for learning, shaping identity, belonging and ambition.

Coe's work further underlines that the quality of education is inseparable from the quality of relationships within it. He argues that "learning depends on what the learner already knows and understands, and on the quality of the interactions they experience" (Coe, 2013, p. 12). This frames education as a relational endeavour, where dialogue, trust and feedback enable teachers to connect new knowledge to prior understanding. For Coe, the teacher's role is not simply to transmit information but to create the conditions in which young people feel known, respected and challenged. In this way, relationships become both the medium and measure of meaningful learning.

More evidence that nurturing relationships is key to human flourishing comes from Harvard University. If flourishing is "a state in which all aspects of a person's life are good," education is one of the few social projects charged with nurturing its full range – happiness and health, meaning and purpose, character and virtue, and close relationships. The *Harvard Human Flourishing Program* helpfully names these domains, while the *Harvard Study of Adult Development* – an 80-plus-year longitudinal study – adds the headline: the single strongest predictor of health and happiness across the lifespan is the quality of our close relationships, not wealth, status or IQ. For us educators, that is both a mandate and a map.

If good relationships are the best long-term 'medicine,' schools must become deliberately relational: time and structures for belonging, mentoring, and collaboration; a sense of strong groups and communities within classes and year groups; rituals that dignify every child; and serious investment in teacher and support staff professional learning and development. A school's relationship-rich culture is not pastoral extra, it is the infrastructure of cognition, wellbeing and character growth.

Aimee Durning, Director of Inclusion at the University of Cambridge Primary School, provides a powerful example of the changes that occur in learning when attention to the relationship between adult and child takes primacy and where listening and observing attentively to understand the individual pays dividends. As you read it, ask yourself what is being valued and how this is being enacted in practice, in the relationship and attention to relationship.

Welcoming Billy

Billy joined our school at the beginning of Year 2 (age 6–7). We had been briefed by Virtual Schools (a supportive intervention for children who do not or find it difficult to access mainstream school) and his social worker about his difficulties in his previous setting. Billy had been caught in a cycle of toxic stress: his earlier school had placed him in isolation for much of the day, supervised largely by adults and restricted to a part-time timetable of just two and a half hours. As a child with experience of the care system, he carried with him multiple layers of trauma, mistrust, and stress.

From the outset, our team made an ambitious commitment: that Billy would not simply be contained but would thrive in our school. This meant resisting external pressure to focus narrowly on academic 'catch up' and instead creating a plan that honoured his need for belonging, trust and play. Ambition here was not only about Billy's academic future, but about believing in his potential as a whole child – capable of friendships, joy and self-discovery.

Inclusion shaped every decision we made. Rather than isolating him further, we designed opportunities for Billy to participate in the daily life of the school. We arranged supported playtimes with peers, stepping back to let him practise social skills and experience acceptance. At first, he could only manage a few minutes in class, but even this was celebrated as progress. We made sure Billy knew he was liked, valued and welcome, even when his behaviour expressed anger, swearing, or aggression. Every day ended with a message of care: that we looked forward to seeing him again, that he belonged.

Innovation was essential. Standard strategies were not working for a child carrying toxic stress. Together with trauma specialists, we reimagined the timetable, embedding play, peer connection and therapeutic practices before formal learning. This creative, responsive approach, challenging the 'one-size-fits-all' model, allowed Billy to gradually dismantle his stress patterns and develop strategies for self-regulation. Even Dr Biddulph, our Headteacher, would work with Billy and I remember one time, they had gone to the Nursery class and soon thereafter they were interacting with the role play area – our tall

Headteacher sitting on a tiny Nursery classroom chair being served imaginary tea and cake and then sometime later, Billy had become a Doctor and was fixing Dr Biddulph's broken arm with a sling and imaginary injection. Billy was being shown care, being taught what positive relationships looked and felt like, and in so doing psychological safety was being formed. Billy was being allowed to learn at a stage not his chronological age and this developed his relationship with authority, with school, with social dynamics, with learning and with challenge in a more connected and profound way.

Over the course of a year, Billy's friendships and confidence grew. He began to recognise his own stress triggers and practise techniques to manage them. By nurturing his spirit with ambition, including him fully in the life of the school, and innovating our practice to meet his needs, we prepared the ground for academic learning to begin. Billy was no longer trapped by his past; he had space to imagine a different future.

One day he came to Dr Biddulph's office with a Lego model of the school's logo. He said, "Look Dr Biddulph this is what I made. It is my school isn't it?" The smile said it all. He felt he belonged.

Reflection from Aimee Durning (Director of Inclusion at The University of Cambridge Primary School)

Billy's story illustrates how what is valued comes alive through the virtues enacted in practice. The value of the ethic of everybody and in being ambitious for Billy meant that he was not defined by his deficits but by his potentials. Inclusive mindsets were valued, ensuring that space was made for him in community, not at its margins. Innovation was needed to disrupt business-as-usual and create new ways of working. Together, these values transformed both Billy's experience and the staff's own understanding of what education can be. It is a reminder that what is valued only matters when lived in behaviours, shaped by the decisions we make, the relationships we form and the futures we dare to imagine for every child.

VanderWeele's (2017) emphasis on meaning and purpose should move from the margins of school life to its centre and suggests that dialogue must be valued in schools. Purpose grows where young people can connect what they are learning to who they are becoming and the problems they long to address.

This suggests enquiry anchored in real community needs; interdisciplinary projects that integrate knowledge with action; reflective practices (journals, advisories, exhibitions) that help young people name what matters. Purpose is not merely picked up from inspirational assemblies; it is constructed through guided encounters with the world and with one's own conscience.

Another aspect from the research that aligns with what we argue is valuable is the development of character (Flutter, 2025). Flourishing requires character – practical wisdom, justice, courage, temperance. Moreover, virtue is formed through practice, not just proclaimed through posters or policies. Schools cultivate virtues when they design repeated, scaffolded opportunities to *do* just, brave, and temperate things: peer mediation, youth leadership of mixed-age teams, assessed ethical reasoning in science and history, and service that includes reciprocal learning rather than charity optics. Crucially, assessment of character should privilege narratives, portfolios, and community testimony alongside any simple self-report scales.

Valuing experiences in the educational encounter

Both the Harvard Study and Vedic philosophy emphasise the importance of experiences in the learning process including in spiritual education. Many learners – religious and non-religious – name experiences of awe, gratitude, lament and transcendence as central to a meaningful life. Flourishing frameworks often under-specify this depth dimension. Education can honour spirituality without proselytising by making space for silence and contemplation; by encountering wisdom traditions alongside philosophy and literature; by inviting learners to articulate ultimate questions ("What is worth suffering for?" "What does a good life ask of me?") and to discern practices that sustain them. Where religious communities are part of young people's lives, respectful partnership can reinforce resilience and civic contribution – consistent with evidence that communal religious participation predicts wellbeing.

Rupert Sheldrake (2017) also emphasises experience as essential in the development of spirituality. In a secular age, spirituality need not vanish, it can be rediscovered as a way of seeing and being that reconnects us with the flow of life. Spiritual practice, as Sheldrake suggests, is less about belief and more about connection: a conscious participation in the web of giving and receiving that sustains existence. Gratitude, meditation and pilgrimage are not mere rituals of faith but doorways into awareness, inviting us to sense our participation in a reality greater than the individual self. Vedic philosophy offers a parallel understanding. The *Upanishadic* vision of *tat tvam asi*, "thou art that," reveals the essential unity between the individual soul (*ātman*) and the cosmic consciousness (*Brahman*). This insight reframes spirituality as an act of remembrance rather than acquisition; we are not seeking connection but reawakening to what has always been true – a feeling of connectedness with others and with something beyond that is unimaginable or conceivable but inculcates awe and wonder. Practices of meditation, reverence for nature and pilgrimage serve to dissolve the illusion of separateness and restore awareness of our participation in the sacred whole.

Sheldrake's emphasis on connecting with the more-than-human world resonates deeply with the Vedic understanding of *ṛta* – the cosmic order that harmonises all beings, animate and inanimate. To live spiritually in a secular world is to realign our consciousness with this rhythm: to see plants, animals and elements as kin; to engage in ritual not as dogma but as continuity with the cosmos. Gratitude becomes an expression of *seva* – service to the whole; meditation a means of stilling the mind to perceive the divine pulse in all things. Thus, spirituality in contemporary life need not depend on religious belief. It can emerge through attention, humility and wonder, through practices that reconnect us with self, others and the living earth. Both Sheldrake's modern synthesis and the ancient Vedic tradition point to the same truth: that the sacred is not elsewhere, but here; woven through every breath, every act of awareness, every journey of rediscovery we make through the ordinary. There is also much synergy with the curriculum design of Richard Dunne (Harmony https://www.theharmonyproject.org.uk/) and the work of King Charles III (King's Foundation https://kings–foundation.org).

For example, the principles of *Harmony* can be understood as natural laws that sustain the dynamic balance and wellbeing of the living world (Dunne and Martin, 2021). Originating from *Harmony: A New Way of Looking at Our World* by HRH The Prince of Wales (now King Charles III), Ian Skelly and Tony Juniper (Prince of Wales, Skelly and Juniper, 2010), these seven principles – cycle, interdependence, health, diversity, geometry, adaptation and oneness – offer a coherent framework for learning from and with nature. Together, these principles invite a way of seeing and living that is attuned to the rhythms of nature, nurturing in learners a sense of belonging, responsibility and reverence for life (Dunne and Martin, 2021, p. 83). Table 14.1 suggests how such experiences might be brought to life in schools.

Table 14.1 Sheldrake's aspects of spiritual development

Practice	Core idea	Vedic parallel	How to practise in daily life	Purpose/ inner effect
1. Gratitude	Cultivating awareness of interconnection through giving and receiving.	Service and selflessness	Begin or end each day naming three sources of gratitude – people, moments or elements of nature. Write a brief note of thanks or offer a silent prayer or words of gratitude before meals. A good friend of the author suggests, "blessings on the food, the farmer and the field and all those who cooked to bring it to our table"	Deepens humility, joy and belonging; nurtures generosity and flow.
2. Meditation	Observing thoughts and sensations to connect with presence beyond the self.	Self-enquiry and introspection	Set aside 10–20 minutes daily for silent sitting, breath awareness or mantra repetition. There are many different forms of mantra or words that could focus the mind, including faith and spiritual options.	Cultivates clarity, peace and awareness of unity with all life.
3. Connection with the More-Than-Human World	Paying attention to the living earth and sensing kinship with all beings.	Living by the principle of non-harm to all living beings. Considering a vegetarian diet.	Spend mindful time outdoors – walk barefoot on grass, observe birds, tend plants or reduce harm in consumption.	Rekindles reverence for nature and responsibility towards the planet.

(Continued)

Table 14.1 Sheldrake's aspects of spiritual development *(Continued)*

Practice	Core idea	Vedic parallel	How to practise in daily life	Purpose/ inner effect
4. Relationship with Plants and Life Forms	Recognising plants as living teachers and symbols of growth and interdependence.	See nature as divine manifestation. As something so incredible, it is unfathomable.	Grow or care for a plant; study its cycles; pause before eating to acknowledge the life that nourishes yours.	Encourages patience, attentiveness and harmony with natural rhythms.
5. Ritual	Honouring continuity with the past and opening to the transcendent.	Consider experiencing sacred rites and acts of offering.	Create simple rituals, e.g. lighting a candle at day's end, marking seasonal transitions, or sharing meals with mindfulness.	Brings sacredness into the everyday; strengthens communal bonds.
6. Singing, Chanting, and Music	Using voice and rhythm to connect body, mind and spirit.	*Kīrtan, bhajan,* yoga of sound.	Sing, chant or hum regularly – alone or with others. Focus on vibration rather than performance.	Opens the heart; fosters unity, joy and emotional release.
7. Pilgrimage	Journeying with sacred intention – externally or inwardly.	*Yātrā* (sacred travel)	Visit a natural or meaningful place with reverence; reflect on the journey as a metaphor for life's unfolding.	Transforms perspective; connects outer travel with inner growth.

We have tried to link various ideas presented herein, also linked with Sheldrake's collation of practices from different faith traditions with the Vedic philosophy. What we can conclude is that spiritual or soul development falls within the domain of intercultural, interrelatedness, harmony, mapping individual and collective growth, linking the inner world of identity, self and purpose with the outer world in nature.

In the next section, the metaphor of a tree is used to present how a Vedic education could be conceived. It is the *Tree of Life* that is used in the discussion about curricula, pedagogy and how the life of school is structured at the Avanti Schools.

The tree of life: a Vedic education for contemporary world

The final concept of the book came about while walking in craggy Swiss forests with His Holiness Sacinandana Swami, a spiritual leader in the Hindu Vaishnava[2] tradition. In Figure 14.1, James Biddulph's journal entry noted the moment.

Figure 14.1 'Tree of life'. Photograph taken by James Biddulph in Kiental, Switzerland, 2024.

It's so important to have strong roots in our lives. Please look at this amazing tree. He decided, "let me grow on top of a rock", but even he needed to have a creative solution what to do with his roots, and he has done masterfully. Look at his strong roots which are supplying him with the nourishment. It teaches us a lesson. In whatever situation we find ourselves, even in an extraordinary situation, it still remains extremely important to look at our roots and to grow them deep. What does this mean?

Deep inside of us, we are not a German, we are not a professor, we are not even a Swami of the Hare Krishna movement. Deep inside of us, in our deepest roots, we are part of Krishna, we are part of the Lord, and in our lives, which are so busy, we require to grow our roots deep. The higher you want to rise, the deeper you have to move. This is a very important aspect, because people nowadays get stuck in their life and stop experiencing spiritual growth. The reason is, or could be, that because of their busyness, and because of a sense of complacency, they forgot to grow their roots deep, have deep roots. Get the inside right and the outside will follow.

(Retrieved on 31st August 2025, from Instagram https://www.instagram.com/reel/DBEEr–gIHVJ/?igsh=MXAwcG41NnY3eGh6aQ%3D%3D)

The image of that tree – precarious yet deeply rooted – became a metaphor that would not leave me. At the time, I was feeling a persistent drumbeat of discontent with aspects of the educational status quo. There was energy, ambition, and creative drive – perhaps the mode of passion at work – but also impatience. I wanted change. I wanted renewal. I wanted systems to shift.

Yet standing before that tree, I recognised something uncomfortable because trying to transform things without having some depth of thinking is dangerous and will be critiqued. Before altering structures, I needed to examine foundations of who I am and what I really believe and also learn from the literature.

> The concept of the soul in education emerged as a leitmotif from that moment we aspire to rise, the deeper we must be willing to grow.
>
> Reflections from James' professional journal (2024)

A tree is both strong and flexible, symbolic of patient growth, life-giving purpose and contribution. Its strength comes from its roots, which sustain the trunk, branches, leaves and ultimately its fruit and seed. Drawing on this image, the *Tree of Life* offers a powerful metaphor for education: spiritual insight as roots, character formation as trunk and educational excellence as crown. Across cultures and traditions, the tree has represented connection between visible and invisible realms, grounding life in deeper meaning and orienting human flourishing toward fruitfulness. Read educationally, the *Tree of Life* becomes a framework for understanding the soul of education.

Within the Vaishnava tradition, Sacinandana Swami reinterprets the *Tree of Life* as the human journey: rooted in spirituality, embodied through identity, branching into diverse expressions, flowering in virtue and bearing fruit in service. In educational terms, the roots of the tree symbolise the spiritual, moral and ethical foundations that nourish learning beyond instrumental outcomes. Though unseen, roots are indispensable. Without such grounding, education risks becoming shallow and fragile, driven by performance rather than purpose. Authentic education requires attention to this inner ground if it is to sustain meaningful growth.

From these roots grows the trunk, representing identity: the recognition of the learner as a whole person with dignity, agency, and depth. The trunk holds together what is hidden and what is visible. When education fragments identity, reducing learners to data or outcomes, the trunk is weakened. When identity is affirmed and nurtured, learners are better able to grow with coherence and integrity, supporting the many directions their lives may take.

The branches extend outward, symbolising the diversity of human expression: vocations, creativity, relationships and citizenship. Each branch grows differently, yet all remain nourished by the same roots and trunk. Education, therefore, must honour plurality without losing coherence, encouraging multiple pathways while remaining grounded in shared values and purpose.

Leaves grow on the branches, representing learning itself: the active process by which knowledge and experience are transformed into understanding and wisdom. Like photosynthesis, learning converts external inputs into life-giving energy. When education is alive, it does more than transmit information; it enables reflection, renewal and contribution to the wider environment.

The tree of life in the context of state funded education

At Avanti Schools Trust, the educational vision is articulated through three core values, conceptualised within the metaphor of the tree of life:

- Educational Excellence,
- Character Formation, and
- Spiritual Insight.

This metaphor captures both the rootedness and the expansiveness of education – anchored in deep philosophical traditions yet continually growing and branching into new contexts of human flourishing. These three values are not discrete compartments but interwoven dimensions of what might be called a holistic education.

Educational excellence represents the intellectual canopy of the tree: the branches and leaves that reach outward in pursuit of knowledge, understanding and wisdom. Excellence is not conceived narrowly as attainment or performance, but as the cultivation of intellectual curiosity, criticality, and creativity. It requires high expectations, rigorous pedagogy and a culture of aspiration, but also recognises that academic flourishing depends upon the health of the whole person (Nussbaum, 1997, 2010).

Character formation constitutes the trunk of the tree – the central strength that supports growth and provides stability. Here, we draw explicitly on the language of virtues: the lived moral qualities that shape who we are and how we act. For Avanti, education cannot be reduced to skills or information transfer; it must also be the deliberate nurturing of dispositions such as compassion, resilience, integrity and respect (Arthur et al., 2017). This is why the daily rhythms of Avanti schools include not only academic lessons but also structured opportunities for reflection, dialogue, service and relational practice. Character is not assumed to form implicitly but is made visible and explicit through curriculum, pedagogy and school culture.

Spiritual insight is represented by the roots of the tree – hidden yet life-giving, drawing sustenance from deep wells of meaning. By spiritual we do not mean adherence to a single religious tradition, but rather the cultivation of awareness, presence and purpose. In Avanti schools, this involves creating spaces where young people can ask ultimate questions, encounter silence and stillness, and connect with something larger than themselves. It also draws upon the Vedic philosophical heritage in which Avanti is grounded, where the search for wisdom, the practice of mindfulness and the recognition of interconnection are understood as essential to human development.

This approach positions Avanti within a broader international conversation about holistic education. UNESCO (2015) has consistently argued that education must integrate cognitive, social, emotional and ethical dimensions to equip learners for the complexities of modern life. To this, we add spiritual dimension as core. Thinkers from John Dewey (1916, 1933, 1934, 1938) to Paulo Freire (1970), and from Nel Noddings (2003, 2005, 2013) to bell hooks (1994, 2003), have emphasised that education is never neutral, as we hope to have shown in this chapter: it always carries implicit or explicit values. By making values explicit, Avanti seeks to provide coherence and integrity to the educational experience. Jessie Yim, Teaching Assistant at an Avanti school, provides a practitioner's perspective on how the Trust valued is enacted and experienced within everyday educational practice.

> It all goes back to 'Our Very First Nativity' that was held at Avanti Court Primary School.
>
> Heart-warming feelings were woven by a series of real life experiences: respectful Headteacher was on the piano ringing out the most angelic tunes, utterly proud parents and families enjoyed every second of the fruits of their beloved children's knowledge and courageous performance, honoured staff members facilitated all activities and transitions diligently and the cutest young learners singing their hearts out in between lines of confident narratives.

The whole entire revitalising performance was surreal as if it had been touched by fairies.

'Our Very First Sports Day' took place on a mildly sunny day. Having no will nor plan to participate in staff running race, of course I nearly tripped over and made myself a total fool in the public eye.

However, the well-meaning cheering parents gave me strength and dignity to finish the race – last perhaps, but it didn't bother me.

I tried my best!

There have been big-hearted people brightening up my path on the way!

Admittedly, I knew very little about the ethos and even the culture some 13 years ago. When I applied for the job, I mistakenly addressed this fine young man (the Headteacher, Dr James Biddulph, he was a Mr then!) as Mrs in writing. During the second part of my interview, the same kind young man whispered that a sticky piece of paper was stuck on my trousers after sitting down closely to the magical young learners on the floor in class. The sweet English gentleman Headteacher cordially invited me to his office for a friendly chat which enlightened my insights regarding the school where I have been serving with my heart for over a decade.

Just before my departure at the end of this job interviewing process, I saw a dear little Chinese girl sat in the chair being sick. Nonetheless, I did not only see a girl feeling unwell. I witnessed the care and genuine love surrounding this child. The same fuzzy feelings I experienced first-hand at our first Nativity.

I could see immediately what the school valued: they wanted good results academically, but it was through being kind, self-discipline, courage to try and risk having a go, and more than this, it was nurturing the spirit of each person. That is what was valued this Tree of education and life.

Reflection of what is valued at Avanti | Jessie Yim, Teaching Assistant, Avanti Court, Redbridge, UK

The *Tree of Life* provides a living metaphor for what a soul-full education would value most deeply. Its branches, trunk and roots symbolise not separate aims but interdependent dimensions of human growth. Educational excellence forms the flourishing canopy that reaches outward, an expression of curiosity, aspiration and the expectation of the highest for every learner. Yet, as with any living tree, its outward vitality depends upon strong inner foundations. Excellence in this sense is inseparable from well-being, imagination and the courage to think critically and compassionately about the world. Character formation, the trunk, connects vision to action. It represents the virtues lived through daily habits. Character cannot be assumed; it must be intentionally modelled, discussed, and enacted in community life. The roots of the tree, spiritual insight, remind us that education is about meaning as much as knowledge. It invites moments of stillness, gratitude, and perspective, allowing learners to sense their interconnection with others and with the wider world. For teachers, this may mean creating time for reflection, nurturing spaces of belonging and framing the curriculum around the enduring questions of human existence.

Notes

1 Pseudonym.
2 A person devoted to Vishnu or Krishna – someone who strives to live with compassion, service and love as expressions of the sustaining Divine.

PART D

Arriving at a new terrain

Reimagining a soul-full education

15 A new landscape for educating the soul

We have travelled a considerable distance in examining a complex philosophical terrain, posing searching questions of ourselves and of society about the condition of education, its purpose and its role in shaping possible futures. These questions arise with particular urgency given the nature of the world in which we educate young people and the considerable pressures on institutions in which they learn. It is a world marked by paradox, quarrel, and hypocrisy, as described in Chapter 4's account of *Kali Yuga*. Yet, it is also a world animated by hope, creativity and social imagination. We suggest that it is precisely this tension that calls for a renewed attention to spirituality and for an education that focuses on the soul.

As a recap: we have explored Vedic inspired beliefs, virtues and what is valued in education as a *Tree of Life* metaphor. Education, we suggest, is constituted through the dynamic relationship between these three aspects:

Beliefs: what we hold to be true or possible about learning and human potential.

- Realising potential
- Empowering choice
- Strengthening interconnection
- Enriching diversities
- Expanding purpose
- Nourishing Loving relationships

Virtues: the cultivated practices through which human flourishing becomes visible

- Respect

DOI: 10.4324/9781003487654-20

- self-discipline
- integrity
- courage
- empathy
- gratitude

Values: what gives direction, coherence and moral purpose to the work

- Education excellence
- Character formation
- Spiritual Insight

We now take a practical turn to understand how we can develop a more soul-full approach in schools and classrooms.

A garden framework

Returning to the literature, we noticed that across philosophical and pedagogical traditions, images of gardens and landscapes have long been used to remind us that education is not a mechanical enterprise (as described in Callahan, 1962) but an organic, living process: cyclical, interdependent and oriented towards growth and renewal. Writers from Tolstoy to Tagore similarly imagined educational landscapes in which freedom, curiosity and nature intertwine, situating learning within a moral ecology of reciprocity and care (see also Dunne and Martin, 2021; HRH Prince of Wales et al., 2010). Most recently, in *Rewilding Education* (2026), Hilary Cremin offers a compelling critique of the industrial logic shaping contemporary schooling. She argues that education's fixation on standardisation and performance has produced ecological, moral and spiritual impoverishment. Her metaphor of 'rewilding' is powerful because it names what many practitioners feel: that education has become over-managed, over-measured, over-standardised and under-loved. This idea is also resonant in the Vedas.

Drawing from previous chapters, Table 15.1 collates the thematic principles; showing how the ideas connect as a coherent understanding of the soul of education. A soul-full approach recognises the human person as a multidimensional being whose development encompasses intellectual, emotional, moral, relational and spiritual dimensions.

From this and using the garden metaphor, Figure 15.1 seeks to hold these beliefs, virtues and values together as an integrated whole because, as we

Table 15.1 Collating the themes within the six beliefs and values

Aspects	Core principle	Key ideas and language	Implications for educational practice
1. The Nature of the Human Person	Human beings possess a deeper dimension often described as the soul.	*An innate human capacity for connection, transcendence, and purpose; the conscious spiritual self.*	Education recognises learners as whole persons with intellectual, emotional, moral and spiritual dimensions.
2. The Human Search for Meaning	People naturally seek coherence, identity, and belonging.	*An inner restlessness; search for meaning beyond the ego; desire for belonging and purpose. This is especially important given the three existential uncertainties worrying children and young people: insecurities about identity, fractured communities and survival of planet earth.*	Schools acknowledge learners' deeper questions about identity, purpose and the meaning of life.
3. Whole-Person Development **Identity, Authenticity and discovering purpose**	Growth occurs across multiple dimensions of human development. Schools have tended to prioritise one or two aspects Learners discover who they truly are.	*Multiple lines of development: cognitive, emotional, moral, interpersonal and spiritual.* *Finding identity; moving beyond labels and achievements; authentic selves revealing talents and vulnerabilities. Purpose beyond the self; seva (loving service); contribution to the wellbeing of the world.*	Curricula integrate knowledge with personal growth, reflection and ethical understanding. Education creates space for self-exploration, voice and personal narrative.

(Continued)

Table 15.1 Collating the themes within the six beliefs and values *(Continued)*

Aspects	Core principle	Key ideas and language	Implications for educational practice
4. Awakening Awareness	Education cultivates higher awareness and discernment.	*Raising consciousness; clarity, compassion, self-control, insight; reflective judgement.*	Practices such as reflection, dialogue, stillness and contemplative disciplines develop attention and awareness. Attention is also given to virtues and how they are acted out in lived ways.
5. Interconnectedness and interrelatedness	Learners recognise interconnection with others and the world.	*Radical interconnectedness; webs of relationship; stewardship and care.*	Learning cultivates responsibility, environmental awareness and social understanding.
6. Diversity	Multiple perspectives deepen understanding of truth.	*Pluralism; diversity as celebration; truth refracted through many perspectives.*	Classrooms value dialogue, cultural understanding and inclusion.
7. Cultivating Social and Moral Emotions	Emotional development supports ethical awareness.	*Awe, gratitude, admiration, compassion, moral elevation.*	Educational experiences foster empathy, wonder and moral responsibility.
8. Love as the Integrating Principle	Compassionate relationships hold the whole vision together.	*Love as the highest form of knowledge; trust, compassion, belonging.*	Education becomes a community of care where teachers and learners flourish together.

Figure 15.1 New landscape of the soul of education. Illustration by Federico Baca.

have shown, they do not exist as parallel tracks but as an entangled, rhizomatic ecology of meaning, each arising through and being intensified by, its relation to the others.

How to read the landscape

Think of this framework as a dynamic landscape rather than a fixed diagram. At different times, different elements come into focus depending on the needs of our learners, the context of the lesson or the challenges we are facing.

At ground level, the "soils" represent the qualities of consciousness that shape how we act in the classroom. Drawing on the three modes of being (see Chapter 8), these range from confusion or disengagement (ignorance), through restless ambition or performance-driven energy (passion), towards clarity, steadiness and moral purpose (goodness). In practical terms, this means noticing the culture we are creating: Are we operating from pressure and compliance, or from thoughtfulness and integrity? The six core beliefs – realising potential, empowering choice, strengthening interconnection, enriching diversities, expanding purpose and nourishing loving relationships – grow from this richer "topsoil" of goodness.

From these beliefs, virtues are planted and start taking shape in daily practice. Respect, self-discipline, integrity, courage, empathy and gratitude are made visible in routines, expectations, language and modelling. Both teacher and learner embody their own *Tree of Life*. The educational encounter, the moment of genuine connection in a lesson, conversation or encounter, becomes the space where these virtues are lived. This is the pedagogical space: structured by clear tools and practices, yet relational at its core.

In practical terms, this means creating classrooms where dialogue matters; where listening is taught and practised; where reflection is built into learning; where the arts and creative expression are valued in every subject domain; and where learners are supported to move through a cycle of listening, reflecting, internalising and acting with intention. When this happens, learning moves beyond simple delivery of content. The classroom becomes a place where identity, purpose and responsibility are explored alongside knowledge and skill.

Beyond the individual classroom lies the wider horizon: a community of many 'trees.' Here, the philosophy of *Acintya-bhedābheda* (difference and oneness held together) becomes practical. Each learner retains individuality, their background, and belief, yet belongs to a shared moral and soul-full community. In school terms, this means fostering interdependence rather than competition alone; intercultural appreciation rather than mere tolerance; shared purpose rather than isolated achievement. It is a movement from narrow self-interest toward contribution and connection.

Seen this way, the framework offers teachers a way of thinking about culture, relationships, pedagogy and purpose as interrelated. It helps us ask: What kind of soil are we cultivating? What virtues are becoming visible? And what kind of forest – what kind of community – is growing as a result?

A soul-full pedagogic approach

In essence, the framework offers a landscape for developing pedagogies to nurture the whole parts of a child, developing their spiritual insight, their character formation through virtues and in realising potential, purpose and interconnection through educational excellence. There are five aspects to consider:

1. Consciousness of educators
2. Importance of relationships, experiences and dialogue
3. Imagination and intercultural creativities
4. Listening, reflecting, meditating and acting within a psychological model of finding meaning
5. Assessing soul learning

First: the consciousness of the educator

Before anything is the consciousness of the educator. A soul-full education cannot be created unless educators raise their consciousness. This is about educators nurturing their own personal relationship, awareness and understanding of the soul. This is where "a philosophical disposition enables such a [person] to continue probing, learning, seeking connections and meanings. In fact, the disposition to find out best equips the human being to bear vicissitudes and pain" (Greene, 1973, p. 108). Biddulph and Baldacchino (2023) write about this powerful pedagogic mindset of reimagining to bring greater consciousness:

> The Social imagination is the capacity to invent visions of what should be and what might be in our deficit society, in the streets where we live and our schools. Social imagination not only suggests but also requires that one take action to repair or renew (Greene, 1998). From that position, if we are strangers in our practice, we take a new position. We become ready for the unexpected. Transformations, openings and possibilities become our ways of being and enacting. And to learn and teach, "one must have an awareness of leaving something behind while reaching toward something new, and this kind of awareness must be linked to imagination" (Greene, 1998: p. 20)
>
> (Biddulph and Baldacchino, 2023, p. 53)

The educators' conscious attitude towards a soul-full education experience can be collated into five dimensions:

- *Wide-awakeness*: attentive awareness of learners' experiences and possibilities
- *Ethical presence*: teaching that is grounded in care, dignity and relational responsibility
- *Reflexive enquiry*: curiosity and continuous questioning of assumptions and practices
- *Imaginative openness*: seeing learners not only as they are but as they might become
- *Professional learning and collaboration*: ongoing learning together as a community of practitioners

Here, the concept of the social imagination has an inherent interest in the soul's learning and development. As we have seen throughout, how we engage in the world shapes the quality of engagement and relationships. If education is a living ecology, then the teacher's inner life is not a private add-on; it is part of the classroom's climate and it must be nurtured in the same way that we nurture the inner life of children and young people. The Vedic language of the *guṇas* or modes (shared in Chapter 8) offers educators a way of noticing what kind of energy is moving through us, and what kind of learning it makes possible. We start, therefore, by refocusing on cultivating the mode of goodness within the teacher. This becomes the soil in which spiritual insight (and the Tree of Life) takes root.

In the mode of goodness is where the soul can develop best. In this mode, there is also a degree of openness and playfulness, space to discover and be curious. Biddulph and Gilbride (2025) refer to 'spaces of uncertainties' in which educators are less fearful of mistakes, confidently humble, purpose-led rather than ego-driven, with reduced hierarchy, adventurousness, aspiration for excellence and a desire for participation (p. 161). When transposed into educational practice, the mode of goodness invites educators to look beyond instructional technique towards the inner dispositions that nourish every interaction with learners.

Personal reflections for being in the mode of goodness

- How do I feel?
- How do I feel about the class I am teaching?
- How do I feel about individuals within the class?
- Who do I give most attention to?
- Who do I inadvertently ignore or find frustrating and do I treat them differently? Not explicitly but implicitly?
- Do the learners know that I care about them? How do they know this?
- What are the long term benefits for the decisions I make now?
- How do I connect with learners beyond their immediate characteristics and see them as unique souls?

A crucial point follows: we do not "arrive" in goodness and remain there. Teachers and learners move between all three modes. The task is not perfection, but cultivation: to choose goodness more often than not; to repair when we fall short; to build rhythms of reflection that keep the soil fertile.

As we will explore in Chapter 16, educators require professional learning about spirituality and the soul that engages both the intellect and the inner life (Erricker et al., 2001). Such development must go beyond abstract theorising to provide embodied opportunities for educators to grapple with ideas of meaning, purpose and transcendence through dialogue and experience. Too often, professional development focuses narrowly on technique or performance (Flutter, 2025; Hargreaves and Rolls, 2021), neglecting the cultivation of wisdom and presence that enable teachers to teach *for* and *from* the soul.

To lead education that is spiritually alive, educators need spaces for enquiry into their own beliefs, values and lived encounters with the sacred and the ordinary. This involves professional and personal learning that is at once cognitive, affective and ethical, holding together knowledge and self-understanding. Professional formation in this sense becomes an act of soul work: a disciplined openness to mystery, to ambiguity and to the shared search for truth.

Second: the core of relationships, experiences and dialogue

The second dimension concerns the primacy of relationship. Soul-focused education is formed through encounter, dialogue, and shared inquiry. As Greene argues, "the classroom situation most provocative of thoughtfulness and critical consciousness is the one in which teachers and learners find themselves conducting a kind of collaborative search" (Greene, 2000, p. 23). In such moments, education becomes a joint pursuit of meaning rather than a transmission of information. As Biddulph and Baldacchino (2023) suggest, it is precisely this shared search that opens a space for deeper questions of identity and purpose.

This emphasis on dialogical relationship resonates strongly with the Vedic tradition. In the *Bhagavad Gītā,* knowledge unfolds not through monologue but through an intimate dialogue between Krishna and Arjuna. At a moment of existential crisis, Arjuna turns to Krishna not merely as a friend but as a disciple to a teacher: "I am your disciple. Instruct me, who has taken refuge in you" (*Bhagavad Gītā* 2.7). The transformative teaching that follows emerges within this relational act of surrender, trust, and guidance. The text later affirms that wisdom is accessed through humility, enquiry, and service: "Approach those who have seen the truth. Inquire from them submissively and render service unto them; they can impart knowledge unto you" (*Bhagavad Gītā* 4.34).

For a soul-full education, this has profound implications. The relationship between educator and learner becomes more than functional or transactional; it becomes the medium through which meaning is awakened. Dialogue is not simply a pedagogical technique but a moral and spiritual practice. Within such relationships, the fundamental questions – Who am I? What is my purpose? What lies beyond me? – are not abstract philosophical puzzles but lived enquiries. The curriculum, in this sense, is the joint pursuit of these questions in the context of trust, intellectual humility and shared search.

Martin Buber's (who was an academic interested in ideas about dialogue) distinction between *I–It* and *I–Thou* relationships offers a powerful lens here. In *I–It* relations, the other is experienced as an object: managed, categorised, evaluated. In *I–Thou* encounters, the other is met as a subject, irreducible and alive. For Buber, "all real living is meeting" (Buber, 1947, p. 11). Education rooted in *I–Thou* acknowledges differences in experience or expertise, but it also refuses reduction. A child's experiences, even though young and forming, are as valid as the adults who may have more maturity in exploring meaning and significance behind their own experiences. The learner is not a data point, or in deficit waiting to be filled up with knowledge, nor the teacher merely a delivery mechanism. Both are participants in a shared process of becoming.

This does not mean abandoning authority or structure. It means reframing authority as relational stewardship rather than control. The teacher brings knowledge, experience and responsibility, but also openness: an orientation of curiosity, presence and ethical attentiveness. Learning, in this sense, is not only cognitive but ontological. It shapes who learners are becoming through the quality of encounter they experience. As we have referred previously, Maxine Greene describes this as *wide-awakeness*: an alertness to one's own existence in relation to others (1995). bell hooks frames it as education rooted in love for the learner's soul (1994). Nel Noddings articulates it through an ethic of care, where attentiveness and responsiveness are the foundations of moral life (2003). Across these perspectives, a shared insight emerges that education forms inner life through relationship before it forms understanding through content. Often times in the busyness of life at school, we skip the relationship making because 'we have to get through the curriculum' and the 'timetable says' we have other matters to deal with.

A vivid example of the importance of relational depth emerged while James was the Executive Headteacher at the University of Cambridge Primary School in the aftermath of the COVID-19 lockdowns. As he and his team of educators reflected on the disrupted routines and learning lost, a deeper question surfaced: how well do we really know our children?

How well do we know them?

We sat in the staff room, unsure how close to sit or whether to wear masks or just open a window. Prior to gathering the whole team, the leadership team had generated a spreadsheet of categories to see how much we knew about the children in our school.

These are some of the categories in the spreadsheet.

- Who do you live with?
- Where were you born?
- Where is your family from?
- Do you have a pet? What's its name?
- What would you like to do when you are older?
- What's your favourite game?
- Who are your friends in school?
- What hobbies do you do?
- What's your favourite food?
- Are your grandparents alive?
- Do you and your family follow a religion?
- Where is the furthest place you have travelled?

We gave the sheet and asked the staff to complete it, teachers and teaching assistants working together. There was some discussion and then increasing silence with a realisation that we hardly knew the children in terms of the categories given. The reason for this lack of knowledge was not because we did not care – indeed our focus was always on relationships – but because, we realised, there was never enough time in lessons or in staffrooms to talk about children, with children, about their lives and the things we needed to do to improve their outcomes – in the full sense of human flourishing not just in terms of their academic scores.

Over the course of the term, the teachers and teaching assistants spent a few minutes wherever they could, having informal chats with individuals, seeking answers for the categories. The result was an A3 spreadsheet of each class.

> A bigger result was that every teacher knew their children much better and informal conversations in the playground, at the school gate, in corridors demonstrated that we had richer relationships with the children – genuine, interested and caring.
>
> "How's your new kitten, Jack?"
> "Did you play cricket with your team, Mandy? How did it go?"
> "When did your grandma go back to India, Rahul? Is she ok? Does it feel strange her not being around?"
> "How's baby Gemma? Are you being a super big brother?"
>
> Journal Reflection by James Biddulph | May 2020 | University of Cambridge Primary School, UK

What does it mean to be known? This question returns us to the concept of the soul and the four aspects that Gor (2025) synthesises: finding identity, raising consciousness, resisting the pressure of materialism and having purpose. To be known is to be recognised; to be recognised is to be invited into responsibility for oneself and others. But what are we recognising about the child? Beyond the labels that so quickly define us (and them), how do we connect at a soul level?

Therefore, the soul is educated *in relationships*. No amount of curriculum design, reflective practice, or contemplative discipline can substitute for the lived encounter between teacher and learner. However, equally, without clear curriculum design, the value given to spiritual or soul development will be compromised. How this is created requires knowledge about the concept of the soul as well as lived experience of spirituality, whether through a sense of awe and wonder, or something more related to faith and relationship with the Divine; however, this is understood. In a soul-full education, this relational space is not incidental to learning; it is the medium through which learning becomes formative.

Relationships through knowledge of others

Relational pedagogy places the learner in dynamic relationship with self, with others, and with the wider world. John Miller (2000), in his work on holistic education, argues that education must integrate body, mind, emotion and spirit, drawing on both inner awareness and external sources of meaning. Without structured engagement with texts, histories, philosophies and spiritual traditions, experiential learning can remain under-theorised and insufficiently grounded.

There are also relationships formed with personalities and inspiring people in history. Learning about the soulful or spiritual experiences of others offers language, metaphors, and conceptual frameworks through which learners can better understand their own inner lives. For example, the mystical visions of Julian of Norwich, the poetic longing of Rumi, the radical compassion of Jesus and the compassionate humility of St Francis provide rich vocabularies for naming experiences of love, suffering, transcendence and hope. Hildegard von Bingen's integration of cosmology, music, theology and healing invites learners to see the soul as inseparable from the natural world, while Bede Griffiths' interfaith contemplative work demonstrates how spiritual identity can be deepened through encounter rather than diluted by difference.

Engaging with these diverse voices builds historical consciousness and cultural literacy, enabling learners to situate their own experiences within wider human narratives. It also fosters respect for different faith and belief systems, countering the tendency to universalise one's own perspective. Table 15.2 draws together some examples of personalities who have lived spiritually focused lives and who could be used within lessons to examine the nature of spirituality, their experiences and to reflect with children and young people's personal experiences.

Ultimately, learning about the soul through others' experiences, writings and life stories, and other texts and narratives, deepens self-awareness precisely because it draws the learner beyond the self. Rupert Sheldrake's work on fields of consciousness and interconnectedness, though contested, further challenges mechanistic understandings of the self and invites learners to consider the soul as participating in a larger, relational universe. Reflection becomes richer when it is informed by traditions; experience gains depth when it is placed in dialogue with history; relational pedagogy becomes transformative when relationships extend across time, culture and worldview. In this way, education for the soul cultivates personal meaning and also a sense of responsibility and belonging within the wider human story and, for many, in relationship with the Universe or the Divine.

Table 15.2 Spiritual personalities

Name of spiritual personality	Century lived in	Personal insights from their spiritual lives
Laozi	6th century BCE (trad.)	Taught harmony with the Tao through simplicity, non-striving (*wu wei*) and alignment with the natural order.
Rumi	13th century	Expressed mystical union with the Divine through poetry; taught love, longing and ego-transcendence as paths to awakening.
St Francis of Assisi	12th–13th century	Embodied simplicity, humility and kinship with all creation; advanced an ecological and relational spirituality.
Hildegard von Bingen	12th century	Integrated visions with theology, music, medicine, and cosmology; emphasised *viriditas* (spiritual vitality) and cosmic interconnectedness.
Julian of Norwich	14th–15th century	Articulated a spirituality of divine love grounded in visionary experience; emphasised hope, compassion and the healing nature of God.
Helena Blavatsky	19th century	Founded modern Theosophy; synthesised Eastern and Western esoteric traditions and emphasised spiritual evolution and universal wisdom.
Thich Nhat Hanh	20th–21st century	Integrated mindfulness with social action; articulated "interbeing" and compassionate presence in everyday life.
Rabbi Abraham Joshua Heschel	20th century	Articulated Jewish spirituality grounded in awe, wonder and ethical responsibility; emphasised prayer, justice and divine pathos.
María Sabina (Mazatec shaman)	20th century	Practised indigenous healing through sacred song and ritual; emphasised communion with the spiritual world for healing and insight.
Indigenous Elders (various traditions)	Across centuries	Emphasise ancestral wisdom, land-based spirituality, relational identity and the soul's embeddedness within community and nature.

Relationships through dialogue

Relationships are developed through experiences and dialogue. In schools, therefore, and supported by the literature about high-quality learning, the development of practices of dialogue are important pedagogic principles upon which a soul-full education must be nurtured. As Earnshaw and Hyman explain,

> The things we say and how we say them can inform, influence, inspire and motivate others and express our empathy, understanding and creativity. It is our ability to communicate that enables us to build positive relationships, collaborate for common purpose, deliberate and share our ideas as citizens.
>
> (British Council, online retrieved on 17th January 2026)

Dialogue is often misunderstood as simply 'more talk' in classrooms. In a soul-full education, dialogue is something much richer: a moral, epistemic, and relational practice through which meaning is co-created and inner life is shaped. Paulo Freire described dialogue as *praxis*, the unity of reflection and action (1970). For Freire, dialogue cannot exist without humility, nor can education be transformative unless teacher and learner become "jointly responsible for a process in which all grow" (1970, p. 89).

Contemporary research strengthens this claim. Robin Alexander's work on dialogic teaching provides a robust pedagogical architecture for dialogue as a central mode of learning. He distinguishes between dialogue as talk and dialogic teaching as the deliberate use of talk to extend thinking, understanding and agency. Dialogic teaching, for Alexander (2020), is inherently cognitive, social, cultural and ethical. It shapes not only what learners know, but how they come to know and how they relate to one another. Alexander identifies six core principles of dialogic teaching:

- Collective – teachers and learners address tasks together
- Supportive – ideas are offered without fear of embarrassment
- Reciprocal – participants listen, share and consider alternatives
- Deliberative – ideas are reasoned, challenged and refined
- Cumulative – contributions build towards shared understanding
- Purposeful – dialogue is structured toward educational goals

These principles align closely with the mode of goodness described earlier. They have potential to cultivate calm attentiveness, ethical listening, and disciplined freedom; conditions in which soul work becomes possible. Neil Mercer and Kate Littleton's concept of inter-thinking adds a sociocultural dimension, explaining why dialogue matters so deeply. Thinking, Mercer and Littleton (2007) argue, is not solely an individual act but a shared one. Through well-structured talk, learners pool knowledge, test ideas, and develop understandings that exceed individual cognition. Dialogue, therefore, is not only expressive; it is generative. It shapes consciousness itself.

This insight resonates strongly with Vedic pedagogical traditions, where debate, logic, storytelling and dialogic enquiry were central to education. Dialogue was not merely a method; it was a discipline for refining ego, testing truth and cultivating humility.

Linked with dialogue is narrative. Spiritual experience is frequently encountered and made sense of through narrative. As Scott argues (1998, 2001), narrative provides a means through which experiences that are ambiguous, affective or resistant to propositional language can be voiced without being finalised (Scott, 2001). Spiritual experiences, particularly those formed in childhood, are often characterised by intensity, relationality and uncertainty, and their telling requires a listening space that is hospitable rather than interrogative. Narrative, in this sense, does not function primarily as explanation, but as an interpretative act through which meaning is gradually formed in relation to an attentive other (Bruner, 1996). A pedagogy for the soul requires, therefore, an appreciation and skill to listen deeply to the narratives that children and young people tell about their spiritual experiences, inner psychological worlds and cultural-religious-belief systems. Importantly so that, "it is necessary to listen to stories openly and without judgement" (Scott, 2001, p. 123).

It is the final ten minutes of the day in a Year 5 classroom. The children are sitting in a circle for what I called, "candle time." A candle sits in the centre of the circle. I light it. This is a signal that this is a time for listening. I begin:

> Today we're not looking for right answers. We're just sharing moments that made us feel something important, something we might not fully understand yet.

There is a pause. Some children stare at the floor, others at the small light in the centre.
After a while, Amir raises his hand.

"I think something like that happened to me," he says hesitantly.
I nod. "Take your time."

Amir continues.

> Last weekend my grandma took me to the park early in the morning. It was really quiet. There was mist over the grass. And suddenly loads of birds flew up together from a tree. It made my chest feel… strange. Not bad strange. Just like everything was really big and I was really small.

He shrugs.

> I don't really know why it mattered. But I keep thinking about it.

This is wonderful I thought but I did not want to interpret the experience or ask probing questions. Instead, gently:

> It sounds like that moment stayed with you.

Amir nods.
A few seconds of silence follow. Then Lily, another learner, speaks.

> Sometimes when I'm in the temple with my mum and everyone is singing, I feel something a bit like that. Like I'm part of something bigger. But I don't always understand what it is.

I look around the class.

> Thank you both for trusting us with those moments.

Pause.

> Does anyone else recognise that feeling…when something ordinary suddenly feels bigger or deeper than usual?

A few nod. One mentions watching the stars with their older brother. Another describes sitting beside their dog when it was ill and feeling very close to it.

I show them a photo of a roof top I used to play on as a child, where my brother, cousins and I would lie down, sticky chins with ice-cream, looking at the stars and shared a little about how I felt.

No one tries to explain the experiences. No one corrects or categorises them.

We breathed in together, deeply and out with ease, in with joy and out with release and then I close the candle time circle by saying:

> Sometimes the most important experiences in our lives are the ones we are still learning how to talk about. Listening to each other's stories helps us notice those moments.

The candle in the centre is switched off, and the class moves quietly into the next activity.

Remembered reflection from James' time as a teacher in Newham, East London, UK

As we have presented above, listening deeply is important for spiritual meaning-making. Brown and Gilligan's work on multiple listenings highlights the ethical responsibility of the listener to attend to voice, relationship and silences, recognising that spiritual narratives may be tentative, incomplete or still in process (Brown and Gilligan, 1991). Such listening honours the lived significance of the experience for the narrator.

All these points raise a pressing question for us all who work in schools: how are spaces created in which children, young people and adults can speak about spiritual experience in ways that are grounded and intimate, yet not exposing or coercive? Such spaces depend not only on pedagogical structures, but on lived beliefs and virtues. Dialogue about spirituality, when rooted in these virtues contributes to ethical orientation and shared meaning-making (Erricker et al., 2001; Kessler, 2000; Mahaffey, 2019).

Third: imagination, the arts and intercultural creativities

The third consideration of a soul-full pedagogy is the development of the imagination through intercultural creativities and the arts (Egan, 2008). We found that not only is there relevant contemporary literature about the place of the arts in school but that this emphasis is also found in the Vedic educational history and philosophy.

Curricula are never neutral. They are moral documents: maps of what a society believes is worth knowing, doing and becoming. When education loses its soul, it is often because the curriculum has narrowed – fragmented into subjects, outcomes and competencies that struggle to speak to the fullness of human life. Across cultures and centuries, however, we find alternative curricular imaginations. Ancient Indian education offers one such vision, not as a blueprint to be replicated, but as a philosophical resource to be reinterpreted.

In the ancient context of India, the arts were vitally important. The human longing for meaning appears wherever people tell stories, make music, create images, dance, sing or shape materials into forms that speak beyond utility. Across cultures, the arts have been humanity's way of grappling with life's deepest questions: love and loss, suffering and hope, belonging and transcendence. In October 2025, tracing the history of Avanti Schools Trust, James visited the ashram of Sandipani Muni at Avantika (modern-day Ujjain), traditionally understood as the place where Krishna and Balaram, two important personalities in the Vedic tradition, were educated. What struck him was not the mythology, but the curricular imagination embedded in the site: an education that integrated sciences, arts, ethics, dialogue, service and spiritual discipline into a coherent way of life. Figure 15.2 is a painted room in the Ujjain ashram, mapping the curriculum of the ancient education.

Notes from James Biddulph's journal | 25th October 2025, Ujjain, India

Even amidst the swirl of motorbikes, bells and temple chants, the Sandipani Muni Ashram seemed to breathe at its own rhythm. In the Ashram, there is a beautifully painted room that explains the type of learning that would have gone on here, including sciences, arts, linguistics, ethics and cosmology.

Figure 15.2 Photo of part of the ceiling in the museum at the Sandipani Muni Ashram, Ujjain, India. Photo of mural taken by James Biddulph on 24th October 2025.

In my mind's eye, children moved between lessons in music, scripture and craft with a natural ease, their learning woven seamlessly with play, devotion and discipline. Indoors, in the shaded classrooms, concentration and care; outdoors, under trees and open sky, I sensed the vitality of learning through experience. It was an education both simple and sophisticated simple in form, yet complex in purpose.

Every act, from sweeping the courtyard to making garlands, from studying the sciences to reciting verses, was charged with intention and presence. It was a full education. Sweeping the courtyard, a lesson in humility, responsibility and community. Making garlands, a lesson in honouring one's elders and in respecting the Divine. Discussions about philosophy, lessons in discernment, criticality and being prepared to change one's position on a topic – evoking qualities to temper the ego!

Journal Reflection by James Biddulph | October 2025

The Vedic tradition speaks of 14 *vidyās* (branches of knowledge) and 64 *kalās* (arts or skills). While mythopoetic accounts describe Krishna mastering them in 64 days, the deeper insight is not speed but scope. Knowledge was understood as multidimensional. Intellectual, aesthetic, practical and ethical forms of knowing were woven together rather than ranked against one another. The *vidyās* encompassed disciplines we would now recognise as sciences, mathematics, linguistics, ethics, governance, cosmology and health. The *kalās* celebrated embodied, relational and aesthetic intelligence: music, dance, craft, dialogue, humour, debate and care. Importantly, dialogue itself was considered both a domain of learning and the medium through which learning unfolded.

To imagine a contemporary curriculum inspired by this vision recovers a principle of integration – to move beyond siloes or disciplinary tribes (Biddulph and Flutter, 2021a and 2021b). A modern soul-full curriculum crafted by this imagination would foreground three interwoven strands:

1. Aesthetic and artistic expression, not as enrichment but as enquiry (educating perception, empathy and imagination)
2. Reasoned dialogue and logic, cultivating discernment, humility and ethical communication
3. Moral and civic formation, oriented toward service, responsibility and compassionate action

Once again, dialogic practices run through all three, connecting inner and outer life, self and society, past and present. Such a curriculum resists fragmentation or obsessive siloing of knowledge content – it is much more transdisciplinary. For example, the relationships between mathematics and music, science and ethics, science and the arts, language and imagination are not isolated silos but mutually informing ways of engaging reality. This is not a new 'watered down' cross-curricular approach to designing the curriculum; rather it strives to find meaningful ways in which domains of knowledge, skills and attributes come together to better construct a meaningful experience, that goes beyond acquisition and towards deeper more sustained curiosity and learning.

Table 15.3 maps selected *vidyās* and *kalās* to contemporary curricular domains. The significance lies not in the categories themselves, but in the educational stance, they imply: that knowing, being and acting belong together. This is in contrast to the current contemporary emphasis on knowing.

Table 15.3 Mapping the *vidyās* and *kalās* to contemporary curricular domains

Ancient domain	Example from Vidyās and Kalās	Contemporary expression	Educational purpose
Performing Arts	*Gandharva Veda, Geet Vidyā, Nritya Vidyā, Nātya Vidyā*	Music, drama, dance and interdisciplinary arts education	Cultivates creativity, empathy, rhythm and expression; integrates body, emotion and intellect
Visual and Material Arts	*Alekhya Vidyā, Mani–bhūmikā–karma, Takṣaṇa*	Visual arts, design technology, sculpture, architecture	Develops aesthetic judgment, craftsmanship and care for form and environment
Language and Logic	*Vyākaraṇa, Nirukta, Prahelikā, Samvāchya, Mlecchita–kutarka–vikalpa*	Grammar, rhetoric, critical thinking, debate and philosophy	Fosters reasoning, dialogue, interpretive skill and ethical communication
Science and Mathematics	*Jyotiṣa, Dhātu–veda, Vāstu Vidyā, Āyurveda*	Astronomy, physics, engineering, health sciences	Integrates empirical enquiry with spiritual and ecological awareness
Ethics and Governance	*Arthaśāstra, Vainayikī Vidyā, Vaijayikī Vidyā*	Citizenship, moral education, leadership, social studies	Encourages justice, discernment and civic responsibility. Compassionate changemakers.
Ecology and Wellbeing	*Vṛkṣāyurveda, Sugandha–yukti, Pushpastaraṇa*	Environmental studies, wellbeing education, horticulture	Nurtures reverence for life and sustainable relationship with nature
Dialogue and Reflection	*Tarka, Vāda, Manasī Kāvyakriyā*	Philosophy, dialogic pedagogy, contemplative enquiry	Promotes reflexivity, intercultural understanding and mindful learning

In such a curriculum, the soul is not an abstract concept added at the margins. It is the animating principle that gives coherence to learning. Learners do not merely acquire skills; they develop ways of seeing, valuing, and responding to the world. One could synthesise that contemporary education, if it is to develop the soul, must be intentionally holistic and formative rather than merely functional. It should cultivate creativity, compassion, the arts, and expression, integrating body, emotion and intellect as dimensions of human flourishing. It must develop aesthetic judgement, craftsmanship, and care for form, language and environment, while fostering reasoning, dialogue and ethical communication through dialogic practices of *inter-thinking*, as articulated by Neil Mercer and Kate Littleton (2007).

We found that neuroscientific research suggests that serious engagement with meaning and purpose expands consciousness and cognitive capacity (Newberg and Waldman, 2009). This aligns with longstanding insights from philosophy and spirituality: meaning making is not an optional extra but central to human flourishing. In this, the arts offer structured yet open-ended ways of engaging uncertainty, ambiguity, and wonder, conditions essential to spiritual and moral development. Maxine Greene's work remains foundational here. Her assertion that "art does not change the world, but it may change people who can change the world" (1995, p. 133) situates artistic experience as a catalyst for transformation. For Greene, imagination is the capacity to see things as if they could be otherwise. This is not escapism; it is ethical perception. Imagination disrupts the taken-for-granted and opens learners to alternative ways of seeing, feeling, and being. Greene's concept of wide-awakeness describes a heightened attentiveness to one's presence in the world and to one's responsibilities towards others. Artistic engagement cultivates this attentiveness by demanding slowness, interpretation and response. Through music, drama, visual art, poetry and movement, learners encounter the "not yet" possibility latent within themselves and their communities.

Parker Palmer (1998) similarly frames spirituality not as belief but as quality of attention, the capacity to be present to beauty, suffering and mystery. From this perspective, the arts operationalise spirituality. Abbs (2003) and Shields (2004) extend this view, describing artistic engagement as relational giving: encounters that invite learners into communion with others, materials, and meanings that exceed certainty. Such encounters often occur in liminal spaces, threshold moments where certainty loosens and transformation becomes possible (Conroy, 2004). They allow learners to experiment, to risk and to play with ideas and identities. Playfulness here is not trivial; it is pedagogically serious. As Biddulph (2025) notes, play enables insights to surface from both conscious and unconscious worlds, revealing inner capacities that remain hidden in tightly controlled environments.

The *International Handbook of Research in Arts Education* captures this orientation powerfully. In relation to the arts, Rita Irwin describes an education of the soul as one in which learners feel "completely alive… experiencing joy, compassion, mindfulness, and a sense of awe for the mystery that abounds" (2017, p. 1401). Irwin further argues that a spiritual curriculum "moves beyond the rational and analytic ways of understanding the world and favours intuitive and emotional ways of knowing as we focus our perceptions on building connections, seeking unity, and feeling centred" (Irwin, 2017, p. 1401). These statements foreground relationship, community, and connection as central pedagogical concerns, an emphasis that resonates strongly with Vedic philosophy, in which *yoga* itself means to connect.

Shaban (2008) says that spirituality in art is, "the connection between the magical unknown and us," describing art as a relational encounter between the soul and a world rendered soulless by excessive instrumentalism. Art, in this framing, restores transparency to inner life, allowing feeling and intuition to re-enter educational spaces often dominated by abstraction and measurement. Importantly, Shaban does not reject scientific understanding, but calls for balance, an integration of intellect, feeling, and meaning that allows the "heart, mind, and soul" to coexist. While such phrases are frequently invoked rhetorically, the challenge remains to make them pedagogically visible and actionable. Creativity emerges at what Nakata (2007) calls the *cultural interface*: spaces where multiple epistemologies meet without collapsing into sameness. Here, difference becomes a resource for insight. Listening precedes judgement; curiosity replaces fear.

In the shaded example that follows, Vergil, the teacher, explains an open-creative learning task. In many ways, it presents all six beliefs in a single educational moment: seeking every learner to see their own potential beyond self-imposed limitations, giving learners choices, which in turn empowered them individually and as a collective. Interconnection was needed because the project was highly dependent on collaboration for success. Diverse ways of working and skills were understood. The purpose was beyond their individual grades and learning. The project created a sense of pride (in the whole school as well as for the group) – it was all done, by teacher and learners, with care and attention.

Reimagining Education: The Avanti Way Through a Go–Kart

It began with a bare metal frame and a dream: to build a go–kart from scratch. For many, it may have seemed like just another school project. But for us, it became a living, moving symbol of the Avanti Way – of character, collaboration, and the power of purposeful education.

From the outset, we knew this wasn't just about engineering. It was about creating space for learners to learn, lead and discover something within themselves. Some came in with knowledge of tools, torque, and brake lines. Others didn't know the difference between a spanner and a screwdriver. But that was never the point. The point was that they showed up, and they stayed.

I remember one student who would take a spanner and try to tighten a screw using the wrong end or attempt to force it onto the completely wrong bolt. He wasn't confident, but he was curious. Rather than dismiss him, one of the more experienced learners simply said, "Come, I'll show you." That moment – a quiet, unforced act of guidance – was character formation in action. What was even more powerful was what followed: the student realised that building might not be his strongest skill, but he still had a lot of fun and took pride in showing up, trying, and being part of something bigger than himself. His joy, humour, and determination became an essential part of the team's spirit.

When I look at the finished kart, I can say with full confidence: *the team did this*. It was not the work of one or two gifted individuals, but the collective sweat and effort of dozens of learners – each one offering what they could, learning as they went. The kart became a shared achievement, shaped by hands and hearts alike. And what has been even more moving is the support from the wider school body. Of course, the learners were the heartbeat of the project, but the encouragement from parents, the practical help from staff, and the buzz from the wider community created a foundation of trust and shared pride. I remember when one of the drivers came into the pit, his face brimming with glee. Or the

Figure 15.3 Go-karting as an example of six beliefs

moment we saw the girls' graphic design for the kart – it blew away the founders themselves. These moments weren't just joyful; they were deeply affirming, reminding us that excellence comes in many forms and that every student has something meaningful to contribute (Figure 15.3).

As we prepare to build on this success next year, I do so with deep hope and gratitude. Not just for the kart we built, but for the values it helped us live out. The Avanti Way isn't just a framework – it's something you can feel in the air when learners collaborate with kindness, when learning is joyful, and when every child, regardless of starting point, is given the chance to make something meaningful. And sometimes, that meaningful thing just happens to have four wheels and a roaring engine. As the African proverb wisely puts it, "Smooth seas do not make skilful sailors." This journey has had its fair share of bumps and learning curves, but it's in those very moments that our learners – and all of us – grew the most.

Reflection by Vergil Wong, Science Teacher at Avanti House Secondary School

Fourth: a framework for conceptualising the development of the soul

We now turn to two complementary frameworks, one psychological, one Vedic, that together offer a language for understanding how inner growth can be cultivated in educational settings. We have argued, from a Vedic perspective, that the soul is not a static entity but with a dynamic potential. Contemporary psychology offers a parallel claim: that human beings actively construct meaning, and that the quality of this meaning making shapes wellbeing, agency, and moral action. In our research, we identified a concept called the Logoplex model (Piedmont and Wilkins, 2020) which provides a useful bridge between these traditions. It describes meaning making along two intersecting dimensions:

- Materialism ↔ Transpersonalism: whether meaning is grounded primarily in possessions, status and achievement, or in connection to something beyond the self
- Intentionalism ↔ Relationalism: whether meaning is derived mainly from individual goals and agency, or from relationships, community and belonging

These dimensions generate a matrix of human functioning. At lower levels, meaning tends to be fragile, contingent and easily disrupted. As awareness expands, meaning becomes increasingly relational and transpersonal – less about accumulation, more about participation; less about separation, more about belonging. The upper quadrants represent a coherence of purpose in which life is experienced as interconnected and morally significant (Figure 15.4).

The Logoplex[1] does not prescribe belief. Rather, it offers a way of noticing where learners and educators may be operating in their search for meaning. The key idea is that spiritual understanding becomes more complex and reflective over time – as is suggested in the Logoplex model. Young children can have genuine spiritual experiences, but they usually experience them without reflection or self-awareness. As people mature, they become better able to reflect on themselves, others, and ultimately on something beyond the self. Further supportive thinking about how spiritual learning takes place is given by Wilber (2000); spirituality is seen as

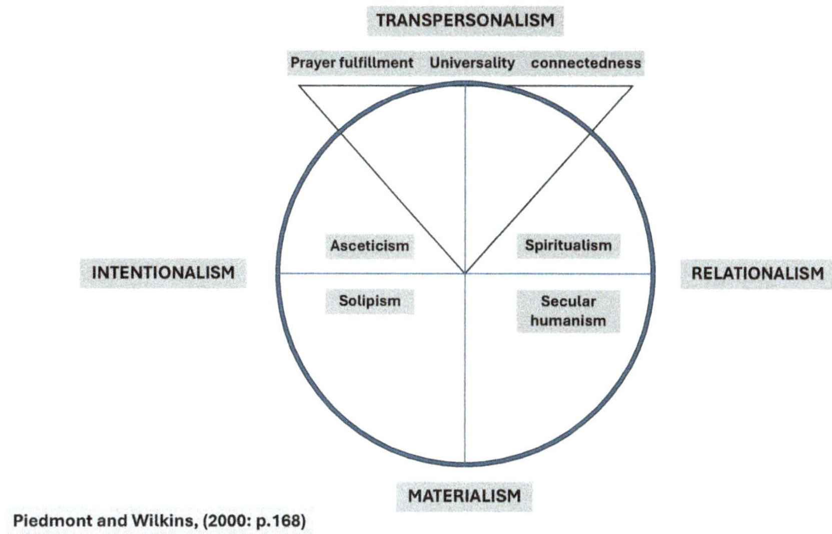

Figure 15.4 Logoplex matrix

something that develops in stages, broadly alongside a child's psychological growth. He argues that difficulties arise when we confuse early, child-like spirituality with later, more mature forms. His model helps teachers recognise that children's spirituality is real, but different in nature from adult spirituality.

Wilber's five stages (paraphrased for our purpose)

1. ***Pre-personal (early childhood)***
   The child experiences wonder, connection, and awe, but without a clear sense of self. Spiritual moments may feel magical or absorbed, but the child cannot yet reflect on them.
2. ***Personal (developing self-awareness)***
   The child develops a stronger sense of "me." They begin to understand rules, stories, values, and beliefs. Spiritual ideas are often understood literally (e.g. God as a character in a story).
3. ***Rational (thinking and questioning)***
   The young person becomes more analytical and questioning. They may doubt, challenge or step away from spiritual ideas as critical thinking grows.

4. ***Transpersonal (beyond the ego)***
   The individual begins to experience a sense of connection that goes beyond the self, combined with reflection and awareness. Spirituality here is conscious and integrated, not naïve.
5. ***Integrated or mature spirituality***
   A deep sense of compassion, meaning, and unity with others and the world. The person understands the limits of the ego and acts with care, humility and responsibility.

Both the Logoplex and Wilber's models provide insight into how a pedagogy for the development of the soul might be created. It also raises a pedagogical question: what kinds of educational experiences support movement toward deeper coherence and relational awareness, towards integrated mature spirituality? Here, the Vedic tradition offers a complementary answer through the fourfold process of *jñāna-yoga*. The Vedic texts present this in three steps with an implicit fourth step to make this explicit. In the same spirit, we have translated the framework to suit a pedagogic framework, recognising that other scholars would use different terms:

1. *Śravaṇa* – deep listening
2. *Manana* – reflection
3. *Dhyāna* – meditation
4. *Praṇidhāna* – intentional or devoted action arising as a natural consequence of direct realisation

Figure 15.5 shows the four practices or processes overlaid onto the Logoplex; this indicates the activating pedagogy to help develop the soul's learning.

These are not religious practices but universal human processes through which understanding matures into wisdom. It is not dissimilar to the transformational arguments made by bell hooks, Maxine Greene, Paulo Friere – help people listen well, help them to be reflective and to sustain their curiosity, support them to meditate on the issue or concept or ideas and not to settle for the first response, and then engage them in reflexivity – to do something with their new learning for the good of all and in the mode of goodness.

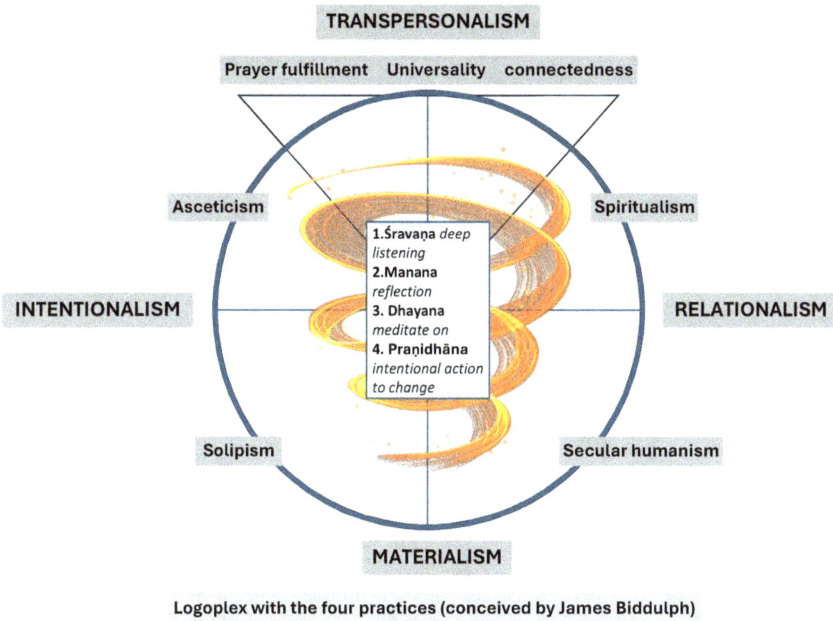

Figure 15.5 Logoplex with four-part Vedic process

When read through the Logoplex, the four processes describe a movement from self-centred meaning towards relational and transpersonal awareness. Figure 15.6 gives more detail of the four-part Vedic process within the Logoplex framework.

There is a movement from materialism through the whole system towards a more spiritual transpersonal awareness – involving for some (for many) the notion of the Divine. The spiral image suggests it is not linear and subjects to the ups and downs of spiritual endeavour. Let us consider each aspect in turn.

Śravaṇa – deep listening (creating the conditions for attention)

Learning begins with listening, not as passive hearing, but as intentional, receptive attention to others, ideas and the world. For teachers, *śravaṇa* is about deliberately designing moments where learners are invited to slow

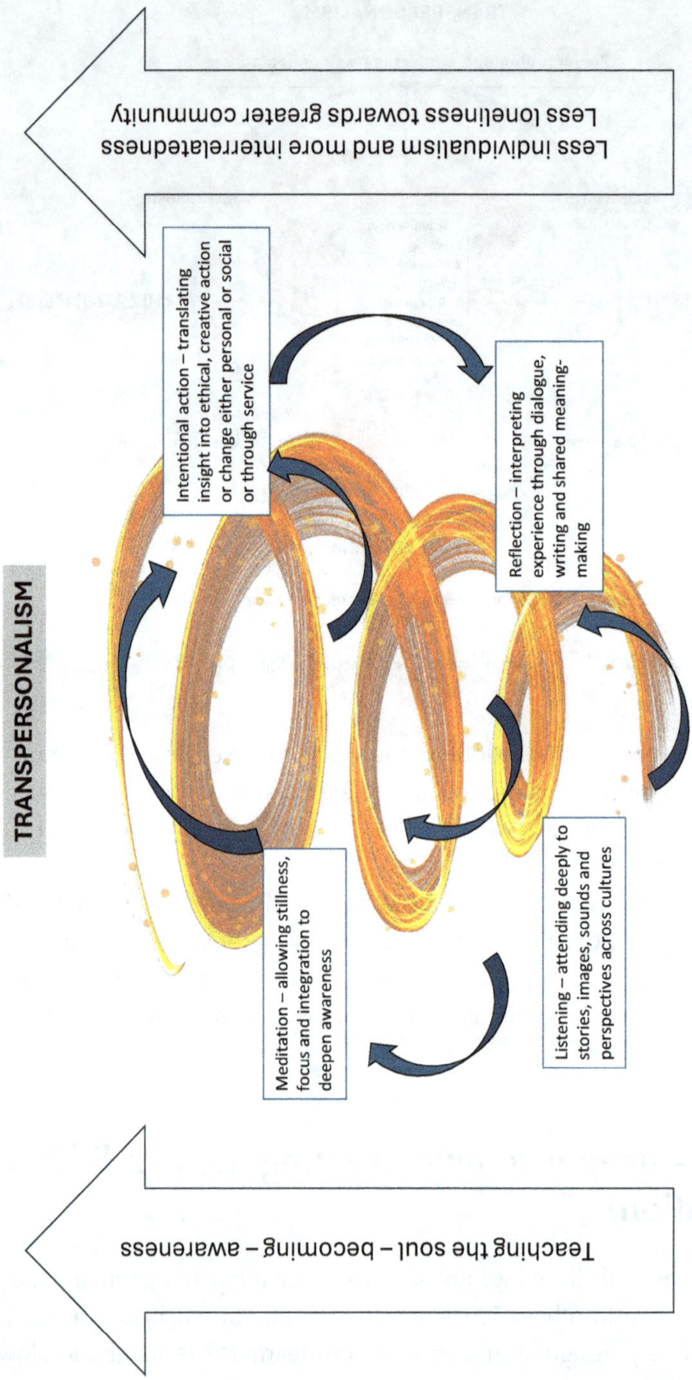

Figure 15.6 Detail of the four-part Vedic process within the Logoplex framework

down, attend and receive before responding. This kind of listening draws learners beyond self-preoccupation and into relationship, marking a shift from individualised performance towards shared meaning.

In practice, deep listening can be built into everyday routines. A primary teacher might begin the day with a short listening circle, where learners hear a poem, piece of music, or a classmate's reflection, followed by a pause rather than immediate discussion. In secondary classrooms, teachers might play a short audio clip, read a powerful paragraph aloud, or present an image, asking learners simply to listen or observe before analysing. In science, this could involve listening carefully to a peer's explanation of an experiment; in geography, to the lived experience of someone affected by climate change.

Teachers can scaffold listening by modelling it themselves, paraphrasing what a learner has said, acknowledging uncertainty, or allowing silence to settle. Over time, such practices cultivate empathy, attentiveness and respect. Listening becomes an act of presence, helping learners move from "What do I think?" towards "What are we noticing together?"

Manana – reflection (making meaning from experience)

Reflection transforms what has been heard into understanding. In pedagogical terms, *manana* is about helping learners process, test and personalise ideas, rather than simply moving on to the next task. Reflection allows learners to connect new knowledge with their own experiences, values and questions, turning information into insight. In classrooms, this can take many accessible forms. Learners might keep short reflective journals, responding to prompts such as: What surprised me today? What did I find challenging? Or What does this idea mean for how people live?

Reflection also happens through talk. Structured pair discussions, think-pair-share, or end-of-lesson circles allow learners to articulate meaning aloud and hear alternative perspectives. The teacher's role is to value the process, not just the conclusion – encouraging thoughtful uncertainty as much as confident answers. Here, learning becomes purposeful and personally meaningful rather than purely task-driven.

Dhyāna – meditation (integrating awareness and attention)

Meditation, in educational contexts, does not mean withdrawal from learning but integration of mind, body and attention. *Dhyāna* helps learners develop the capacity to focus, to notice their inner states and to remain present, skills increasingly vital in fast-paced, overstimulated environments.

In schools, this can be introduced gently and inclusively. Teachers might use one or two minutes of quiet breathing after breaktime, before a test, or at the start of a challenging lesson. In art or design, learners may be invited to work in sustained silence for a short period, noticing texture, colour or form. In outdoor learning, learners might pause to observe natural sounds or patterns before recording observations.

Such moments are brief but powerful. They help learners regulate emotions, settle their attention, and reconnect with themselves. Over time, learners learn that stillness is not empty time but fertile space for insight. Within the Logoplex, these practices support movement toward transpersonal awareness, where learners begin to experience themselves as part of something larger than immediate outcomes or performance.

Praṇidhāna – placing intentional action (learning embodied and lived out)

The cycle completes with *praṇidhāna*: turning insight into action. Pedagogically, this is where learning becomes ethical, relational, and purposeful. Learners are supported to ask: *What do I know? How might this shape what I do?* In this phase, the learner embodies the new insights – they become new ways by which they live and engage in the world around them.

In practice, intentional action can be woven into curriculum and school life. A class studying environmental science might design and implement a recycling initiative. Learners exploring kindness or justice might engage in peer mentoring, community projects or acts of service within the school. In creative subjects, learners might produce work intended for a real audience, reflecting on the responsibility that comes with being heard.

Even small rituals matter, like writing thank-you notes, acknowledging contributions, or reflecting on how classroom agreements are lived out. These actions help learners experience learning as participation in shared wellbeing rather than individual achievement. Knowledge, reflection and awareness are embodied as compassionate practice.

Together, the Logoplex and the fourfold Vedic process offer a possible framework for soul-full education. The Logoplex maps where meaning may be located; the Vedic process offers how movement towards deeper coherence can be cultivated. Importantly, neither framework requires adherence to a belief system. Both invite educators to nurture universal human capacities: awareness, curiosity, reflection, gratitude and compassion. Education becomes the art of creating conditions in which learners can move from fragmentation toward wholeness, from ego toward relationship, from knowledge towards wisdom.

Fifth: pedagogic toolkit for the soul and its assessment

What arises from both the Vedic philosophy and contemporary thinking are key pedagogic principles that draw from arts, creativities, relational and dialogue research and theory. When James Biddulph was the Executive Headteacher at the University of Cambridge Primary School, he worked with colleagues to define a research-informed pedagogic toolkit which very much align with his current thinking as CEO of Avanti Schools Trust (Biddulph, 2025; Biddulph and Burnard, 2022; Biddulph and Flutter, 2021; Coltman and Rolls, 2021). Together these pedagogies have the potential to cultivate deep understanding, purposeful agency and compassionate participation in the world. What is not needed is a wholesale acceptance of (often uncritiqued) technocratic 'pedagogic toolkits' which can result in automated deliverers of content and not the conscious, wide-awake and curiously engaged teachers who can open up a soul-full educational experience.

Building on previous learning: depth, continuity and meaning

Soul-full learning recognises that understanding grows through continuity and coherence. Learning sequences are deliberately designed to revisit, connect and deepen prior knowledge so that new learning rests on secure foundations. Retrieval, reflection, and assessment are used not as endpoints, but as acts of meaning-making, supporting learners to see how their learning fits into a larger narrative over time Praetorius et al., 2018; Rosenshine, 2010).

Pedagogies of engagement: curiosity, wonder and joy

At the heart of soul-full teaching is engagement that arises from curiosity and intrinsic motivation. Learning sequences begin with rich, inviting experiences, stories, drama, practical exploration, dialogue, creative media and educational visits, that awaken wonder and invite children into learning as active participants. These pedagogies acknowledge that attention, emotion and cognition are deeply intertwined. By designing learning that resonates with learners' interests and lived experiences, teachers create conditions in which engagement is not coerced but cultivated, supporting sustained focus and a love of learning (Dehaene, 2020; Fredricks, Blumenfeld and Paris, 2004; Moore, 2013; Reeve et al., 2004).

Productive challenge: courage, growth and wellbeing

The belief in nourishing loving relationships involves creating learning that requires productive challenge. Soul-full learning embraces challenge as a vital condition for growth, while holding children in care. Learning experiences are designed with appropriate 'desirable difficulty,' allowing for multiple pathways and outcomes. Through independent and collaborative challenges, learners encounter uncertainty, develop resilience and learn that struggle can be meaningful rather than threatening (Bjork and Bjork, 2011; Kapur, 2011; Hattie, 2012).

Language, talk and oracy: voice, relationship and belonging

Language is central to soul-full pedagogy because it shapes thought, identity, and relationship. Explicit vocabulary teaching across all subjects ensures that learners are given the words they need to think, express and participate fully. Learning environments act as living language spaces, where vocabulary is introduced dynamically and used purposefully in context (Baines et al., 2008; Gersten, Baker and Shanahan, 2007; Gillies, 2016; Mercer, Wegerif and Dawes, 1999; Nash and Snowling, 2006; OECD, 2015; Quigley, 2018; Slavin, 2014; Wegerif, 2017; Wegerif et al., 2017).

Intelligent practise: fluency, mastery and purpose

Practise is purposeful rather than repetitive. Learners are given frequent opportunities to rehearse, apply and consolidate learning across subjects so that knowledge becomes fluent and transferable. Daily practise in reading, writing, mathematics and subject-specific skills is integrated with opportunities to apply learning creatively and across the curriculum (Bjork and Bjork, 2011; Ericsson, 2009; Gu et al., 2004; Soderstrom and Bjork, 2015). One lesson about spirituality a week, for example, will not provide the knowledge or experiences to deepen awareness and reflection about the nature of the soul.

Responsive teaching: attunement and trust

Soul-full pedagogy requires attentiveness. Teachers continuously elicit evidence of learning through questioning, dialogue, tasks and reflection, using this insight to adapt teaching responsively. Planning is iterative rather than fixed, shaped by what children reveal about their understanding and needs.

Learning environment: space as the third teacher

The physical and relational environment is understood as a 'third teacher,' shaping ethos, communication, and belonging. Learning spaces are intentionally designed to support exploration, collaboration and play, enabling children to apply knowledge in meaningful ways (EEF, 2019; Muijs et al., 2014; Praetorius et al., 2018; Strong-Wilson and Ellis, 2007).

Metacognition and self-regulated learning: agency and purpose

Soul-full learning aims to develop reflective, self-directed learners. Children are explicitly taught metacognitive strategies that help them plan, monitor and evaluate their learning. This develops self-discipline. Teachers model thinking aloud, scaffold reflection and facilitate dialogue that supports children to make sense of their experiences (Donker et al., 2014; Panadero, 2017; Quigley, Muijs and Stringer, 2018; Vansteenkiste et al., 2004).

Table 15.4 brings together the eight pedagogic principles, aligned with examples of what teachers might do within each principle.

Table 15.4 A soul-full pedagogy framework (Integrating TLRP principles with classroom design and the consciousness of the teacher)

Pedagogical orientation	What arises	Design principle	What happens in the lesson	Soul lens (human formation)
Building on Previous Learning *(Pedagogy recognises prior experience and learning)*	Depth, Continuity, Meaning	Learning is cumulative and coherent.	Lessons begin with retrieval connecting prior knowledge to big ideas. Prior concepts are revisited through low-stakes quizzes, dialogue and reflection. Teachers narrate the learning journey and conclude with synthesis.	Learners experience learning as a meaningful unfolding narrative rather than disconnected tasks.
Pedagogies of Engagement *(Pedagogy promotes the active engagement of the learner)*	Curiosity, Wonder, Joy	Engagement is cultivated rather than imposed.	Lessons may open with a story, image, artefact or dilemma. Learners speculate before explanation. Teaching integrates creativity, dialogue, exploration and lived experience. Space is preserved for awe and reflection.	Attention becomes emotionally alive and intrinsically motivated. Behaviours are positive and prosocial because learning is interesting and allows for co-construction of meaning. Learners see the purpose beyond passing exams or doing it for the teacher.
Productive Challenge *(Learning requires scaffolding and growth through difficulty)*	Courage, Growth, Wellbeing	Growth requires challenge held within care and structure.	Teachers design tasks with desirable difficulty. Struggle is normalised. Scaffolds support thinking without removing it. Learners collaborate to solve problems and explore multiple pathways.	Challenge becomes a pathway to growth rather than a threat to confidence. Learners know that challenge is learning and learning is challenging and accept failure because it advances their learning. This strengthens their self-esteem and confidence.

Language, Talk and Oracy *(Pedagogy fosters social processes and dialogue)*	Voice, Relationship, Belonging	Language shapes thinking, identity and community.	Teachers explicitly teach vocabulary, model sentence structures and scaffold dialogic talk. Learners articulate ideas in full sentences, justify reasoning and respectfully challenge one another's thinking.	Language and voicing truths, identities and cultural ways dignifies the learner's voice and builds intellectual belonging.
Intelligent Practice *(Pedagogy engages with valued forms of knowledge)*	Fluency, Mastery, Purpose	Practice cultivates mastery and freedom.	Learners move from guided practice to independence. Practice is purposeful rather than repetitive. Knowledge is applied across contexts through reading, writing, mathematics and disciplinary thinking.	Fluency frees the mind for deeper reflection and creative thought.
Responsive Teaching *(Assessment congruent with learning)*	Attunement, Trust	Teaching responds to learners in real time.	Teachers use hinge questions and formative assessment to diagnose understanding. They listen carefully, adjust pace and treat misconceptions as opportunities for insight.	Attentiveness communicates care and cultivates trust. Feedback is meaningful and does not include 'good, well done' but rather is evaluative and constructive and moves learning to the next stage.
Learning Environment *(Policy and structures supporting learning)*	Belonging, Aspiration, Exploration	The environment communicates the values of learning.	Displays reinforce vocabulary and big ideas. Spaces invite exploration and collaboration. Materials are purposeful. Beauty, order and calm are visible. Relationships feel respectful and safe.	The classroom becomes a place of work focus, celebration, aspiration and possibility.
Metacognition and Self-Regulated Learning *(Learners equipped for life)*	Agency, Purpose, Reflection	Learners become reflective authors of their own learning.	Teachers model thinking aloud. Learners plan before beginning tasks, pause to reflect during learning and evaluate their strategies afterwards through dialogue and journaling.	Learning becomes an act of self-formation and conscious growth.

Assessment

Having explored the relational, dialogic, imaginative, creative and pedagogic tool kit, we now turn towards the challenge of assessing the development of soul. As Layard (2015) writes, if you treasure something, you should measure it – which means that if we value spirituality/soul work as a core aspect of education, then, to give it worth, it needs to be assessed. Whilst there is value in this statement, it is important to note the cautionary words of historian and educator, Anthony Seldon,

> "We are human beings…in the same way that you can't measure the beauty of a sunset in a numerical way or what makes your heart sing…what makes your life worth living…just because you cannot measure it does not mean it does not matter. For human beings, often the most important things in our life, when we look back at the end of our lives, the things that we'll be thinking about, most of them will be by their very nature immeasurable. So how can we respect those things that never, never under the sun, will ever be measured?"
>
> (Seldon, A. *Examined Life Podcast* with Kenny Primrose. Retrieved from YouTube. https://www.youtube.com/watch?v=COF5tUKzRdI retrieved on 1st January 2026)

Assessing spiritual or soul-full development in education presents a significant conceptual and methodological challenge (Biddulph, 2024). Although schools in England are required to promote pupils' spiritual, moral, social and cultural (SMSC) development, practical approaches to assessing spirituality remain underdeveloped and contested. Teachers face constraints arising from accountability systems, dense curricula and a lack of confidence in engaging with spirituality in diverse classrooms (Casson, Cooling and Francis, 2018). The challenge lies in developing coherent frameworks that respect plural understandings of spirituality while remaining workable within the realities of school life (Biddulph, 2024).

As we have explored, spirituality and the soul resists definitive categorisation. It may be understood as an awareness of transcendence, an inner sense of meaning or a relational consciousness that connects self, others and the world (Holmes, 2021). Fisher (2009) emphasises that spirituality can only be inferred from its expressions and consequences; it cannot be directly measured. Hence, assessment must focus on indicators that suggest spiritual awareness or growth, while recognising that such indicators are partial and interpretative.

The first aspect is to focus on the possible components of soul development, perhaps linked with the Logoplex. In another way, Vickery (2019) identifies three interrelated components useful for teachers: spiritual capacities, spiritual contexts and spiritual experiences. Spiritual capacities refer to dispositions or qualities – such as empathy, courage, wonder, forgiveness and reflective awareness – that can be fostered through curriculum and pedagogy. Contexts refer to the environments and relationships that enable these capacities to emerge, such as classroom ethos or opportunities for contemplation. Experiences refer to moments of awe, stillness or deep connection that prompt reflection or transformation. Used together, these components could provide a balanced framework for observing and planning for spiritual/soul development. Cooper (1999) argues that spiritual growth arises through self-enquiry rather than accumulation of knowledge. Assessment, therefore, should focus less on outcomes and more on evidence of reflective engagement. Teachers might assess how young people articulate meaning, make connections between personal experiences and broader moral or existential questions, or demonstrate curiosity and attentiveness. And these expectations require development in literacy, in reading and dialogue especially as precursors to writing.

Dialogic approaches offer a productive methodology. Drawing on Biddulph and Burnard (2022), assessment can emerge through structured conversation – philosophical dialogue, reflective journals, or peer discussion – that allows learners to externalise their inner thinking. Teachers can then assess the *quality* of reflection rather than its content, noting depth, openness and capacity for empathy. Such methods align with current formative assessment practices, emphasising ongoing feedback and self-regulation (Wiliam, 2017). To make reflection assessable, teachers might use guiding questions such as:

- How has this experience changed the way you see yourself or others?
- What do you find most meaningful or puzzling about this idea?
- How might you respond or act differently as a result?

Responses could be analysed qualitatively, using rubrics that describe levels of reflective depth or emotional awareness.

Importantly, such tools should inform pedagogy rather than serve as instruments of comparison. All major spiritual traditions highlight the importance of the teacher or guide. In secular education, the teacher's role in modelling reflective and ethical engagement remains central. Fisher (2009) and Moberg (2002) both note that assessments of spirituality inevitably reflect the assessor's worldview. Consequently, professional learning is foundational. Teachers require not only theological or philosophical knowledge but also personal and experiential understanding of reflection, silence, and dialogue. Professional development might therefore include opportunities for staff to experience spiritual learning – through retreat, reflective writing or dialogic enquiry – so that assessment practices are informed by lived understanding. Such work helps educators to distinguish between assessing *belief* (which is inappropriate in public education) and assessing *capacity for reflection or connectedness*, which is pedagogically legitimate.

Practical tools can help translate conceptual understanding into classroom assessment. The Church of England's model of "windows, mirrors, and doors" (Mills, 2019) offers a simple structure compatible with plural contexts:

- *Windows* provide opportunities to look outward – to notice and wonder about the world, encountering its beauty, mystery and challenge.
- *Mirrors* invite inward reflection – considering how experiences relate to one's feelings, values or beliefs.
- *Doors* encourage outward action – expressing learning through creative, ethical or community-focused responses.

Used alongside Vickery's capacities, contexts and experiences, these metaphors enable schools to plan, observe and evaluate spiritual development in a coherent way. Teachers can collect qualitative evidence – reflections, artwork, dialogue transcripts or project outcomes – to illustrate spiritual engagement. Assessment, in this sense, becomes documentation of growth rather than measurement of attainment.

Despite these frameworks, assessing spirituality (and the soul's development) remains inherently problematic. As Wiliam (2017) notes, assessments often underrepresent the things they are meant to assess. Spirituality, being interior and relational, resists simplification into measurable indicators. Overemphasis on observable behaviour, such as stillness or politeness, risks conflating spirituality with compliance. Similarly, attempts to quantify emotional or reflective depth may reduce complexity to checklists. Therefore, the goal should not be precision but discernment: professional capacity to notice patterns of awareness, empathy or connectedness that signal spiritual growth. Such discernment relies on teacher judgement supported by shared professional dialogue rather than formal grading. In practice, effective assessment of spirituality involves several interdependent processes:

- Creating contexts for spiritual experience – through curriculum design that values wonder, silence and ethical questioning.
- Fostering reflective dialogue – providing structured opportunities for learners to articulate meaning.
- Documenting evidence – using journals, displays or portfolios that capture narrative and creative responses.
- Engaging in professional reflection – teachers sharing observations to build collective understanding of spiritual progression.

As we grappled with the challenge of assessment, we asked: how can the Logoplex and four-part Vedic process be used to develop our approach to assessment? The former has an implied route map for advancing the spiritual development of a person. The latter gives a pedagogic framework to support the development.

Table 15.5 illustrates how such progression can be observed and supported in practice, making visible the learner's journey towards coherence, wisdom and compassionate participation in the world. This framework integrates the Logoplex, a model of spiritual and moral development, with a four-part pedagogical cycle to reimagine assessment as a process of growth rather than measurement. It recognises that learning unfolds through stages of awareness, reflection, integration and contribution, each revealing the learner's inner and outer transformation.

Assessment of the spiritual aspects of learning must remain qualitative, dialogic and context sensitive. It cannot capture the essence of spiritual experience, but it can help teachers recognise and value the dispositions, relationships and insights through which the spiritual life of education becomes visible. It is complex and complicated. If we treasure it, however, grappling with the challenges is a worthy pursuit – even if impossible to achieve in its entirety – and keeping some of the personal aspects hidden from assessment has a place to be honoured and respected. As Seldon reminds us, we cannot assess the quality of a sunset nor our feelings on seeing it!

Table 15.5 Approach to assessment

Aspect of learning	**Purpose and focus**	**Connection to Logoplex**	**Practical examples of assessment**	**Advancement of the soul (observable in the learner)**
Listening and attending	Understanding where the learner is, cultivating openness, curiosity, and receptivity. Assessment begins in attention to the learner's voice, ideas and experiences.	Awakening of self-awareness and perception of interconnection.	Reflective journals, learning conversations, baseline self-assessments, observation of engagement and disposition.	The learner begins to show attentiveness, curiosity and presence. They listen more deeply, ask genuine questions and demonstrate an emerging sense of self as part of a shared learning community.
Reflecting and Making Meaning	Supporting the learner to think critically, connect ideas and question assumptions through reasoning and dialogue.	Growth of insight and discernment; movement from knowledge to understanding.	Peer dialogues, collaborative reasoning tasks, structured reflection prompts, debate with reflective debrief. Narratives and storytelling.	The learner articulates connections between ideas and experiences, expresses thoughtful uncertainty and demonstrates respect for multiple viewpoints. They move from opinion to considered reflection.
Integrating and Deepening	Encouraging synthesis across domains – linking intellectual, emotional and ethical learning. Assessment focuses on depth, creativity and coherence.	Development of coherence and relational wisdom – integration of mind, heart, and will.	Portfolios, creative interdisciplinary projects, teacher–student conferences, reflective essays. Narratives and storytelling.	The learner demonstrates coherence between thought and action, shows empathy and Self-discipline (self-regulation), and connects learning across contexts. Their reflections reveal an emerging moral and aesthetic awareness.
Acting and contributing	Applying learning through ethical action, creativity or service. Assessment recognises transformation through lived practice.	Embodiment of wisdom; the flowering of learning into compassionate action.	Community projects, mentoring roles, public exhibitions, self and peer evaluations of contribution.	The learner demonstrates maturity through initiative, compassion and a sense of responsibility. They act with integrity, contribute positively to others and see learning as a means of service and collective wellbeing.

Summary

The soul of education is not an optional spiritual supplement to 'real' schooling, nor a soft alternative to rigour, knowledge or excellence. It is a fuller account of what education is for. It begins from the conviction that human beings are more than performers of outcomes: they are meaning-making, relational, moral and spiritual persons whose learning shapes not only what they know, but who they are becoming.

A soul-full education therefore recognises the learner as a whole person. It attends to knowledge and intellectual development, but also to identity, awareness, character, belonging and purpose. It asks not only, 'What has been learned?' but also, 'Who is this learner becoming through the experience of learning?' In a contemporary context shaped by accountability, fragmentation, performativity and speed, this matters greatly. When education is reduced to metrics alone, it risks becoming efficient but spiritually thin: capable of producing attainment, yet less able to cultivate wisdom, compassion or meaning.

This chapter has argued that soul-full education offers a response to that narrowing. It does so first through its view of the human person. Learners are not empty vessels, data points or future economic units; they are persons with inner lives, histories, questions, gifts and vulnerabilities. They seek coherence, belonging and significance.

Secondly, soul-full education is fundamentally relational. The soul is educated through encounters: by being known, listened to, challenged and invited into responsibility. Relationships are not simply the conditions that make learning possible; they are themselves part of learning's substance. In the everyday life of classrooms, this means that dialogue, trust, care and recognition matter educationally, not just pastorally. Learners grow through the quality of attention they receive and the quality of presence they are invited to offer to others.

For this reason, the consciousness of the teacher is foundational. A soul-full classroom begins before any technique is used, in the teacher's way of seeing. Maxine Greene's idea of wide-awakeness is especially important here: the educator who remains attentive to learners, alert to possibility, and unwilling to take the world for granted. Reflexivity, ethical presence and imaginative openness are preconditions for pedagogy that forms rather than merely instructs. In practice, this means teachers noticing the atmosphere they create, the assumptions they carry, the learners they draw towards them and the learners they may inadvertently overlook.

From this foundation arises a practical pedagogy. Soul-full teaching builds on prior learning so that knowledge feels coherent and meaningful. It cultivates engagement through curiosity, wonder and relevance rather than compliance alone. It embraces challenge, but within structures of care and scaffolding. It values language, dialogue and oracy because voice is central to thought, identity and belonging. It creates spaces for reflection, creativity and metacognition, so that learners become more aware of themselves and their learning.

The chapter has also shown that imagination, the arts and dialogue are central to this work. They enlarge perception, deepen meaning and create openings through which learners can encounter ambiguity, beauty, difference and possibility. They help young people ask deeper questions about themselves, others and the world. This is not a retreat from academic seriousness. It is a reminder that serious education must include the cultivation of perception, discernment and moral imagination if it is to remain equal to the complexity of contemporary life.

Taken together, these strands suggest that the soul of education is present when schools hold together intellectual excellence and human's spiritual depth; when teachers combine rigour with care; when classrooms become places not only of instruction but of awakening. In such spaces, learners are helped to grow in knowledge and also in self-understanding, connectedness, courage and purpose. The soul of education could thus be defined as:

> The disciplined, relational and hopeful work of forming whole human beings through knowledge, reflection, creativities, dialogue and care. It seeks not merely to expand what learners can do, but to awaken who they may become: more attentive to the world, more compassionate toward others, and more purposeful in shaping a better future.

From a spiritual perspective, we could further tune this statement, thus:

> The disciplined, loving work of forming whole human beings, awakening the soul to attend deeply to the experience of living, loving generously, inclusively and respectfully, and live with purpose, responsibility and meaning.

From a policy perspective:

> Education is the disciplined, relational formation of the whole person, equipping every learner with the knowledge, character, and agency to thrive and contribute to a just, cohesive society.

As has been the motivation of the book, we seek collaboration of ideas and invite you to consider your own definitions, focused on the existential questions that have threaded through each chapter; it is through the personal reflections, inner work of one's own identity and relationship with the world, with others and with beyond, that the richness of ideas will bring new imaginative possibilities and a relentlessness to ask again and again: who am I (really)? What is my/our purpose? Where and how do I/we create meaning? What is beyond?

Note

1 Defining the terms

- Materialism is the doctrine that nothing exists except matter and its movements and modifications.
- Relationalism is the theory that the nature and identity of things are constituted by their relations rather than by intrinsic properties alone.
- Intentionalism is the philosophical theory that mental states are defined by their intentionality, that is, their capacity to be about or represent something.
- Transpersonalism is an approach to psychology or philosophy that studies experiences in which the sense of identity extends beyond the individual self.
- Solipsism is the philosophical view that only one's own mind is certain to exist and that knowledge of anything outside it is uncertain.
- Asceticism is the practice of severe self-discipline and abstention from indulgence, typically for religious or spiritual reasons.
- Secular humanism is a system of thought that prioritises human values and reason without reference to religious belief or supernatural authority.
- Spiritualism is a metaphysical belief that the world is made of matter and spirit.

Oxford University Press. (n.d.) *Oxford English Dictionary* (online). Available at: https://www.oed.com (Accessed 17 Jan. 2026).

16 Educators as gardeners of the soul's education

Parents (and grandparents) are seen as the first educators in children's lives. Educators in school are the second. In this chapter, we focus on educators and in the next we focus on parents.

Becoming 'spiritually educationally wise' requires educators to experience, learn and reflect on their own spiritual identities and personal seeking prior to nurturing it in children and young people. Gert Biesta (2013) asks, "How might we become educationally wise?...The first implication is that teacher education should be concerned with the *formation of the whole person*" (Biesta, 2013, p. 134). Typically, professional development focuses on knowledge and skills whereas we argue that it must also focus on the inner world of the educator, building from Biesta,

> Teacher education is not just about the acquisition of knowledge, skills and disposition or just about doing as other teachers do but starts with the formation and transformation of the person, and it is only from there that questions about knowledge, skills and dispositions, about values and traditions, about competence and evidence come in, so to speak
>
> (Biesta, 2013, p. 135)

We used the metaphor of a tree to describe Vedic education in a contemporary context – the *Tree of Life*, rooted in educational excellence, character formation and spiritual insight. Yet one single *Tree of Life* becomes truly powerful only when it grows into a *Forest of Life*, representing the wider flourishing of society. Walking through the redwood forests in North America, Radhanath Swami, a monk from the Vaishnava Hindu tradition,

 DOI: 10.4324/9781003487654-21

reminds us that trees do not necessarily stand alone, paraphrasing him: just underground, the redwood tree roots grow out, and they reach for the roots of other trees. And when two redwood tree roots meet, they wrap around each other. They embrace and create a permanent bond. In this way, the trees support each other.

This metaphor invites us to consider not only the growth of individual learners but also the networks of educators, parents, and communities of practice which sustain them.

Education, like a living ecosystem, depends on the careful tending of those who nurture it. This chapter explores educators as gardeners of the soul, cultivators of wisdom, virtue and relational flourishing. Drawing on the imagery of trees and forests, we consider how the growth of one child, or one teacher, is sustained through the roots of many: the rhizomatic networks of care, dialogue and practice that form a forest of life.

Professional learning for soul-led education

We found in previous chapters that the seeking to find purpose and meaning is an ongoing quality of being a human. For teachers to teach for the soul in education, engagement in an ongoing process of professional and spiritual formation that enables them to navigate, rather than avoid, the ambiguities and complexities of human meaning (Chia and Holt, 2007). Beyond religion, there are scientists, like Lisa Miller, Andrew Newberg and Mark Waldman, who emphasise that many forms of spiritual practice affect our brains in fundamentally healthy ways,

> It doesn't matter how you believe in God, and there is considerable evidence that such practices work even if you don't believe [in a religion]. Part of the reason for this is that spirituality is often defined in terms of personal values and the search for meaning and truth, and thus, spiritual practices can take on many forms.
>
> (Newberg and Waldman, 2009, p. 149)

Wright (2000) argues that "the core educational challenge is to grasp the nettle and acknowledge that the issue of ultimate truth is a controversial one, about which there is no public consensus" (p. 93). Rather than viewing this as a problem, Wright invites educators to see it as an opportunity for critical and dialogic engagement with questions of value, purpose and identity. Such an approach requires teachers to cultivate the courage, language, and conceptual literacy to hold spiritual ambiguity as pedagogical potential rather than professional threat. We must remain ignorantly wise.

Wills (2011) furthers this argument in her discussion of the spiritual and existential dimensions of learning through the arts, suggesting that education should foster both "belonging, identity and not negating the externally set learning objectives of 'standing out'" (p. 104). This dual movement, of belonging and distinctiveness, mirrors the teacher's inner work of reflexivity and authenticity. It is also coherent with the Vedic philosophy of oneness and difference. The reflexive practitioner, as Adams (2010) suggests, moves beyond reflection-on-action to consider "one's own beliefs, attitudes, assumptions, prejudices and suppositions" and how these inform teaching (p. 130). Spiritual teaching and leadership in education, then, is inseparable from reflexive enquiry into one's own interior life and ethical positioning.

Cultivating professional communities of practice: rhizomatic wisdom

Newberg and Waldman explain that the 'top two' ways to exercise the brain (beyond smiling (yes, it is good for the brain!), staying intellectually active, consciously relaxing, yawning (another fascinating discovery), meditating and aerobic exercise) are: having dialogue with others and faith. They explain that if we don't exercise our language skills, through dialogue, large portions of the brain will not effectively interconnect with other neural structures (Newberg and Waldman, 2009, p. 162). With faith,

> No matter what choice we make concerning our physical, emotional and spiritual health, we'll never know for certain if we are absolutely correct in our beliefs. We can make educated guesses about the world, but some degree of uncertainty will always remain. This is true for medicine and science, and it's certainly true when it comes to our religious beliefs
>
> (p. 163)

Developing awareness of spirituality and faith (and a healthy scepticism to remain curious) is good for the brain. For teachers and school leaders (and parents as first educators) who are to lead soul in education, it is therefore important to engage in the lifelong task of becoming more human through dialogue and consideration of our faith (whatever that might be) – cultivating inner stillness, critical consciousness, and professional wisdom in the service of collective flourishing. What is fascinating in understanding the neuroscientist's perspective is how aligned it is with the Vedic philosophy conceived thousands of years ago, "Truth is one; sages call it by many names" (*Ṛg Veda* 1.164.46; version translated by Schweig, 2010), which emphasises the need for faith and most importantly dialogue.

John Dewey (1916) and Gert Biesta (2023) assert the view of education as communication; the notion that education is conducted through educational questions, in particular those questions about the interaction between teacher and learner. They both see communication as, "a process of sharing experience till it becomes a common possession…which insures participation in a common understanding" (in Biesta, 2023, p. 29). Moreover, what is needed in schools is professional learning that does not occur in isolation but within *communities of practice* (Wenger, 1998) where dialogue about spiritual experience, ethical challenge and educational purpose is legitimised and shared. Within such communities, teachers may develop the "spiritual literacy" (Wright, 2000, p. 94) required to respond to both the transcendent and the troubling aspects of human experience. In this example, James records his reflections of working with a secondary history teacher, creating a sense of share responsibility and collaboration – an example of a rhizome being made between two educators, strengthening thinking and awareness of the qualitative aspects of one lesson.

Email: October 2024

I was thinking about the lesson we taught. And that although not intentionally planned, we did include the four aspects of listening, reflection, meditation and intentional action.

The Year 9 History class gathered to explore how propaganda shaped men's decisions to enlist during the Second World War. We framed the lesson through intercultural creative learning (although at the time we did not call it that), inviting learners to consider not just *what* people believed, but *why* and *how* those beliefs were shaped by culture, language and emotion.

The lesson began with deep listening. We showed them a scene of the famous performer who persuaded men to sign up. (In reflection, we could have also dimmed the lights slightly and play a collage of authentic wartime propaganda: Churchill's speeches, radio broadcasts, and enlistment appeal from India, the Caribbean and Canada. This would have further brought a multicultural dimension to the learning as an act of decolonising the knowledge). We invited the learners to close their eyes and listen deeply.

Alongside these, we showed posters from different nations, each with its own tone of pride, duty, fear, or belonging. Learners are asked to listen not only to the words but to the silences and emotional pull beneath them. What feelings are being stirred? Who is being addressed, and who is left out? This listening becomes a relational act, an entry point into the lived experience of persuasion across cultures.

The class then moved into reflection. In small groups, they discussed how propaganda might have felt to young men from different backgrounds. It is the feeling aspect we wanted to elicit here. They examined how imagery, colour and symbolism vary across cultures, comparing British posters invoking honour and empire with Indian recruitment materials promising equality and recognition. One thing we could have done is to include some journal writing. For example, learners could write brief reflective journal entries: "What message would have spoken to me?" or "What emotions are these posters trying to shape?" Through this, learners begin to interpret propaganda not as static content but as a dynamic conversation between power, identity and belonging.

To honour the four-part process, meditation would have enhanced the lesson further. After the reflection section of the lesson, we could have begun a short period of meditation. Something like this:

> The whole class close their eyes and imagined being a young man in 1940 (perhaps in London, Kingston, or Lahore) hearing the call to serve. They are asked to visualise the posters, the voices, the sense of uncertainty and duty. This quiet moment

helps them to inhabit the human dimension of history, fostering empathy rather than judgement. They are asked to visualise leaving their homes, shutting the front door, leaving their families and joining their friends as they visualise walking joyfully to the subscription posts. Breathe in deeply. Breath out calmly. Finally, the class engage in intentional action. Each group designs a contemporary propaganda poster – not to promote war, but to critically expose how persuasive techniques work.

What struck me is the power of the relationships you have with your learners. It seems that through this process although we did not follow it completely, knowledge is developed through relationship, an encounter between historical understanding and moral imagination, between the past and their present. The lesson ends not with memorisation, but with awareness: how persuasion shapes identity, and how empathy can resist it. The learners left the class deep in conversation about how social media influences them and they consider the propaganda in Instagram, TikTok and other social media.

Note from James Biddulph after a History lesson
with Gauranga Purohit, History Teacher | 2024

The image of a *Forest of Life* illustrates that human flourishing is never solitary but deeply relational. The redwoods embody what Deleuze and Guattari (1987) described as the rhizome – roots spreading laterally rather than vertically, producing non-hierarchical networks of growth and exchange. From a Vedic perspective, this interconnectedness reflects the paradoxical philosophy of oneness and difference: each tree distinct, yet each sustained by and sustaining others. Like rhizomes, the redwoods embody plurality, resilience and connectivity; they each stand alone and yet they each stand together.

Instead of a single taproot of authority, there is a living system of mutual reinforcement. Teachers do not work in isolation. They are part of a school community. They are part of a wider community of educators, through organisations like the Chartered College of Teaching. What happens in one classroom can connect or disconnect children and young people from a wider purpose of learning. One teacher can bring out the virtues in the same way that just one interaction with another can damage them. As a metaphor, the rhizome emphasises the interconnectedness, interrelatedness and mutual support found within community life of a school and indeed the (potentials in) wider education system. Rhizomatic community is thus both diverse and unified, a living system in which collaboration strengthens individuality and individuality enriches the whole; an ecology of support that embodies unity through multiplicity.

Yet, as Marx and Engels observed, nature is not only harmony but also conflict: "'Man' could also observe a great many other things in nature, e.g., the bitterest competition among plants and animals; he could see, for example, in the plant world, in his 'forest of tall and stately oaks', how these tall and stately capitalists consume the nutriment of the tiny shrubs…" (Marx and Engels, 1998, p. 498). It is perhaps in the tensions of harmony and disharmony, in the age of quarrel and hypocrisy, that a spiritually educated person can make a difference – and choose for greater harmony.

This turns us to wisdom. Aristotle's notion of *phronesis*, practical wisdom, adds another layer to our understanding of ethical life. Just as Redwood trees hold one another through their interwoven roots, human communities flourish when they are grounded in discernment, cooperation and ethical care. Stephen Kemmis (2012) offers a contemporary rendering of *phronēsis* as a quality of mind and character and action, a disposition that grows through reflection on experience and a readiness to act wisely for the common good. Such a person, he explains, "thinks critically about a given situation … and then practically about what should be done here and now." If schools are to nurture the soul of education, they must therefore become spaces where reflective dialogue about purpose, what is worth doing and why, is alive and ongoing. Aristotle's understanding of practical wisdom has long guided reflection on moral reasoning and the good life (Flutter, 2022; Flutter, 2025). *Phronēsis* involves bringing together knowledge, moral character and experience to guide action towards *eudaimonia* – a life of flourishing. The wise person acts not by rigid rules but by discerning what is right in complex situations, uniting thought and action through moral sensitivity.

Management researchers Robert Chia and Robin Holt describe such wisdom not as the accumulation of knowledge, but as a disciplined practice of unlearning, what they name a form of learned ignorance, "…a cultivated humility, meekness of demeanour, and openness of mind that is distinct and different from the aggressive and relentless pursuit, acquisition, and exploitation of knowledge. Rather than associate wisdom with learning, we argue that it is ironically unlearning that is the path towards genuine wisdom and insight" (Chia and Holt, 2007, p. 505).

Uncertainty and a vagueness are not failures of learning but markers of its deepest form. This insight resonates strongly with Carl Jung's psychological understanding (2009), which reminds us that the unconscious, the symbolic and the mythic are not distractions from education but vital sources of creativity, healing and wholeness. From uncertainty, questions emerge; from the vague, imagination and creativity open new awareness and insight. We suggest that the qualities of humility, openness, comfort with uncertainty and symbolic depth are essential dispositions to nurture within school communities, for the benefit of all who learn and work within them (Biddulph and Gilbride, 2025). Cultivating a shared practice of *unlearning* runs counter to the dominant educational culture, which privileges certainty, standardisation and linear progress (Hargreaves and Rolls, 2021).

However, long before Aristotle, the Vedic traditions of ancient India explored parallel questions about wisdom, knowledge and right action. In this worldview, wisdom is not simply an intellectual skill but a deeper form of knowing that brings together reason, intuition and an awareness of life's interconnection. The ancient texts known as the *Upaniṣads*[1] distinguish between two kinds of knowledge: one concerned with worldly learning and technical skill, and another directed towards insight into what is enduring and unchanging. This distinction parallels Aristotle's separation between theoretical and practical wisdom but goes further. While Aristotle aims at contemplation of universal truths, the Vedic tradition seeks direct realisation of unity between the individual self and ultimate reality, a recognition that wisdom is not only about right action but about right perception.

The *Bhagavad Gītā* brings these ideas into the realm of everyday life. It teaches that wisdom involves the integration of knowledge, action and devotion. The person of steady wisdom acts with focus and compassion but without attachment to personal gain. Here, wisdom entails calmness, perspective and freedom from ego – qualities that resonate with Aristotelian moderation but also add a spiritual dimension of self-transcendence.

The integration of relational care and professional knowledge finds expression in theories of *communities of practice* (Flutter, 2025; Wenger, 1998). In such communities, teachers continually construct and reconstruct their professional identities through participation, dialogue and shared meaning-making. Expertise, in this view, is not static but socially and ethically embedded. Teachers learn from one another and from their learners, negotiating knowledge within a living professional ecology. The relational landscape of education thus extends beyond the classroom: it encompasses the networks of colleagues and mentors through which the teacher's wisdom is continually renewed.

More recent analysis of this desired collegiality is by Julia Flutter (2025), in *Empowering Teacher Professionalism: Collegiality and Practical Wisdom in Education*, who similarly highlights opportunities for professional learning rooted in "dialogue, professional wisdom and collegial sharing" (p. 112). It is what she and James Biddulph sought to nurture in the *Unlocking Research* (Routledge) series (Biddulph, Rolls and Flutter, 2023; Biddulph and Flutter, 2021; Black-Hawkins and Grinham-Smith, 2023; Burnard and Loughrey, 2022; Durning, Baker and Ramchandani, 2025; Hargreaves and Rolls, 2021) and what Biddulph and Emily Shuckburgh extend in the new *Education Visions* series (Cambridge University Press) (Biddulph, Shuckburgh and Pearse, 2026): crafting dialogue between different forms of knowledge, between academic research and practitioner wisdom, and acknowledging the diverse spaces in between.

Professional spaces for collective thinking, being, engaging and enacting possibilities can be understood through the lens of *phronēsis* that unfolds like a dance between different forms of knowledge, balancing ethical judgement, moral purpose and relational responsibility. Such spaces are not static but dialogical, requiring conditions that invite teachers, leaders, support staff and learners alike into collaborative exploration. As Flutter (2025, p. 4) reminds us:

> Fostering practical wisdom requires us to review and evaluate the conditions of teaching and learning in our education systems. Education spaces, whether physical, virtual or social, should be built in ways that generate a spirit of collegiality for teachers and learners, reflecting American educator Maxine Greene's call for school communities that question and seek out possibilities for social justice, equality and transformative change (1995). Practical wisdom flourishes in spaces that nurture dialogue. It is important to support teachers' and learners' empowerment as transformative changemakers who possess capacities of practical wisdom. Values, morality, and character need to infuse in our educative efforts so that learners and teachers can develop practical wisdom, becoming active members of learning communities in which relationships and dialogue are framed as collaborative, constructive and respectful. Far from being an abstract or cerebral ideal, practical

> wisdom is about taking action: it envisions schools of the future as spaces where both learners and teachers develop and hone capacities for practical wisdom that can direct us towards a more hopeful future.
>
> (Flutter, 2025, p. 4)

For spirituality and the soul of education to be central to school life and teachers' and teaching assistants' practices, this type of professional development, through communities of practice, is so important. Learning and being able to teach about the inner world of the soul cannot come purely from reading a book like this, or in only doing a course, or attending a place that inspires awe and wonder: instead, we suggest, it comes with all those things and importantly through a professional space for exploring, navigating and discovering together.

The following example, describes the Avanti Schools central office as a space for dialogue about the self, the soul and the relationships: the impact is a powerful reminder for everyone who works with children and young people – to feel connected, to be open to explore and to be vulnerable enough to share.

The Soul in the Stairwell

I walk up the flight of stairs to our central office, expecting the familiar chorus of the workplace, the clatter of keyboards, the overlapping hum of Teams calls, the steady pulse of busyness. But instead, I hear something different. Three colleagues leaning over mugs of tea, sharing how the practice of daily gratitude journalling has reshaped their mornings and their sense of meaning. One speaks of how noting three small blessings a day has softened the edges of her anxiety; another smiles as he describes how gratitude helps to be intentional, how it opens a door to purpose. The third listens quietly, her eyes lit with a glow that comes from being understood in the language of the heart. And I think, this is not ordinary office talk. This is spirit in conversation.

At Avanti, spirituality is not an agenda item or a box to tick after 'safeguarding' or 'budget review.' It is the quiet undercurrent that moves through our day, shaping how we see, speak and serve the community. The values that ground us. Empathy, self-discipline, integrity, gratitude, courage and respect are not displayed just as slogans on corridor walls. They live instead, in the ways we connect with each other, in the pauses we take before a meeting to reflect, in the laughter shared over lunch.

At my previous workplace, talk of the spirit was something to be whispered about, tucked away for fear of seeming unprofessional. At Avanti, it is the opposite: to speak of meaning, purpose or faith is to speak in our shared mother tongue. It is what connects the teacher in the classroom to the Receptionist behind the desk, the cook in the canteen to the student sitting exams. We are each invited to bring our whole selves to work, not only our skills and efficiency, but our questions in pursuit of self-discovery.

There is something profoundly liberating about this. To be in an environment where the inner life is not sidelined but celebrated, where it is natural to discuss spirituality as easily as KPIs, or to reflect on stillness as much as strategy. The curriculum of Avanti cannot be limited to a policy document or lesson plan. It lives in the invisible spaces: the moments before the school gates open, when staff reflect on their way to work; the soft word of encouragement from the principal; in the humility to admit we are still learning.

What makes Avanti different is how its people live by our values when no one is watching. It is the understanding that success is not measured only in tasks, but in the emotional and spiritual transformation we witness daily. And so, as I find a desk to start my day's work, I pause. The conversation about gratitude has moved on, but its echo lingers steadily. In that moment I feel the pulse of something sacred: a Trust alive with purpose.

And I realise, this simple moment is what it means for spirituality to come alive. Not in ideals, but through living it.

Ravi Talsania | Head of Communications and Marketing, Avanti Schools Trust

To make sense of how we might develop soul work in schools, with professionals, it is helpful to return to the theoretical thinking tools developed by Bourdieu (1977): *field, habitus* and *capital*. He drew attention to what he called the *habitus* of an individual which is related to the cultural and familiar roots from which a person grows. For our purpose, how does a person become soul-aware, given that Miller (2015) strongly affirms that developing spirituality is key to thriving and human flourishing for children and young people in their current lives and for their futures? To this, Hodgkinson (1996) also observed that,

> Lifestyle and habitus are inseparably interrelated – one is the manifestation of the other. They evolve, partly though choice and partly through changing circumstances, as life progresses. They are constrained and enabled by the social and cultural conditions within which a person lives, which are, in turn, influenced by the actions of that individual.
>
> (Hodgkinson, 1996, p. 147)

How can we develop the *spiritual habitus* of an individual that is not indoctrination but about growing awareness, curiosity and empowerment? There is a habitus of discourse that Ravi evidences in his reflection – a way of being/living that engages people in discussion about spirituality, faith and belief. The idea of *spiritual capital* (drawing from the notion of cultural capital) is relevant here, to rethink the position of young people from diverse backgrounds and their perspectives on spiritual matters and the soul. Ravi's example notes the value in spirituality, 'We are each invited to bring our whole selves to work, not only our skills and efficiency, but our questions in pursuit of self-discovery.' The Avanti Schools Trust culture values the whole self not just the work self or the roles we take at work. As with Bourdieu's view that cultural capital is acquired and inherited, we remain curious how spiritual capital, knowledge, awareness and skills arise as inherited capital (which schools cannot influence nor should they) and the acquired capital (which schools provide as a matter of purpose)?

The last concept, *the field,* is also useful to conceptualise as a 'configuration of relations' between individuals and institutions (the family, the school, the workplace for example). Returning to Ravi's anecdote, 'To be in an environment where the inner life is not sidelined but celebrated, where it is natural to discuss spirituality as easily as KPIs, or to reflect on stillness as much as strategy,' suggesting the field of the workplace of Avanti is one that mediates the capital of spiritual development for all. Relations are mediated by different forms of capital.

For a manifesto about the soul in education, we consider how we raise the value of spiritual life so that it becomes a form of capital, engaged in the field of relations and becomes a new evolved habitus to sustain children and young people as they navigate their lives – the ups and downs of which are predicted to become more complex and complicated. When schools make time and space for reflective professional learning, they affirm that teaching is a profoundly human and social endeavour. In the *Unlocking Research Series* (Biddulph and Flutter, Routledge, 2021a, 2021b), there are various examples of professional collaboration and learning through communities of practice: lesson study (Rolls and Seleznyov, 2021), about the art of reading (Cremin and Durning, 2021), developing excellence in music (Kirkman, Long and Robin-Ross, 2021) to name but three. Flutter (2025) pays attention to the impact of the series on nurturing a sense of collegiality and shared practical wisdom.

As Hargreaves and Fullan (2012) remind us, improving teaching at the individual level is insufficient; what matters equally is the environment in which educators work, one that supports learning, collaboration and shared purpose. "At its best," they write, "culture doesn't give you a good teacher here and a weaker teacher there, but many strong and capable teachers working passionately together, under visionary leadership, so all learners succeed" (p. 21). In such a culture, professional development becomes a space for exploring the inner landscape of teaching, the emotions, values and relationships that underpin professional action. Reflection becomes not merely an evaluative act but a creative and ethical one, an invitation to explore how we connect, respond and make meaning.

However, as Flutter cautions, this kind of professional learning and the advocacy of *phronēsis* in educators' professionalism must not translate into "neatly created systems of metrics, impact analysis and bureaucracy" (Flutter, 2025, p. 134). Kemmis (2012; Kemmis, Edwards-Groves, Wilkinson, and Hardy, 2012) adds that calls for *phronēsis* arise because we seek resources "to confront the unimaginable, unspeakable void of uncertainty we face in this fragile world – a void inhabited by horrors and monsters like the obstinate ineradicability of professional malpractice, our enduring impotence in the face of the sufferings caused by war, and our gathering frustration in the face of the global environmental crisis" (Kemmis, 2012, p. 152). Such challenges, shaped by scientism, technocratic rationality and instrumentalism, undermines its capacity to serve the common good.

From a Vedic perspective, however, transformation rests in recognising the soul as eternal, moving through *karma* (the consequences of our actions) and guided by dharma (our individual true purpose) towards full consciousness of its relationship with the Ultimate (seeing oneself as connected with others and also seeing beyond to something bigger than the ego self). Transformation, then, is not episodic but part of a longer unfolding, shaped by our collective actions and oriented towards our ultimate relationship with the Divine. This vision invites us to imagine educational and social structures that honour both oneness and difference, recognising the interdependence of all beings. Rupesh Hirani, a long-standing teacher at Avanti, wrote a reflection about how professional learning resulted in transformation, within a culture of care and collaboration.

Growth of Colleagues

It has been an absolute privilege and joy to witness the incredible growth and development of colleagues across many of our schools. What began as a journey for some as Early Career Teachers, Newly Qualified Teachers, trainee teachers or Learning Support Assistants has blossomed into something truly inspirational. Through dedication, passion and an unwavering commitment to their craft, many have progressed into pivotal roles such as Progress Leads, Subject Leaders, Phase Leaders, Assistant Principals and Principals.

Seeing colleagues grow in confidence, capability and leadership has been one of the most rewarding aspects of this journey. Their stories are a powerful reminder of the strength and richness within our educational community, and a testament to what is possible when talent is nurtured with care, opportunity and belief. I count myself truly blessed and honoured to have witnessed such remarkable professional journeys unfold. It gives me great pride to celebrate the milestones achieved and the bright future that lies ahead for so many of our educators.

An emailed reflection by Rupesh Hirani | Class Teacher, Avanti House Primary School, UK

Summary

The imagery of trees and forests illuminates the idea of democratic communities, which at best are not hierarchical but rhizomatic, "a network of connections where diverse voices are sustained and strengthened through their relations with one another" (Biesta, 2010, p. 62). Stability and longevity emerge not from centralised authority but from "mutual support, interdependence, and shared responsibility" (Biesta, 2010, p. 63). Schools, likewise, need not be rigidly hierarchical. By fostering professional agency and collective enquiry, they can become rhizomatic communities – dialogic spaces where teachers, support staff and leaders explore joys, creative possibilities, challenges and complexities together.

Note

1 The *Upaniṣads* are a collection of foundational Indian philosophical texts composed between roughly 800 and 200 BCE, forming the concluding portion of the Vedas. They explore the nature of ultimate reality (*Brahman*), the self (*Ātman*), and liberation (mokṣa), emphasising inner knowledge, contemplation and ethical living. Rather than ritual practice, the *Upaniṣads* focus on insight and direct experience, shaping later Hindu philosophy and enduring reflections on consciousness, purpose and the unity of existence.

17 Parents as gardeners of the soul's education

Parenting is increasingly recognised not only as a determinant of childhood wellbeing but as a foundational influence on lifelong development, as are schools (Layard, 2015).

In both ancient Vedic philosophy and contemporary developmental science, the parent-child relationship is viewed as central for shaping emotional resilience, moral clarity and spiritual insight. While modern frameworks often emphasise psychological traits such as independence, confidence, self-regulation and curiosity, Vedic-inspired parenting offers a complementary perspective, one that sees these traits as expressions of the soul's unfolding journey. This section explores how Vedic principles align with and enrich contemporary research on parenting and life preparedness. It is not a critique of parenting nor is it a parent guide. Instead, we offer aspects from the Vedic philosophy to invite discussion.

Anthony Seldon speaks passionately about the value of spirituality in childhood, "if one doesn't recognise that the spiritual is what makes life worthwhile, for any professed atheist to understand the sense of awe and wonder, seeing a sunset, seeing an extraordinary seascape, being in love, the love of one's children, the love of one's partner. We cannot define life in purely rational, logical ways, in sequential ways" (https://www.moneymazepodcast.com/blog/anthony-seldon).

Yet, it can happen that parents' desire for a particular life for their child blindfolds them to the reality of the child in front of them. Parenting becomes linked with expectations that are based on preconceived ideas of what it means for a child to flourish, what society thinks and how it

DOI: 10.4324/9781003487654-22

judges success and how parents project their own hopes for their own life on to the lives of their children. These are socially and culturally bound and often hard to shift. In a world full of the contradictions of *Kali Yuga*, in which uncertainties are the only certainty, then old ways of thinking about education and parenting must be reimagined. Seldon holds a strong critical view,

> British children are facing a mental health crisis, according to Seldon, who has now been a headmaster at three schools and who has been an adviser to the government. "I think a really sick ideology has swept this country and the Pisa [Programme for international student assessment] studies, which compare children's academic attainment internationally, are responsible for it," he says. "Ofsted inspections make it worse. Exams have become a mania, a frenzy, an obsession. We now validate a school, a child or a teacher only on their passes and we think the way to do well is to cram children with often senseless material they then have to regurgitate."
>
> As a result, he thinks children appear to be less content and teenagers more psychologically disturbed. "My sense is that children are not getting happier, their distress is growing and it's deeply troubling. They often aren't helped until it's too late. Parents, teachers and universities are a disgrace in their lack of regard for the wellbeing and mental health of students. We need to embed good habits when children are young and let them develop naturally, instead of forcing them through this factory schooling.
>
> (Alice Thomson, The Times, retrieved on 1st February 2026 https://www.thetimes.com/travel/destinations/uk-travel/sir-anthony-seldon-pushy-parents-are-abusing-their-children-z9pm5lbpct0?msockid=3a68e9eb6e7a62d815ffff306fca63d9)

James recently visited a school and was shown a piece of writing from a child in Year 5 (9-year-old). It was a letter written as part of a Religious Education lesson in which the child was writing to God. The letter shows how parents can close pathways of possibilities with unintended consequences.

> Dear God,
>
> I am sorry (sic.) I have not prayed to you much because I have been busy. My parents make me do tutoring every day for maths and English and I don't even get time to play cricket. I know I should pray to you so please make me have less tutor so I can be less stressed and have friends to play. My parents want me to get to grammar school so that is why I can't do much.
>
> Sorry and please let me pass the grammar tests, so they are proud of me and don't think I am not good.
>
> K.

The obsessive competition inherent in our education systems gives rise to the battle for school places and an almost aggressive focus on very narrow forms of knowledge and skills. Sam Freedman, political analyst and adviser explains that the improvement of exam results mean more people have access to the labour market and so there is more competition,

> Another reason that concern [in education] is dropping is that more people are succeeding, at least in terms of accessing qualifications. This does not, given grade inflation, necessarily mean standards are improving, but it does mean more people are leaving the system with better hopes of labour market access. And it also means, given the greater awareness in both higher education and amongst employers of arguments about social mobility and fairness, that we are starting to see access to top career pathways opening up
>
> (Freedman, 2024, p. 44)

How can we limit this vicious cycle? How can adults nurture children to grow and open possibilities? How do we learn to see the child in front of us and, with them, imagine a future that *they* want to pursue?

There is, however, evidence that spirituality and the themes we present here are not in conflict with contemporary contexts and views can be found in the annual survey from *ParentKind*, a UK charity that supports parents and schools to build better partnerships with one another. In the

National Parent Survey 2025, parents' views on education extend well beyond academic performance, showing that wellbeing, identity and confidence are central to what families hope schools will nurture. Parents consistently emphasise the importance of their children feeling happy and confident, with 86% ranking wellbeing as the most important outcome of education (Parentkind, 2025). Many highlight that learning should foster resilience, a sense of self-worth and opportunities for children to express themselves as individuals.

Spirituality and meaning making also feature implicitly, with parents suggesting that education should guide children to discover values, purpose and belonging in an increasingly complex world (Jenkins, 2008; Kessler, 2000; Miller, 2015). This is reinforced by parents' expectations that schools actively cultivate kindness, respect and love in classrooms. For example, over two-thirds of parents state that equality, diversity and inclusion should be central to the school ethos, demonstrating that families see moral and relational development as inseparable from intellectual growth. In this way, schools are viewed not only as academic institutions but as formative spaces where identity is shaped, spiritual wellbeing is nurtured, and love and community can flourish (Parentkind, 2025). We set out these preoccupations in chapter two: equality, diversity and love. Where do they feature at home and where in school?

The survey also shows that parents regard education as a pathway to confidence and social justice. Almost three-quarters of respondents (72%) believe that schools should place as much emphasis on confidence and personal growth as on academic grades, suggesting a shift towards holistic conceptions of success. Parents from ethnically diverse backgrounds especially emphasise the importance of inclusion and equality: 59% of ethnic minority parents report worrying about discrimination against their children, compared to just 13% of white parents, underscoring the deep need for schools to foster safe and equitable environments.

Parents stress the value of love, care and respectful relationships between children and teachers, viewing these as vital to them developing a positive sense of identity and belonging. In particular, families express a desire for schools to model compassion and acceptance as part of everyday practice, linking this directly to their child's confidence and ability to thrive. Collectively, these findings highlight that parents want education to be soul-enriching as well as skill-building: a space where children grow in love, learn to honour diversity and find confidence in who they are and can become (Parentkind, 2025). Making sense of love in the formal context of state education is where the challenge lies.

The soul-centred view of the child

As we have explained, Vedic philosophy presents the view that each person is an eternal soul, born with a unique nature and purpose. This view contrasts with tabula rasa models that treat children as blank slates shaped entirely by environment. Remembering John Locke's view that education was about influencing and making the mark on the blank state of the child, whereas in the Vedic position, a person already has an innate quality that needs to be nurtured to its completion – to its realisation. This is the education that Krishna was giving to Arjuna in the midst of the looming battle. Instead, the Vedic tradition encourages parents to act as stewards, guiding the child's inner potential with reverence and wisdom. This aligns with contemporary developmental theories that emphasise the importance of autonomy-supportive parenting in fostering self-determination and intrinsic motivation (Ryan and Deci, 2000). By recognising the child's spiritual individuality, Vedic parenting naturally supports traits such as independence and curiosity. Rather than imposing rigid expectations, it encourages exploration and self-discovery, principles echoed in modern educational psychology, which links autonomy and competence to lifelong learning and wellbeing (Deci and Ryan, 1985).

Parenting is deeply contextual, shaped by enduring human needs yet evolving with cultural, social and psychological understandings. The Vedic model of parenting articulated by *Chanakya*[1] (c. 350 BCE) continues to offer a profound framework for raising children, structured in three phases: early childhood suffused with love, formative years disciplined with care and adolescence guided with friendship. Contemporary research since 2015 affirms many of these principles while extending them in ways that address the challenges of modern life. Integrating insights from developmental psychology, neuroscience and educational theory allows us to reimagine parenting as a process of nurturing complete human beings. The themes of love, tough love, nurturing independence and building confidence through non-violent communication bring together Vedic and modern perspectives in a way that balances authenticity to the philosophy with contemporary evidence and relevance.

Love: building emotional security

Chanakya's first stage, "treat the child as a prince or princess" from 0–5 years, highlights the role of unconditional love and affection in building deep emotional security. The Vedic tradition recognised that early love is not indulgence but the foundation for resilience, discipline and spiritual growth later in life. This is echoed by attachment theory, which shows that children who experience secure attachment in infancy are better able to regulate emotions, handle stress and build relationships. Consistent affection fosters trust and a sense of worth, shaping the child's neurological and psychological development (Butcher and Tempest, 2026).

Whitebread (2019) argued that early childhood experiences of love and play are not luxuries but essential for cognitive, social and emotional growth. Playful interactions between parent and child not only express love but also build the foundations of executive function, problem-solving and empathy. In this light, love during early years must be embodied through presence, play, and acceptance, not just words. Anthony Seldon (2016) reinforces this, noting that "education – and by extension parenting – is about helping young people discover who they really are." That discovery is only possible when children feel held in unconditional love, where their value is intrinsic, not conditional on performance. This does not mean a *laisse faire* approach where 'anything goes' and where there are no boundaries. David Whitebread (2019) and Whitebread and Coltman (2016) show that research on parenting and teacher-child relationships highlights three contrasting interaction styles: authoritarian, permissive (or uninvolved) and authoritative, each producing different outcomes for children which we think important when considering how to develop the soul.

Authoritarian parenting emphasises strict control, obedience and authority with little warmth or explanation. Children raised in this environment may follow rules but often develop lower confidence, weaker self-regulation and less independence. Permissive or uninvolved parenting, by contrast, offers warmth but few clear boundaries or expectations. Without guidance or consistent standards, children may struggle with discipline, persistence and responsibility. These are in contrast to authoritative parenting which combines emotional warmth with clear expectations and consistent boundaries. Adults explain rules, listen to children and encourage autonomy. This balanced approach supports stronger self-regulation, higher self-efficacy, better learning outcomes and more positive relationships with peers and adults.

In her book *The Spiritual Child,* Lisa Miller argues that children are born with a capacity for spirituality defined not simply as formal religion but as an inner sense of relationship to something greater than themselves: a higher power that is loving and guiding. According to Miller, this capacity is hard wired: children naturally display wonder, connection to nature, empathy and a sense of the numinous long before formal faith is introduced. Her message to parents is that rather than trying to "make" children spiritual, the task is to cultivate their innate spiritual potential by creating the space, language and relational ground in which that capacity can flourish.

Miller identifies that one of the key factors is what she calls the "field of love" an environment where children feel deeply loved, accepted and seen. In such a field, their spiritual capacities grow. She also describes how adolescence brings a surge in spiritual capacity and existential questions, making the parental role of companion and guide all the more important.

Modern example:

A parent working remotely pauses between meetings to join their toddler in a brief moment of play, noticing the child's curiosity instead of rushing to correct or direct. The act may last only minutes, but it builds a foundation of belonging that no toy can replace.

Questions for reflection:

- When my child seeks attention, do I respond with presence or productivity?
- What does love 'look like' when I am tired or distracted?
- How can I make affection feel like a language of safety, not reward?

Tough love: allowing mistakes and failure

The second stage, ages 5–15, is described by Chanakya as "discipline them like a servant." The language may sound austere, but the principle is clear: childhood requires boundaries, responsibility and resilience. In Vedic tradition, children were educated in the Gurukula system, often away from luxury, where even princes lived simply, undertaking chores and study alike. This was not about punishment but about cultivating character, self-reliance and an orientation towards dharma (moral duty).

Contemporary research supports this notion of "tough love," understood as setting clear expectations while allowing children to encounter difficulty and even failure. Seaton and Beaumont (2015) found that parental overprotection undermines children's psychological needs for autonomy and competence, leading to anxiety and lower motivation. Conversely, allowing mistakes within a supportive environment fosters resilience and adaptive coping. Carol Dweck's (2017) work on growth mindset further underscores that children who are encouraged to learn from failure, rather than shielded from it, develop stronger perseverance and creativity.

Here, the work of Swami and Steinborn (2025) is especially resonant, "avoidance of experience plays a key role in the development of mental illness. When avoidance of experience is used as a coping mechanism for unpleasant and challenging feelings, a person retreats from the signals coming from their body, mind and emotions, and in that way loses contact to their inner world. This contributes to the typical experience of overwhelming numbness in depression" (p. 379). This highlights why difficulty must not be prematurely removed from children's lives. Parents who intervene too quickly deny their children the chance to process frustration, disappointment or failure in constructive ways or to be bored. By holding back, parents allow children to develop resilience, emotional intelligence, and authentic confidence in their ability to navigate adversity. Unfortunately for parents, this is where the emotional pain arises (for the parent especially!).

As Seldon (2019) observed, children need to experience both success and failure if they are to grow into whole human beings. Failure, framed constructively, becomes a teacher, shaping resilience and humility. The Vedic insistence on discipline resonates here, reminding us that structure and self-control, when combined with love, are not restrictions but enablers of flourishing.

Modern example:

A parent resists the urge to email a teacher after their child receives a poor grade. Instead, they ask, "What did you learn about yourself from that?" The child may cry or resist and yet, in that discomfort, resilience is born.

Another example might be a child has forgotten their PE kit and knows that the teacher will talk to them about this. Does the parent change their own plans, rush home to get the PE kit and return to school or does the parent accept that their child will have to learn from the discomfort of speaking with the teacher about being more organised and remembering their PE kit? Which will serve the child better?

Questions for reflection:

- Do I protect my child from pain, or prepare them to meet it with courage?
- How do I respond when they fail with fear, or with trust that this is part of the learning?
- What lessons might I be interrupting by rescuing too soon?

Nurturing independence: trust and letting go

From 15 years onwards, Chanakya urged parents to "treat them as a friend," or as a mentor, signalling a fundamental shift in parental role. Adolescence and early adulthood are times for autonomy, self-definition, and exploration. In Vedic terms, this stage was about preparing for independence and wisdom, often through deeper engagement with study, spiritual reflection, and social responsibility. Parents were expected to let go, trusting the young person to make choices, mistakes, and discoveries.

Contemporary research reinforces this emphasis on autonomy. Ryan and Deci's (2017) self-determination theory demonstrates that autonomy, competence and relatedness are core psychological needs that underpin wellbeing and motivation. Adolescents thrive when parents move from control to guidance, providing scaffolding but also freedom. Miller et al. (2018) note that nurturing independence must also be sensitive to inequalities and diversity: young people from minority backgrounds may face systemic barriers, and parents play a crucial role in affirming identity and confidence amidst these challenges.

David Whitebread's (2019) insights into play extend into adolescence, where exploratory learning, creativity, and choice remain vital. He cautions against over-standardisation in education, arguing that genuine independence requires spaces for curiosity, risk-taking and collaboration. Parenting that fosters independence, then, is less about letting go entirely and more about cultivating environments of trust, dialogue and shared responsibility.

Modern example:

A parent who once dictated bedtime now finds themselves waiting up while their teen returns from a volunteer project. Instead of enforcing old rules, they talk over tea about what the young person is learning about life, purpose and limits.

Questions for reflection:

- Can I trust my child's unfolding more than my own timeline?
- How do I respond when their choices differ from my ideals?
- What does letting go look like, in love rather than fear?

Building confidence: non-violent communication and constructive language

Confidence is central to the transition from dependence to independence. Chanakya's framework, with its emphasis on modelling behaviour and open friendship in adolescence, aligns with modern approaches to communication. Non-violent communication (NVC), developed by Marshall Rosenberg and increasingly supported by research, highlights the importance of empathy, constructive feedback and language that avoids judgment or labelling. Parents who use NVC report improved family cohesion and children with higher self-esteem and emotional intelligence (Housman, 2017).

Language shapes identity. When parents label children ("you're shy," "you're not good at maths"), they restrict possibilities and create fixed self-concepts. By contrast, constructive language focuses on effort, process, and feelings: "you worked hard on that problem," or "I can see you're feeling frustrated – how can I support you?" This empowers children to define themselves rather than being defined by external judgments. Whitebread (2019) noted that confidence also develops through play and exploration, where children can take risks without fear of harsh criticism. Here, the Vedic notion of modelling values through lived example converges with modern psychology: children learn how to treat themselves and others by observing how parents communicate.

Modern example:

Instead of saying "You're so clumsy," a parent pauses and says, "That cup slipped – what do you think happened there?" The focus shifts from blame to belonging. Over time, such language builds emotional intelligence and self-trust. Similarly, instead of saying "She is the clever one and he is more practical" you could resist comparing and say, "they each have such different qualities."

Questions for reflection:

- What words do my children hear most from me?
- Do my corrections carry compassion as well as clarity?
- How can my language create the atmosphere of friendship Chanakya envisioned?

Rather than imposing belief, Miller encourages meeting children and young people where they are: noticing wonder, repairing relationships and fostering purpose. The following ideas translate her findings into practical ways families can weave spiritual awareness into ordinary life

Ideas drawn from *The Spiritual Child: The New Science on Parenting for Health and Lifelong Thriving,* Lisa Miller (2015)

1. Use spiritual language daily.
   Miller recommends that parents speak about spirituality in everyday language – not just in formal religious moments – and invite children into conversations about meaning, purpose, connection and the transcendent. For example, noticing moments of awe ("Did you see that rainbow? What does it make you feel?") or discussing acts of kindness ("Why do you think you felt moved to help her?") helps children develop a spiritual awareness. In practical parenting terms, then: try setting aside a weekly "wonder walk" with your child – perhaps in a park or garden, where you

notice together things that evoke awe or mystery (a spider web glistening, the sound of wind in leaves), prompt gentle questions and then share how you each feel about it. Avoid turning it into a quiz or moral lecture, instead allow the space for silence, reflection and simply being together.

2. Share your own spiritual journey and be transparent.
   Children benefit when parents model vulnerability, curiosity, and authenticity regarding their own spiritual lives. Miller suggests sharing experiences of wonder, mystery, loss and hope, as this gives children permission to ask big questions and feel safe in their own search. Also, share your own mini-stories of wonder or struggle: "When I was your age I got very upset that I wasn't picked for the team – I asked myself, 'What does that mean about me?' and I found myself trying to listen for a deeper voice in me that said, 'What is the gift here for me?'" Opening your story helps children see that spiritual growth is part of everyday life, not only Sunday mornings.
3. Meet the child where they are.
   Rather than impose a rigid belief system or expecting children to adopt an adult-level spiritual understanding, Miller advises parents to attend to the child's current level of meaning-making: their language, their sense of wonder, their questions. Meeting them where they are builds trust, rather than creating a gap between parent and child.
4. Build a spiritual practice together.
   Practices needn't be elaborate. Miller suggests shared rituals, meditative moments, nature walks, sitting quietly, noticing breath, exploring art or music – whatever invites the child to reflect on transcendence and connection. Regular shared practice helps children internalise a sense of something beyond the everyday.
5. Nurture relationships with nature, animals and the world.
   Part of spiritual growth, according to Miller, is connection beyond the self: to other people, to nature, to a "higher power." Encouraging children's affinity with nature or caring for animals opens pathways to wonder, empathy, beauty and transcendence.

6. Tend to the "field of love" by repairing and caring for relationships. Spiritual development doesn't happen in the absence of relational conflict or hurt. Miller underscores that loving relationships, and also the willingness to repair them when they fracture, are central. A home where mistakes are owned, forgiveness is practised, and relationships are restored cultivates the soil in which children's spiritual capacities grow. When difficulties arise (conflict between siblings, disappointment, anxiety), you might say: "I wonder what this moment might be inviting us to learn or to grow in?" rather than jumping straight into correction. This invites a deeper layer of conversation about meaning, values and relationships.
7. Encourage striving toward an inspired life.
   Finally, Miller points to the value of helping children develop a sense of calling or purpose – a "beyond-the-self" orientation. Whether that is service, creativity, learning, caring for others or exploring their gifts, helping children ask "How can I make a difference?" links their spirituality with flourishing and resilience.

Summary

Parenting plays a vital role in the development of a child's wellbeing, character and sense of purpose. Both contemporary research and Vedic philosophy emphasise that parents are the first educators, shaping emotional resilience, moral understanding and spiritual awareness. Effective parenting begins with love in early childhood, where affection, play and secure attachment build confidence, trust, and a sense of worth.

As children grow, parents must introduce clear expectations and boundaries while allowing mistakes and challenges, helping children develop resilience, responsibility and perseverance. During adolescence, the parental role shifts towards guidance and friendship, supporting independence, identity formation and thoughtful decision-making. Research also shows that an authoritative style of parenting, combining warmth with clear standards, best supports self-regulation, confidence and healthy relationships.

Additionally, compassionate communication and language that encourages effort rather than labels help nurture self-belief and emotional intelligence. Ultimately, soul-centred parenting seeks to recognise each child's unique inner nature, guiding them with love, wisdom, and trust so their deeper potential can gradually unfold. Most importantly, parents and schools working together will help release the imagination and celebrate the art of the possible for every child to achieve, thrive and flourish.

Note

1 *Chanakya* (c. 350 BCE), also known as Kautilya, was an Indian philosopher and strategist whose *Arthashastra* and *Chanakya Niti* offered insights into ethics, governance and human conduct. His writings on parenting emphasised discipline balanced with wisdom, urging parents to guide children through love, moral instruction and preparation for independent, responsible adulthood.

18 Reclaiming the soul of education

This book has carried us across a widening landscape, philosophical, historical, spiritual and practical, as we have explored what it might mean to reclaim the soul of education. Four parts shaped the arc of our journey, each illuminating a different facet of this enquiry.

Why pick up a book for modern education that draws on an ancient Indian philosophy? It is the very question we asked ourselves at the outset. Is this a book only for faith schools? For one type of faith school? Or only for those educators who follow an Eastern religious tradition? Does it offer a narrow, culturally bound perspective? We hope that you agree that to each, our answer is a clear and wholehearted 'no.' Most recently, Kat Eghdamian, human rights expert and writer about religions, says that schools that cultivate the mind but neglect spiritual education leave children unanchored in a challenging world. Spirituality and its development are not a luxury or a bolt on (Eghdamian, 2026; Miller, 2015), and there is increasing contemporary interest and relevance in spirituality, faith, identity, belief and religions. This book is responding to this new zeitgeist.

At first glance, drawing on ancient Indian philosophy to think about contemporary (and future) education might seem distant from the preoccupations of modern schools and policy. Yet, the approach shared within this book invites us to look beyond subject knowledge and performance measures (while we accept that they are also important parts of education and not to be dismissed), towards questions of meaning, dignity and human flourishing that lie at the heart of the educational task. Even for those who do not share the scriptural or spiritual frameworks of the Vedic texts, your own insights into beliefs, values and virtues will contribute to the discourse.

DOI: 10.4324/9781003487654-23

Figure 18.1 Arjuna understands his purpose and prepares to fight. Photo taken of *Bhagavad Gītā* mural on 24th October 2025 by James Biddulph in the Sandipani Muni Ashram, Ujjain, India.

We started on the battlefield of Kurukshetra and that is where we now return. Figure 18.1 shows Arjuna bending down, almost in slow motion and picking up his bow. He is no longer afraid because he has understood a deeper purpose and a fuller awareness of the meaning of life.

Krishna listened to Arjuna's trembling heart and spoke with a calm that cut through the roar of war. He did not promise him an easy path, nor escape from sorrow, but a way of seeing more deeply. Life, he said, will always bring choices tangled with love and loss. What matters is not to run from them, but to act with clarity, with courage and with care for the whole. This is when profound learning happens and people transform.

Slowly, Arjuna's despair lifted. He began to see that the battlefield was also a place of learning. What Krishna gave him was not only counsel for war but the soul of education itself: to wake up, to discern what is true, to serve something greater than oneself. Education was no longer just lessons remembered but wisdom lived, a steadying light when the world turned dark.

At last, Arjuna raised his bow, not in anger, not in blind duty, but with a new steadiness. He had learned that strength is not domination, but in understanding; that the truest victory is to act from the heart of wisdom.

As the armies surged forward, Arjuna carried a powerful new weapon, a new vision of life: that every field, whether of battle or of learning, can be a place where the soul grows, where virtues are nurtured to provide the courage to guide us to compassion.

Retold by James Biddulph from *Bhagavad Gītā (18.73)*

At the outset, Arjuna froze in fear and did not want to do what he was duty bound to do: to protect his people. He tried to respond with the rational mind. Krishna, however, teaches that the mind is like a feather in a storm, it is blown here, there and everywhere. To quieten the storms of life, our purpose is to deepen our abilities to listen with a wide-awakeness, to reflect, to meditate upon and then to engage in action in the mode of goodness. Our dear spiritual friend and guru, His Holiness Sacinandana Swami, says that if we want to change the world, we must first change the world within. If we want to clean up the environment, we have to clean the internal environment. If we want to stop wars, we must address the battle within. If we want schools to be joyful, creative, dialogue rich places, we have to attend to the places of joy, creativity and discourse within ourselves as well as developing new rhizomatic communities of practice where collaboration not competition exists.

Rewriting our narratives: seeking the soul again and again

The world is essentially storied (Atkinson, 2015). We tell stories about ourselves, our past, present and futures. We spin yarns to explore our purpose in the world and examine the purpose of our histories, both personal and collective, and look forward to stories of our futures (Biddulph, 2017; Biddulph and Burnard, 2022). We author and co-author narratives about who we want to be, how we want to be and define our existence through these multiple (auto) biographies: and the stories told, bound together by cultural, social, political, religious narratives, guide how we choose to live our lives. With all stories there are moments of crisis, conflict, confusion and the ups and downs of living are written; they are etched in our memories and reverberate in the tales we tell one another, around fires, around tables, on trains, with friends, with strangers, in our heads. This story telling and the stories we read and retell are important ways to make sense of life and its purpose. Bruno Bettelheim (1976), educator and psychologist, emphasises our human struggle for meaning, "if we hope to live not just from moment to moment, then our greatest need and most difficult achievement is to find meaning in our lives" (1976, p. 3).

In the 21st century, the invention and expansion of social media have brought a new genre into our story telling. As we engage with the fast developing forms of social interaction online, our reality is distorted and exhorted into a space which is disembodied, becomes lived in two dimensions on a screen, where there are additional selves, versions of our self, of our story that is edited, photoshopped and presented in a way that can remove the grittiness of life. These raise profound questions about the nature of the self and identity and on how we decide what the desired qualities of living ought to be. It is incumbent on anyone interested in education to narrate our diverse stories and to craft together a hopeful narrative for education, our future and our humanity.

One powerful way to reconnect with 'Soul purpose' in education is by engaging with our own personal/professional stories – examining the experiences, motivations and contexts that have shaped us as educators, and the hopes that guide our next steps. As John Elliott suggests, educators' narratives can provide new insights for guiding future practice:

> Educational research, which involves teachers sharing and developing their practical insights into the problems of realising their educational values in concrete teaching situations and their judgments about how these are best resolved, can yield useful summaries of the universal significance of insights and judgments to guide further reflection and action.
>
> (Elliott, 2006, p. 177)

Personal narrative is one means of expressing spiritual experiences allowing meaning to be constructed and co-constructed (Scott, 2001). We can take much from professional and personal stories: take Alison Peacock's story of Mary in the foreword or Aimee Durning's story of Billy or of James' reflections about education. The sharing of their stories exemplars the motivation behind their actions; a passionate commitment for inclusion and changing how we view children, reimagining how we support the most vulnerable children by taking bold decisions in the face of more technocratic views of achievement and success, and exploring how we spend time in schools and defining what truly matters. Sharing these narratives helps us make sense of ourselves and our place in the world.

There are also the stories we hear from others, in our immediate social contexts and also across time and place. In the opening chapters, we welcomed William Blake, William Shakespeare, Maxine Greene, Charlie Chaplin and Lisa Miller, to name but a few, to our uncovering of the soul; we asked what the soul might mean, recognising that it has a vital place in education not solely for the betterment of the individual learner but because society and the future is in need of a more energising and hopeful narrative – and that this arises from educating to navigate the questions of meaning, purpose and identity. When we write and speak our narratives (not relying on the mind forged manacles of an unfettered, lazy use of artificial intelligence to do the work and thinking for us) and slow down, just a little perhaps, we might hear the whispers of new stories that could transform us.

Another story from James. Before he finalised the conception of this book, he was on a sabbatical in India. On 14th February 2024, while in Bodhgaya in Northern India, where Lord Buddha was enlightened, he met Pawan, a taxi driver, who wanted to build a school for his family's village. James' personal story was tinted with the story of Pawan. In James' journal, he noted the experience, his position as a westerner, white, male educator, foregrounding his questioning and problematising the issue of education's purpose. The emphasis on place is important, as a reflection on how we create educational place from cultural, contextual, social and personal spaces.

14th February 2024. Pawan. Taxi. School.

Pawan, the taxi driver, had in his idea that I could help build a school. He wanted me to see his village.

He said it was 20 to 30 minutes away, but after two hours we arrived. On the (very) bumpy rickshaw drive, I got thinking about education and its sole purpose. Seeing children heading to school as we passed by, their neat uniforms, their tidy hair, I can't help but think how little I know and how naïve I feel. In my work at the University of Cambridge Primary School I have talked and written about 'reimagining education and celebrating the art of the possible.' What does reimagining education mean for children here, in this community, in a remote part of India? It seems so Global North and middle class to talk about creativity, possibility thinking, and spirituality when families I meet here in remote villages in Bihar are focused on providing the basics for their children.

When I spoke with Pawan, mediated by google translate, I learnt that for many in the village, like so many villagers (I imagine), the purpose of life and education is to continue supporting the family by working on the fields; Pawan told me it's all farming here.

Around shop fronts groups of young men gather, their phones out, either playing music or on social media; the great pull from social media (to be richer, faster, fitter) means there is great tension – between tradition and modernity, between cultural values and modern values, between desires and opportunities.

We drove through mountains shrouded in low cloud and rain splash, palm trees framing each vista, splashes of bright orange, green and blue scarves as women carrying water, *puja* items, or their children walked along the damp path. We eventually arrived. He looked so pleased to welcome me to his home. They offered me water, tea, and lunch. I resisted because I didn't want to add burden to them, but they looked disappointed, so I accepted their generous hospitality.

To build a school, to educate children, to nurture a future society, what does this mean in a community, in a remote village?

As teachers, we are constantly building communities and sometimes rebuilding them. But what does that really mean in practice? What does it mean in the UK today? In the former coal-mining towns of Durham, in coastal communities in Cornwall, or in the diverse neighbourhoods of inner-city Birmingham for example? And how might those questions echo in schools across the world?

When we pause to look outward, the contrasts can be striking. A child growing up in a small rural village in India may experience schooling very differently from a child in the UK. Their daily lives, opportunities and expectations may not look the same. But behind those differences lie deeper questions that teachers everywhere wrestle with.

What are the dreams of the children we teach?
What do they hope their futures might hold?
What do their parents want for them…security, opportunity, belonging, purpose?
And just as importantly: where do we find the similarities between children across contexts, and where do we need to honour the differences?

The challenge for us as educators is not to assume we already know the answers. Instead, we need to keep asking questions together.

Yet, this is not easy. Schools are busy places. The demands of the education system, accountability measures, timetables, assessments and the daily intensity of teaching can leave little space for reflection. So, we might ask ourselves:

Where, in the life of our schools, do we create space for curiosity?
Where are the moments of pause; the places where teachers and learners can reflect on what really matters?

Community is not built only through policies or structures. It grows through the rituals and encounters that shape daily school life: the way we welcome children in the morning, the stories we share, the traditions we create, and the conversations we allow ourselves to have. These are the place-making activities of schools, the small, human practices that help a community feel like it belongs to the people within it.

But there is a tension here. In the urgency to *do* (to deliver lessons, meet targets and manage systems) we can lose sight of something essential. Are we becoming *human doings* rather than *human beings*?

> Rebuilding school communities asks us to return to this question again and again. Because underneath everything lies a bigger challenge: what is education really for? Where do we begin when we ask that question seriously?
>
> And how do we make education more deeply human at a time when technology, particularly artificial intelligence, is rapidly reshaping the landscape of learning? I am worried about this drive for faster efficiencies when we might be walking headlong into unintended consequences – how can we slow down learning, to deepen it, to deepen reflections about purpose, identity and the world in which we live, which we share? AI offers extraordinary possibilities, but it also brings uncertainty and raises profound questions about what it means to learn, to think and to be human.
>
> In this moment of change, perhaps the most important work for teachers is not simply to adapt to new tools or systems. It is to keep returning to the human heart of education, to nurture curiosity, belonging and purpose in the communities we build together.
>
> James Biddulph | Journal entry February 2024

These are profound and demanding questions. How many of us, after a long and busy term marked by rising absences, increasing needs and shrinking budgets, have the space to truly dwell on them? Yet, such reflection is essential. Without it, we risk teachers and leaders becoming deskilled and automated – technicians rather than thinkers, executors rather than creators. When our sense of purpose fades, energy and imagination drain away.

But when we narrate a return to the *why* of education (wherever we might be teaching), new possibilities emerge. With the *why* explored, we begin to reimagine the *how* – how learning might feel, how schools might flourish, how communities might thrive. Our hope is that this book becomes a spark: an invitation for educators to pause, to wonder, and to rediscover the deeper callings that brought them to this work in the first place. If we think of the teachers in the Global South, where pay and conditions, facilities and professional development opportunities may be less favourable than in the North, the challenge of including spirituality in education may become even more challenging, if not impossible.

Is this possible for our fellow educators across the world, in small village schools in India, in the well-established private (fee paying) schools, in inner city schools, in schools without classrooms, in schools without a regular teacher, in schools where the expectations of government and society is for academic excellence at all costs? For all other and various schools in the diverse communities in which they exist?

News about education is often peppered with negativity. Our duty is to cultivate a new meliorist[1] movement in education; to show that between optimism and pessimism lies an agential opportunity to act, with a hopeful narrative. We must write and rewrite narratives of possibilities, especially for children and young people who need guided pathways for future thriving and flourishing. The story of Pawan and his dream to build a school is one such unfolding narrative. It reminds us that education is, at its heart, a deeply personal and sacred act, an invitation to consider what kind of world we wish to bring into being. What these reflections about story telling remind us is that "narrative requires a listening space for this interpretative work to occur" (Scott, 2001, p. 120). It is a space that allows for the qualities of indirectness, implication and ambiguity; a space that allows us to say – 'we just don't know.' That is the starting point for soul awareness and soul-full learning; for all manner of possibilities, dialogues and new narratives to be spoken, crafted and written down.

This is what Mark Nichols does. He loves teaching. In one reflection of his classes' learning, he narrated his experiences and insights; it is his story and the story of his young people. We are sure, however, that it connects rhizomatic-like with educators in other contexts. It is a narrative that shows his learners becoming awakened, in this case, to a sense of Romanticism in literature and its affective nature.

The End of a Journey, The Start of Something Greater

There are moments in the life of a teacher when the noise of the job quiets for just long enough to let something more profound be heard – an echo, perhaps, of the deeper purpose we all hope to fulfil. Today was one of those moments. I've spent the day reading my Year 9 learners' end-of-year assessments – an open-ended question on Romanticism and whether it truly belongs only to the 18th century. They were invited to respond by drawing upon any of the texts they've studied this year: Shakespeare's *Romeo and Juliet*, Van Gogh's letters, poetry, drama, prose. And what I've encountered is not just analytical skill or refined writing – it's thought. Real thought. The kind of thought that lingers, matures and dares to take itself seriously.

These essays mark the culmination of a Key Stage 3 curriculum that was conceived three years ago – not to mirror the national curriculum, but to transcend it. This wasn't designed to be a checklist of topics or a recycled sequence of 'what's always been taught.' It was built with aspiration in mind. It is a curriculum forged from long evenings, rigorous debate, quiet persistence and the refusal to settle for convenience. It stands as an act of defiance against educational complacency – and today, it proved itself.

What I read today moved me. Some learners wrote with fierce precision and poetic lyricism:

> *To say that one's love is as deep and immense as a sea should be considered a blessing due to the absolute love and passionate desire displayed here.*

Others saw the Romantic movement alive in the everyday:

> *You come to a realisation that the loud, chaotic phone calls and the dramatic coffee spills don't matter. That's what Romantics believe.*

Many embraced the moral force of Romanticism in the modern world:

> *If we deny nature, then nature will not hesitate to fight back without doubt.*

And some, quite simply, wrote with a truth that pierced:

> *Nature is something innately rooted in our hearts, and when such a thing is ripped away, a dull and dreary ache is left within ourselves.*

> Because teachers who are romantically fascinated with the past have always taught learners about romantic texts and ideals, romanticism has never really died, as it has awoken in learners the innate reverence for nature that is inside all of us as humans who are born and descended from the earth, whether we choose to embrace that or not.

And one, beautifully, almost prophetically, declared:

> *Romanticism can save people's lives – not only that, but it could also help people connect with nature as it can help them in the future.*

Reading these words, I realise: the curriculum wasn't just taught. It was lived. Internalised. Wrestled with. These learners weren't parroting facts or mimicking model paragraphs as is the norm in many schools I have worked with in the past. They were thinking independently, feeling deeply and writing with clarity and conviction. They had become philosophers, poets, cultural critics and quiet revolutionaries – something that could only be achieved through working for a school and trust that gives the freedom to exercise an educational philosophy that is rooted in ethics, virtues and the arts.

This isn't just about the essays. It's about the legacy of a curriculum that dared to be more – more ambitious, more challenging, more human. I am proud – undeniably, deeply proud – of what they have achieved. Not because they got the "right answer," but because they made meaning. And if the measure of a curriculum is what learners carry forward from it – not just in knowledge, but in how they see the world and how they live in the world – then today, I have all the evidence I need.

By Mark Nichols, Assistant Principal |
Avanti Grange School, Bishops Stortford

Narratives yet to be told: limitations of the book

What the book has not done is as revealing as what it has sought to do. To write about the soul is to enter a conversation that resists closure; to explore education through this lens is to accept that much will remain unfinished, provisional and open to reinterpretation. This is not a deficiency, but a necessary humility, a recognition that our work stands within a wider landscape of enquiry and practice, one that continually invites deeper questioning.

Firstly, we have only begun to engage with the complex and unpredictable futures being shaped by artificial intelligence (AI). Our emphasis has been on the human, the animating pulse of purpose, creativity, and care, yet we have only gestured towards the entangled relationship emerging between AI, HI (human intelligence) and SI (spiritual intelligence – and/or spiritual habitus and capital). How might education evolve when intelligence itself is being redefined; especially when new technologies have dual possibilities – and the 'dark side' of these is yet to be fully explored or understood? What forms of discernment, ethical imagination, and spiritual literacy will be needed as these intelligences converge? We acknowledge that these questions lie ahead of us, demanding courage and interdisciplinary collaboration.

Secondly, our reflections have been situated primarily within the UK context, its histories, tensions and possibilities. This has given our enquiry depth and focus but also narrowed its horizon. How might our understandings be enriched or disrupted by deeper dialogue with global and Indigenous traditions, those that have long conceived of learning as relational, ecological and sacred? The soul of education cannot be claimed by one culture or system; it is a shared human inheritance, spoken in many tongues and shaped by diverse ways of knowing. There are also the very real challenges of developing soul education in conditions of poverty and disadvantage.

Thirdly, we recognise that our engagement with the Vedas and the wider corpus of Indian philosophy is necessarily partial. The Vedas constitute an immense and layered body of insight – philosophical, poetic, ritual and metaphysical – whose study demands both depth and devotion. While we have identified key texts as a foundation, we have not delved into the full richness of this tradition. How might a more sustained encounter with this vast inheritance further illuminate what it means to educate the whole being, mind, heart and spirit, in dialogue with contemporary life?

Fourth, our focus on one Multi-Academy Trust within the UK has offered a living laboratory for reflection, yet it also raises questions of scope and generalisability. There are however other trusts, schools, and communities exploring similar questions, sometimes through different philosophical or linguistic frameworks. What might be learned if we held these differing articulations in conversation, not as competing claims to truth but as varied perspectives on a shared search for meaning? The soul of education, perhaps, is best understood not as a single viewpoint, but as the light refracted through many lenses. To name these absences is to reaffirm our commitment to enquiry, dialogue and from a position of humility.

Returning to equality, diversity and love

Throughout this book, equality, diversity and love have been interwoven as essential foundations for education. A Vedic lens offers a distinctive contribution to this conversation by locating human flourishing not only in social structures, but in the inner life. Within *Kali-Yuga*, the material world is inherently imperfect and contradictory – marked by injustice, competition and fragmentation. Attempts to reform society without attending to inner transformation therefore tend to be partial and short-lived. The first insight, then, is simple but demanding: lasting social change and personal change are inseparable.

A second insight concerns identity. Beyond the body, the restless mind, and the conditioned ego, the Vedic tradition points to the *ātman*, the enduring self. Whether understood metaphysically or metaphorically, this idea is profoundly empowering. It invites a reframing of purpose: life is not only about managing the world, but about understanding who we are and how we relate to others, to nature, and to meaning itself. Practised as mindfulness, ethical attention and lived virtue, this orientation is non-sectarian and universally accessible. For some, this evolves into religious practices, ways of being and strengthened by faith.

From this follows a third insight: agency. When individuals act from inner clarity rather than fear or comparison, they are less dominated by external pressures and more capable of compassion and wise action. Difference is no longer experienced as threat, but as contextual and relational. In this way, equality becomes recognition, diversity becomes richness, and love becomes the active practice of seeing ourselves in one another.

Final thoughts

What might be the impact of a book like this? In a UK context, as we enter the second quarter of the 21st century, where financial resources are limited, where the complexity of educating children and young people is challenging the status quo, in which accountability structures seem to be intensifying, and where there seems little political appetite for substantial change – more evolution than revolution in the words of politicians in 2026, the possibility that our book is dismissed as naïve or quixotic is possible and real. However, we wrote it as a resistance to the heaviness of the era; a resistance against a system that does not give primacy to the whole child's education. We wrote it as a new clarion call against the rising unchecked wave of AI which has a potential stripping away of humanity's capacity for creativity, imagination, joyful expression of the awe and wonder in the world and a deeper connection with the transcendence. Instead, we advocate for a wave of Spiritual Intelligence (SI perhaps?) to ensure we all move from only survival towards thriving and flourishing. It is in recognising the wisdom in religions, to tell the full story separate from fanaticism and choosing language rooted in humility, inquiry and hope (Eghdamian, 2025) that we get close to talking about beliefs to engage meaningfully with honesty and depth.

The *Soul of Education* is not a final word but an invitation, a gesture towards a richer conversation about what it means to educate for life, in all its complexity and possibility (see Appendix I). A discussion framed around these questions, the others we asked on the journey and the ones you generate in your own workplaces, schools or homes could reawaken public and professional discourse about the moral and spiritual purposes of education, inviting educators, leaders and families to reconsider what it truly means to nurture the whole human being. It could offer a language of the soul that bridges secular and spiritual traditions without imposing dogma, creating space for dialogue grounded in shared human values and virtues. Such conversations might inspire a cultural movement within education, one that reclaims stillness, reverence and compassion as essential dimensions of learning and leadership. In doing so, they challenge dominant paradigms built on utility, competition and data, opening pathways towards a more humane, consciousness-centred vision of schooling. A soul-led education is less certain and more spacious; less uniform and more diverse. It unfolds not in straight lines, but in cyclical or spiral movements, where meaning deepens over time and wisdom grows through attentiveness, patience and being fully present in the moment.

...and farewell

We began with three concerns – equality, diversity and love – and we end with three profound opportunities. Firstly, to shape an education that honours the boundless potential of every child. Secondly, to embrace diversity not as a problem to be managed but as a gift that expands our shared humanity, free from the narrow politics of nationalism, religiosity and paternalism. And thirdly, and perhaps most importantly, to place love at the very heart of education: love as practice, as knowledge, as the bridge between self and other, between humanity and the beyond, with the Divine.

Simply put, without love in education – without learning how to hold ethical boundaries, to cross differences with curiosity and humility, and to create pathways into genuine relationship – with one another, with the living world and with the Sacred (by whatever name it is known: Krishna, Christ, Allah, Yahweh, Truth, Nature, the Holy Name) – education loses its depth and direction. Learning becomes transactional rather than transformational, and we, at the level of our truest selves, become hollowed, diminished and exhausted.

With love, education reclaims its sacred and practical purpose. Love shows up as care, as rigour that is humane, as classrooms that are psychologically safe yet intellectually brave. It invites dialogue across difference, honours interdependence, and treats each learner as a whole human being rather than a container for information. In this way, education engages, awakens, liberates, empowers and heals.

Through relationship, learning gains meaning. Through relationship, responsibility, purpose and hope take root.

This is the work of spiritually grounded, compassionately courageous changemakers, those educators and learners who understand that transformation is not produced by content alone, but by the quality of presence we bring to one another and to the world.

This, we humbly suggest, is the soul of education.

With love.

Note

1 Meliorism is the philosophical belief that the world, while not perfect, can be made better through human effort and positive action, positioning itself between naive optimism and cynical pessimism. Rooted in the Latin word *melior* ("better"), it emphasises that progress isn't automatic but is achievable through deliberate choices, intelligence and dedicated work to improve society, morality and the human condition.

Afterword

The soul of education in a world that needs it more than ever

When I was introduced to the House of Lords in February 2025, I felt the weight of responsibility that comes with service as I have always done working with people. Standing beneath the vaulted ceilings of Westminster, I thought not of politics, but of purpose and service. Leadership, whether in Parliament, faith or education, must always be an act of service. In my maiden speech, I spoke of community integration, recalling Robert Putnam's insight that unattended diversity can fracture communities. He was right. But I have also seen that when diversity is met with intent and leadership, it becomes a source of strength. Inclusion is not passive; it takes effort, humility and heart.

That conviction comes from my own story. My grandfather, Manishankar, left India at fifteen as a cook's assistant, alone and impoverished. Through hard work, he rose to become a general manager of a large export business. Beside him was my grandmother, Kantaben, resilient, wise and unshakeable. Their journey is my inheritance: a testament to courage, faith and perseverance.

In 2007, I founded *Faith in Leadership* (FiL) to bring together diverse faith leaders, imams, rabbis, priests, monks, nuns, humanists and public servants, to learn and grow together. Since then, we've shared meals, stories, silence and disagreement. Again and again, I've witnessed that difference does not have to divide. Dialogue, when practiced with sincerity, becomes a sacred space of encounter. Over the years, our faculty has trained senior and emerging leaders to engage with faith and the public sphere, to transform conflict, to lead with authenticity and to heal trauma in their communities. Perhaps most moving of all are our programmes for young leaders, people of faith and no faith, who discover through dialogue that they share a common human longing: to live meaningfully, to belong and to serve.

And that is where my reflection on the soul of education begins. For what we have learned in interfaith work is equally true for schooling: that education, at its best, awakens the soul as much as it informs the mind.

Too often, education has become transactional. James and Nitesh have shown how over time, the education system has focused on academic excellence, at a cost to the inner growing of the soul. Under pressure from tests and targets, we have risked reducing young people to outcomes rather than beings of depth and dignity. We have seen in this book that the soul is a complex thing to define. It is the part of us that knows, however faintly, that we are part of something larger. When we neglect that dimension, we produce clever minds but anxious hearts. When we honour it, we nurture resilience, empathy and hope. The world needs that more than ever. Amid growing division, loneliness and disconnection, education must once again become a place where the inner life is cultivated, where we learn not only *what* to think, but *how* to live.

In the House of Lords, we debate and we do it often. True education begins with dialogue: the courage to listen, the humility to learn and the grace to disagree well. Dialogue is not weakness; it is strength expressed through curiosity. When children are taught to speak honestly and listen deeply, they become citizens capable of building bridges. When they learn to hold difference with dignity, they become leaders of peace. Dialogue, then, is not an optional skill, it is the grammar of coexistence.

I have seen how faith leaders, grounded in their traditions yet open to others, have been agents of transformation. During the Ebola crisis, it was local faith leaders who helped communities trust medical science. In the global fight against modern slavery, faith communities are again at the forefront. Faith, when guided by compassion and wisdom, is a force for human flourishing. And education must learn from that. Not by teaching doctrine, but by inviting understanding. The secular and the sacred need not be adversaries, they can be partners in shaping conscience, character, and compassion.

We are living through an age of fracture, of politics that divides, media that polarises and communities that drift apart. But I remain hopeful. And this book is certainly hopeful in its message. I have seen reconciliation happen in the most unlikely places: in shared meals between those who once mistrusted each other, in classrooms where learners from different backgrounds find friendship, in moments of shared silence where words fall away and humanity remains. Healing begins with encounter. A teacher who makes room for every voice, a school that values belonging as much as

achievement, a community that sees its diversity as strength, these are the quiet revolutions that restore the human spirit.

As I look back on my own journey, from my grandparents' courage to my work with communities across faiths, I am convinced that the renewal of our world depends on reawakening the soul of education. That is the exciting offer that James and Nitesh give us in this book: the opportunity to delve deep into our own consciousness, ways of thinking, being and acting, and to ask bigger, better, bolder questions about the future for our children and, indeed, for us all. It is also an opportunity to open up the rich Indian heritage to a wider audience, relevant in its ideas for a contemporary world. It is an opportune time given the closer political relationship the UK has with India.

We must teach young people to imagine, to care, to stand firm in conviction yet soft in heart. We must help them to navigate a noisy world with stillness and to meet difference not with fear but with curiosity. The soul of education is not a luxury. It is the quiet force that holds societies together. It teaches us that knowledge without wisdom is hollow, and that success without service is empty.

If we can restore that sense of soul to our classrooms, our communities and our leadership, we may yet raise a generation capable not just of succeeding, but of healing, of building a world where the mind, the heart and the spirit move together in harmony. This is because the true purpose of education is not only to make a living, but to make a life.

And in a world that needs it more than ever, that is the education worth fighting for.

Lord Krish Raval OBE
Member of the House of Lords

APPENDIX I

List of questions from the book

The questions that follow form the living heart of this book. They are not intended to be answered once, nor resolved conclusively, but to be returned to, personally, collectively and across time. Taken together, they provide enquiry pathways through which teachers, learners, leaders and communities can develop rhizomatic communities of practice: relational, non-hierarchical and responsive networks of shared meaning-making. Engaged seriously, these questions do not merely generate knowledge; they cultivate phronesis, the 'ignorant wise' discernment required to act well in complex, uncertain and ethically charged conditions. They invite pauses, dialogue, discomfort, imagination and courage, anchoring education in purpose, relationship and moral agency.

We envisage that you could use them to explore the development of the soul-led education in your own contexts with your own people and communities. They could be the start of sangha groups or communities of practice.

They could be the questions that provide space to breath and consider: *what if?*

1. Identity, Becoming and Purpose

Questions of selfhood, direction and meaning across a life

- Who am I?
- Who am I becoming?
- Why am I here?
- What is the point?
- What do I value most deeply in my own life, and how do these values shape the way I relate to others?

- When I pause and turn inward, where do I sense the source of meaning in my life – in achievement, relationship, service or something deeper still?
- In moments of challenge, personal suffering, hardship or stillness, what helps me remember my connection to something larger than myself?

2. Reality, Transcendence and the Nature of Existence

Questions that stretch beyond the immediate and instrumental

- What is the nature of this life, and what lies beyond it?
- What is this Universe?
- What is beyond this Universe?
- What else might be?

3. Awareness, Listening and Inner Practice

How attention, stillness and receptivity shape knowing

- What practices of listening, reflection, meditation or devotion draw me from self-focus towards openness and wonder?
- When I truly listen to another, to the world or to silence, what becomes possible in me that was not there before?
- How might learning itself become an act of awakening: a movement from information towards insight, from doing towards being?

4. Interconnectedness, Oneness and Difference

Holding individuality and unity together

- In a world that emphasises individual identity and self-expression, how do we also honour our deep interconnectedness with others and with the natural world?

- How might holding together both oneness and difference help us navigate tensions around diversity and unity in schools, communities or nations?
- In relationships, what does it mean to see the other as both distinct and yet inseparably connected to ourselves?
- On a personal level, when have you experienced a moment of "oneness" with nature, another person or a community, and how did that coexist with your own sense of individuality?

5. Ethics, Responsibility and Action in the World

From awareness to moral agency

- How shall we act?
- Where and how can we be bold and respond positively, hopefully and imaginatively?
- How might our collective work serve something beyond us, a greater harmony, a more compassionate world or what the Vedas might call the unfolding of the Self?
- How might recognising our shared essence with all beings change the way we respond to issues such as climate change, inequality, food choices or conflict?

6. Education, Learning and the Formation of the Person

Reclaiming purpose beyond performance

- What is education for?
- In education, how do we teach children to value their uniqueness without fostering individualism at the expense of community?
- How far do our current policies and institutional priorities reflect "information without wisdom" and "connection without communion"?
- What structural changes would be required to re-anchor schooling in meaning?

7. Kali Yuga, Crisis and Systemic Disruption

Diagnosing modern fragmentation and reclaiming wisdom

- How is it that societies are advancing in wealth and technology, yet rates of loneliness, anxiety, and suicide are rising, especially among the young?
- In your own life, do digital connections make you feel closer to others, or strangely more isolated?
- Do you sense that truth and lies are more tangled than ever, making it harder to discern what is real?
- If Kali Yuga is an age marked by noise, fragmentation and the eclipse of wisdom, in what ways has our education system internalised these qualities through workload, accountability structures, curriculum design or digital saturation and how might we disrupt them?
- Kali Yuga exposes a crisis of purpose: to what extent has our system reduced education to credentialing, compliance and competition, and what would be the system-level consequences of reorienting it towards moral agency, character and the flourishing of the whole person?

8. Society, Trust and Collective Wellbeing

Reading the moral climate of our times

- Do you feel that political leaders today act with integrity, consistency and sincerity, or do you notice hypocrisy and contradictions?
- Does your community feel hopeful and joyful, or does it carry a heaviness and confusion, even without clear reason?
- Do you find it harder today to trust institutions, neighbours or even yourself?
- Are you content with the state of the natural world, its forests, rivers, air and climate, or do you sense decline?

9. Values, Integrity and Intergenerational Responsibility

Alignment between belief, practice and consequence

- What values do I hope to pass on, whether as a teacher, parent or role model, and how do I make them visible in practice?
- What values should shape the society we are building together, and how do schools contribute to that formation?
- What values do we need to guide our responsibilities to the planet, to future generations and to those we may never meet?
- Who benefits from the values I live and teach, and who might be excluded or harmed by them?
- Are the values I claim to hold the same as those I enact in practice? Where do they align, and where do they fracture?

References

Abbs, P. (2003) *Against the flow: Education, the arts and postmodern culture*. London: Routledge Falmer.

Adams, K. (2010) 'Childhoods past and present', in: Watson, J. (ed.) *Children and spirituality: Searching for meaning and connectedness*. London: Continuum, pp. 128–133.

Alexander, R. (2010) *The Cambridge primary review*. Abingdon: Routledge.

Alexander, R. (2020) *A dialogic teaching companion*. Abingdon: Routledge.

Alexander, R. and Flutter, J. (2004) *The national curriculum in action: Pupil voice and consultation*. Cambridge: University of Cambridge Faculty of Education.

Andreotti, V. (2014) *Education, conflict and development: Rethinking the relationships between education and the economy in the global South*. New York: Bloomsbury.

Argyle, M. (2000) *Psychology and religion: An introduction*. London: Routledge.

Aristotle. (2016) *De anima (On the soul)*. Translated by C.D.C. Reeve. Indianapolis: Hackett Publishing Company.

Arthur, J. (2003) *Education with character: The moral economy of schooling*. London: Routledge.

Arthur, J., Kristjánsson, K., Harrison, T., Sanderse, W. and Wright, D. (2017) *Teaching character and virtue in schools*. London: Routledge.

Atkinson, P. (2015) *Ethnographic research*. London: SAGE Publications.

Ayers, W. and Miller, J. (eds.) (1998) *A light in dark times: Maxine Greene and the unfinished conversation*. New York: Teachers College Press.

Baldacchino, J. (2009) *Education beyond education: Self and the imaginary in Maxine Greene's philosophy*. New York: Peter Lang.

Baines, E., Blatchford, P. and Kutnick, P. (2008) *Promoting effective group work in the primary classroom*. London: Routledge.

Bauman, Z. (2005) *Liquid life*. Cambridge: Polity.

Beauregard, M. and O'Leary, D. (2007) *The spiritual brain: A neuroscientist's case for the existence of the soul*. New York: Harper Collins Publishers.

Beck, I.L., McKeown, M.G. and Kucan, L. (2013) *Bringing words to life: Robust vocabulary instruction*. 2nd edn. New York: Guilford Press.

Beck, U. (2006) *The cosmopolitan vision*. Cambridge: Polity.

Bergin, C. and Bergin, D. (2009) 'Attachment in the classroom', *Educational Psychology Review*, 21(2), pp. 141–170.

Bettelheim, B. (1976) *The uses of enchantment: The meaning and importance of fairy tales*. New York: Knopf.

Bhaktivedanta Swami Prabhupāda, A.C. (1983) *Bhagavad-Gītā as it is*. Los Angeles: Bhaktivedanta Book Trust.

Bhaktivedanta Swami Prabhupāda, A.C. (2013) *Śrīmad Bhāgavatam*. Los Angeles: Bhaktivedanta Book Trust.

Biddulph, J. (2017) *The diverse diversities of creative learning at home: three case studies of ethnic minority immigrant children*. PhD thesis, Cambridge University.

Biddulph, J. (2020) Compassionate citizenship and whole child development at the University of Cambridge Primary School. *University of Cambridge Faculty of Education*. [online] Available at: https://www.educ.cam.ac.uk/people/staff/biddulph/ (Accessed 31 Jul. 2025).

Biddulph, J. (2022) 'Intercultural creative learning: New spaces for nurturing compassionate global citizenship', *Journal of Supranational Policies of Education*, 16, pp. 13–28. https://doi.org/10.15366/jospoe2022.16.001

Biddulph, J. (2024) 'Exploring the assessment of spirituality in primary education', in *Primary First* (Issue 40). UK: NAPE

Biddulph, J. (2025) 'Play is for children not for school' in Durning, A., Ramchandani P., and Baker, S. (eds.) *Unlocking research: Empowering play in primary education*. Abingdon: Routledge.

Biddulph, J. and Baldacchino, J. (2023) 'Wilful strangers in a possible democracy', in Biddulph, J., Rolls, L., and Flutter, J. (eds.) *Unleashing children's voices in democratic primary education*. Abingdon: Routledge, pp. 43–61.

Biddulph, J. and Burnard, P. (2022) 'Storying the journey to new spaces of intercultural creative learning', in Burnard, P. and Loughrey M. (eds.) *Creativities in primary education*. Abingdon: Routledge, pp. 45–60.

Biddulph, J. and Flutter, J. (eds.) (2021) *Inspiring primary curriculum design*. Abingdon: Routledge.

Biddulph, J. and Flutter, J. (2021a) 'Unlocking research: To new possibilities', in Biddulph, J. and Flutter J. (eds.) *Inspiring primary curriculum design*. Abingdon: Routledge, pp. 167–181.

Biddulph, J. and Flutter, J. (2021b) 'Considering the possibilities', in Biddulph J. and Flutter J. (eds.) *Inspiring primary curriculum design*. Abingdon: Routledge, pp. 13–25.

Biddulph, J. and Gibride, N. (2025) 'Playful school leadership: Being serious about leadership playfully', in Durning, A., Baker, S. and Ramchandani, P. (eds.) *Empowering play in primary education*. Abingdon: Routledge, pp. 147–166.

Biddulph, J., Rolls, L. and Flutter, J. (eds.) (2023) *Unleashing children's voices in democratic primary education*. Abingdon: Routledge.

Biddulph, J., Shuckburgh, E. and Pearse, H. (eds.) (2026) *Education visions: Thriving on planet earth*. Cambridge: Cambridge University Press.

Biddulph, M. and Hewitt-Clarkson, S. (2023) 'Exploring LGBT+ identities and their relationship to inclusive practice in the primary school', in Black-Hawkins, K. and Grinham-Smith, A. (eds.) *Expanding possibilities for inclusive learning*. Abingdon: Routledge, pp. 61–76.

Biesta, G. (2010) *Good education in an age of measurement: Ethics, politics, democracy*. Boulder: Paradigm.

Biesta, G. (2013) *The beautiful risk of education*. Boulder, CO: Paradigm Publishers.

Biesta, G. (2017) *The rediscovery of teaching*. Abingdon: Routledge.
Biesta, G. (2020) *World-centred education: A view for the present*. Abingdon: Routledge.
Bils, M. and Klenow, P.J. (2000) 'Does schooling cause growth?', *Journal of Political Economy*, 108(5), pp. 1160–1183.
Bjork, R.A. and Bjork, E.L. (2011) 'Making things hard on yourself, but in a good way: Creating desirable difficulties to enhance learning', *Psychology and the Real World: Essays Illustrating Fundamental Contributions to Society*, 2, pp. 56–64.
Black-Hawkins, K. and Grinham-Smith, A. (eds.) (2023) *Expanding possibilities for inclusive learning*. Abingdon: Routledge.
Blake, W. (1863) 'Auguries of Innocence'. Available at: https://www.poetryfoundation.org/poems/43650/auguries-of-innocence (Accessed 3 Jan. 2026).
Bohm, D. (1980) *Wholeness and the implicate order*. London: Routledge.
Bourdieu, P. (1977) *Reproduction in education, society and culture*. London: Sage.
Boyer, E. (1996) 'The scholarship of engagement', *Journal of Public Service & Outreach*, 1(1), pp. 11–20.
Boyle, P.A., et al. (2010) 'Purpose in life is associated with a reduced risk of Alzheimer's disease', *Archives of General Psychiatry*, 67(3), pp. 304–310.
Braidotti, R. (2013) *The posthuman*. Cambridge: Polity Press.
Bresler, L. (ed.) (2008) *International handbook of research in arts education*. Dordrecht: Springer.
Briggs, A. and Reiss, M.J. (2021) *Human flourishing: Scientific insight and spiritual wisdom in uncertain times*. Oxford: Oxford University Press (OUP).
Brighouse, T. (2006) *Keys to success: A handbook for schools and LEAs*. London: Routledge.
Bronk, K.C. (2014) *Purpose in life: A critical component of optimal youth development*. Dordrecht: Springer.
Brown, L.M. and Gilligan, C. (1991) 'Listening for voice in narratives of relationship', *New Directions for Child Development*, 34, pp. 43–61.
Bruner, J. (1996) *The culture of education*. Cambridge: Harvard University Press.
Buber, M. (1947) *I and thou*. Translated by R.G. Smith. Edinburgh: T. & T. Clark.
Burnard, P. (2020) *Musical creativities in practice*. Oxford: Oxford University Press.
Burnard, P. and Biddulph, J. (2025) 'Editorial', *Impact*. Issue 25: A Broad and Varied Curriculum, October. Online.
Burnard, P. and Loughrey, M. (eds.) (2022) *Sculpting new creativities in primary education*. Abingdon: Routledge.
Butcher, I. and Tempest, S. (2026) 'The Biology of Stress', in Biddulph, J., Shuckburgh, E. and Pearse, H. (eds.) (2026) *Thriving sustainably on planet Earth: Inspiring innovation in children's education*. Cambridge: Cambridge University Press.
Callahan, R.E. (1962) *Education and the cult of efficiency: A study of the social forces that have shaped the administration of the public schools*. Chicago: University of Chicago Press.
Cambridge Dictionary. (2024) *Soul and spirit*. Cambridge University Press. Available at: https://dictionary.cambridge.org (Accessed 31 Jul. 2025).
Casson, A., Cooling, T. and Francis, L.J. (2018) *Lessons in spiritual development: Learning from leading Christian-ethos secondary schools*. Coventry: University of Warwick. Available at: https://warwick.ac.uk/fac/soc/impact/policybriefings/1_lessons_in_spiritual_development.pdf (Accessed 29 Apr. 2024).

Challen, A., Machin, S. and Gillham, J. (2019) *The impact of a wellbeing programme on academic outcomes: Evidence from a randomised control trial*. London: Education Endowment Foundation.

Chia, R. and Holt, R. (2007) *Strategy without design: The silent efficacy of indirect action*. Cheltenham: Edward Elgar Publishing.

Church of England. (2016) *Vision for education: Deeply Christian, serving the common good*. London: Church of England Education Office.

Cixous, H. (1994) 'To live the orange', in Sellers, S. (ed.) *The Hélène Cixous reader*. Oxford: Routledge.

Clark, A.E., De Neve, J.E., Layard, R. and Ward, G. (2018) *The origins of happiness: The science of wellbeing over the life course*. Princeton: Princeton University Press.

Coe, R. (2013) *Improving education: A triumph of hope over experience*. Durham: Centre for Evaluation and Monitoring, Durham University.

Coltman, P. and Rolls, L. (2021) 'Nurturing compassionate citizens of the future: Weaving together pedagogy and curriculum', in Biddulph, J. and Flutter, J. (eds.) *Inspiring primary curriculum design*. Abingdon: Routledge, pp. 27–43.

Conroy, J. (2004) *Betwixt and between: The liminal imagination, education and democracy*. New York: Peter Lang.

Cooper, D.A. (1999) *Silence, simplicity and solitude: A complete guide to spiritual retreat*. Woodstock: SkyLight Paths.

Cremin, H. (2026) *Rewilding education*. Oxon: Routledge.

Cremin, T. (2021) *Reading for pleasure: A research overview*. Milton Keynes: Open University.

Cremin, T., Mottram, M., Collins, F., Powell, S. and Safford, K. (2014) *Building communities of engaged readers*. London: Routledge.

Cremin, T. and Durning, A., (2021) 'Inspiring a love of reading: professional learning to develop a culture of reading for pleasure' in *Unlocking Research: reimagining professional development in schools*, Hargreaves, E. and Rolls, L. eds, Abingdon, Routledge.

Cross, R., Rebele, R. and Grant, A. (2016) 'Collaborative overload', *Harvard Business Review*, 94(1), pp. 74–79.

Custodero, L. (2005) 'Observable indicators of flow experience: A developmental perspective on musical engagement in young children from infancy to school age', *Music Education Research*, 7(2), pp. 185–209.

Damasio, A. (2003) *Looking for Spinoza: Joy, sorrow, and the feeling brain*. Orlando: Harcourt.

Damon, W. (2008) *The path to purpose: Helping our children find their calling in life*. New York: Free Press.

Damon, W., Menon, J. and Bronk, K.C. (2003) 'The development of purpose during adolescence', *Applied Developmental Science*, 7(3), pp. 119–128.

Das, A. (2026) 'Spirituality and science', in Biddulph, J., Shuckburgh, E. and Pearse, H. (eds.) *Education visions: Thriving on planet earth*. Cambridge: Cambridge University Press.

Das, B. (Warren Weinstein) (2020) *The art of teaching: A guide for training our children in Krishna consciousness*. Vrindavan: VIHE Publications.

Deci, E.L. and Ryan, R.M. (1985) *Intrinsic motivation and self-determination in human behavior*. New York: Plenum.

Dehaene, S. (2020) *How we learn: Why brains learn better than any machine… for now*. London: Viking.

Deleuze, G. and Guattari, F. (1987) *A thousand plateaus: Capitalism and schizophrenia*. Translated by B. Massumi. Minneapolis: University of Minnesota Press.

Descartes, R. (1637) *Discourse on the method*. Translated by I. Maclean (2006). Oxford: Oxford University Press.

de Souza, M. and Halafoff, A. (eds.) (2018) *Re-enchanting education and spiritual wellbeing: Fostering belonging and meaning-making for global citizens*. London: Routledge.

Dewey, J. (1916) *Democracy and education*. New York: Macmillan.

Dewey, J. (1933) *How we think: A restatement of the relation of reflective thinking to the educative process*. Boston: D.C. Heath.

Dewey, J. (1934) *Art as experience*. New York: Minton, Balch & Company.

Dewey, J. (1938) *Experience and education*. New York: Macmillan.

Dharma, K. (2000) *Mahabharata*. USA: Torchlight Publishing.

Domash, L. (2021) *Imagination, creativity and spirituality in psychotherapy: Welcome to wonderland*. Abingdon: Routledge.

Donker, A.S., de Boer, H., Kostons, D., van Ewijk, C.D. and van der Werf, M.P.C. (2014) 'Effectiveness of learning strategy instruction on academic performance', *Educational Research Review*, 11, pp. 1–26.

Dorling, D. (2023) *Seven children: The inequality of opportunity in the UK*. London: Verso.

Douglas A. MacDonald (2000) 'Spirituality: Description, measurement, and relation to the five factor model of personality.' *Journal of Personality*, 68(1), pp. 153–197.

Dunne, R. and Martin, E. (2021) 'Learning to learn from nature: How principles of harmony in the natural world can guide curriculum design', in Biddulph, J. and Flutter, J. (eds.) *Inspiring primary curriculum design*. Abingdon: Routledge, pp. 87–104.

Durlak, J.A., Weissberg, R.P., Dymnicki, A.B., Taylor, R.D. and Schellinger, K.B. (2011) 'The impact of enhancing students' social and emotional learning: A meta-analysis of school-based universal interventions', *Child Development*, 82(1), pp. 405–432.

Durning, A., Baker, S. and Ramchandani, P. (2025) *Empowering play in primary education*. Abingdon: Routledge.

Dweck, C. (2006) *Mindset: The new psychology of success*. New York: Random House.

Dweck, C. (2017) *Mindset: Changing the way you think to fulfil your potential*. Updated edn. London: Robinson.

Ean. (2024) Available at: https://www.optionstheedge.com/topic/people/epsom-college-uk-head-sir-anthony-seldon-education-meeting-changing-needs (Accessed 1 August 2025).

Easterlin, R.A. (1981) 'Why isn't the whole world developed?', *Journal of Economic History*, 41(1), pp. 1–19.

Easwaran, E. (2007) *The upanishads*. Tomales: Nilgiri Press.

Edmundson, M. (2010) 'William Blake's America, 2010', *The Chronicle of Higher Education* (The Review), 24 October. Available at: https://www.chronicle.com/article/william-blakes-america-2010/ (Accessed 3 Jan. 2026).

Education Endowment Foundation (EEF) (2019) *Improving behaviour in schools*. London: Education Endowment Foundation.

Edurio (2025) *Pupil Experience Report 2025*. London: Edurio.

Egan, K. (2008) 'Education, spirituality, and the arts', in Bresler, L. (ed.) *International handbook of research in arts education*. Dordrecht: Springer, pp. 1495–1500.

Eghdamian, K. (2025) What if the world's religions aren't competing but rather one unfolding truth? Available at: https://www.theguardian.com/commentisfree/2025/jun/29/what-if-the-worlds-religions-arent-competing-but-rather-one-unfolding-truth (Accessed 18 Mar. 2026).

Eghdamian, K. (2026) Schools that cultivate the mind but neglect spiritual education leave children unanchored in a challenging world. Available at: https://www.theguardian.com/commentisfree/2026/feb/09/children-schools-spiritual-education (Accessed 18 Jan. 2026).

Eisner, E.W. (2002) *The arts and the creation of mind*. New Haven: Yale University Press.

Elliott, J. (2006) *Educational research: Its nature, methods and uses*. London: Routledge.

Ericsson, K.A. (2009) 'Development of professional expertise: Toward measurement of expert performance and design of optimal learning environments', *Educational Researcher*, 38(6), pp. 412–423.

Erikson, E.H. (1950) *Childhood and society*. New York: Norton.

Erricker, J., Ota, C. and Erricker, C. (eds.) (2001) *Spiritual education: Cultural, religious and social differences – New perspectives for the 21st century*. Brighton: Sussex Academic Press.

FFT Education Datalab. (2025) The educational outcomes of disadvantaged white pupils. [online] Available at: https://ffteducationdatalab.org.uk/2025/07/the-educational-outcomes-of-disadvantaged-white-pupils/ (Accessed 10 Sep. 2025).

Favors, J.E. (2002) *Leadership for an age of higher consciousness*. Vol. 2. India: Krishnapada Press.

Fisher, J. (2009) 'Getting the balance: Assessing spirituality and wellbeing among children and youth', *International Journal of Children's Spirituality*, 14(3), pp. 273–288.

Flutter, J. (2006) *Teacher development and phronesis in practice*. Cambridge: University of Cambridge Faculty of Education.

Flutter, J. (2022) ''What can be otherwise': Embodying a collective *phronesis* (or practical wisdom) for sculpting new creativities in primary education and beyond', in Burnard, P. and Loughrey, M. (eds.) *Creativities in primary education*. Abingdon: Routledge, pp. 203–220.

Flutter, J. (2025) *Empowering teacher professionalism: Collegiality and practical wisdom in education*. The Netherlands: BRILL.

Flutter, J., Biddulph, J. and Peacock, A. (2023) 'Raising voices: Journeying towards a new democratic education', in Biddulph, J., Rolls, L. and Flutter, J. (eds.) *Unleashing children's voices in democratic primary education*. Abingdon: Routledge, pp. 7–25.

Frankl, V.E. (1969) *The will to meaning: Foundations and applications of logotherapy*. New York: World Publishing.

Frankl, V.E. (2004) *Man's search for meaning*. London: Rider.

Fredricks, J.A., Blumenfeld, P.C. and Paris, A.H. (2004) 'School engagement: Potential of the concept, state of the evidence', *Review of Educational Research*, 74(1), pp. 59–109.

Freedman, S. (2024) Lessons learnt? Reflecting on 20 years of school reform in England [online]. Available at: https://www.suttontrust.com/wp-content/uploads/2024/10/Lessons-learnt-1.pdf (Accessed 1 Feb. 2026).

Freire, P. (1970) *Pedagogy of the oppressed*. New York: Continuum.

Freire, P. (1994) *Pedagogy of hope: Reliving pedagogy of the oppressed*. New York: Continuum.

Friedman, H., Krippner, S., Riebel, L. and Johnson, C. (2024) '7 models of spiritual and transpersonal development', in Miller, L.J. (ed.), *The Oxford handbook of psychology and spirituality*. Oxford: Oxford University Press, pp. 149–172.

Fromm, E. (1976) *To have or to be?* New York: Harper & Row.

Gaunt, A. and Stott, A. (2019) *Transform teaching and learning through talk*. USA: Rowman and Littlefield.

Gergen, K.J. (2009) *Relational being: Beyond self and community*. Oxford: Oxford University Press.

Gersten, R., Baker, S.K. and Shanahan, T. (2007) *Effective literacy and English language instruction for English learners*. Portsmouth: RMC Research Corporation.

Gillies, R.M. (2016) *Cooperative learning: Review of research and practice*. Canberra: Australian Council for Educational Research.

Gilligan, C. (1982) *In a different voice: Psychological theory and women's development*. Cambridge: Harvard University Press.

Goleman, D. (1996) *Emotional intelligence: Why it can matter more than IQ*. London: Bloomsbury.

Goodall, C. and Ward-Sinclair, J. (2023) 'Taking account of neurodiverse learners in the classroom: Supporting inclusive classroom practices', in Black-Hawkins, K. and Grinham-Smith, A. (eds.) *Expanding possibilities for inclusive learning*. Abingdon: Routledge, pp. 45–60.

Gor, N. (2025) *Before religion: Remembering ancient India's vision for universal spirituality*. India: Harper Collins.

Greenberg, M.T., Kusché, C.A., Cook, E.T. and Quamma, J.P. (2003) 'Promoting emotional competence in school-aged children: The PATHS curriculum', *Prevention & Treatment*, 6(1), pp. 1–29.

Greene, M. (1973) *Teacher as stranger: Educational philosophy for the modern age*. Belmont, CA: Wadsworth Publishing.

Greene, M. (1978) *Landscapes of learning*. New York: Teachers College Press.

Greene, M. (1988) *The dialectic of freedom*. New York: Teachers College Press.

Greene, M. (1995, 2000) *Releasing the imagination: Essays on education, the arts, and social change*. San Francisco: Jossey-Bass.

Griffiths, B. (2003) *The golden thread: The classical tradition of spiritual wisdom*. London: Darton, Longman & Todd.

Gu, Y., Park, J. and Bjork, R.A. (2004) 'Optimal scheduling of retrieval practice', *Journal of Experimental Psychology: Learning, Memory, and Cognition*, 30(4), pp. 862–876.

Guggenbühl, A. (2008) *The power of imagination: The importance of fairy tales in education and therapy*. London: Karnac Books.

Habermas, J. (1984) *The theory of communicative action. Volume 1: Reason and the rationalization of society*. Translated by T. McCarthy. Boston: Beacon Press.

Hacker, D.J., Dunlosky, J. and Graesser, A.C. (eds.) (2009) *Handbook of metacognition in education*. New York: Routledge.

Hallam, S. (2013) *Ability grouping in education*. London: SAGE.

Hargreaves, A. and Fullan, M. (2012) *Professional capital: Transforming teaching in every school*. London: Routledge.

Hargreaves, E. and Rolls, L. (2021) *Unlocking research: Professional learning and development in education*. Abingdon: Routledge.

Harper, D. (2024). *Online etymology dictionary*. [online] Available at: https://www.etymonline.com (Accessed 31 Jul. 2025).

Hart, S., Drummond, M.J., Dixon, A. and McIntyre, D. (2004) *Learning without limits*. Maidenhead: Open University Press.

Hattie, J. (2009) *Visible learning: A synthesis of over 800 meta-analyses relating to achievement*. London: Routledge.

Hattie, J. (2012) *Visible learning for teachers: Maximizing impact on learning*. London: Routledge.

Hattie, J. and Timperley, H. (2007) 'The power of feedback', *Review of Educational Research*, 77(1), pp. 81–112.

Hay, D. (1982) *Exploring inner space: Is God still possible in the twentieth century?* Harmondsworth: Penguin.

Hay, D. and Nye, R. (2006) *The spirit of the child*. London: Jessica Kingsley.

Hillman, J. (1996) *The soul's code: In search of character and calling*. New York: Random House.

Hodgkinson, P. (1996) *A new theory of career decision-making*. Unpublished monograph, Manchester Metropolitan University.

Hollis, J. (2000) *Finding meaning in the second half of life: How to finally, really grow up*. Toronto: Inner City Books.

Holmes, D. (2021) Exploring spirituality in the primary school. Available at: https://www.peacefulschools.org.uk/application/files/9716/2886/9553/Exploring_Spirituality_in_Primary_Schools_by_D_Holmes_.pdf (Accessed 29 Apr. 2024).

hooks, b (1994) *Teaching to transgress: Education as the practice of freedom*. New York: Routledge.

hooks, b (2003) *Teaching community: A pedagogy of hope*. New York: Routledge.

Housman, D. (2017) 'The importance of emotional development for young children', *Early Child Development and Care*, 187(11–12), pp. 1856–1863.

Howe, C., Hennessy, S. and Mercer, N. (2019) *Dialogue, argumentation and education*. Cambridge: Cambridge University Press.

Immordino-Yang, M.H. (2007) 'A tale of two cases: Lessons for education from the study of two boys living with half their brains', *Mind, Brain, and Education*, 1(2), pp. 66–83.

Indian National Congress. (2024) *Election manifesto 2024*. New Delhi: INC.

Irwin, R.L. (2017) 'A/r/tography as living inquiry', in Leavy, P. (ed.) *Handbook of arts-based research*. New York: Guilford Press, pp. 134–151.

James, L. and Wilks, J. (2018) *The game changers*. Los Angeles: Netflix.

Jenkins, P. (2008) *Nurturing spirituality in children*. New York: Atria Books.

Jennings, P.A., Frank, J.L., Snowberg, K.E., Coccia, M.A. and Greenberg, M.T. (2017) 'Improving classroom learning environments by cultivating awareness and resilience in education (CARE): Results of a randomized controlled trial', *School Psychology Quarterly*, 32(3), pp. 384–401.

Johnson, D.W. and Johnson, R.T. (2002) 'Learning together and alone: Overview and meta-analysis', *Asia Pacific Journal of Education*, 22(1), pp. 95–105.

Jung, C.G. (2009) *The red book: Liber novus*. Edited by S. Shamdasani. New York: W.W. Norton & Company.

Kahneman, D. (2011) *Thinking, fast and slow*. New York: Farrar, Straus and Giroux.

Kafka, J. (2019). Inequality in education. In J. L. Rury & E. H. Tamura (Eds.), *The Oxford Handbook of the History of Education*. Oxford University Press.

Kant, I. (1785) *Groundwork of the metaphysics of morals*. Translated by M. Gregor (1997). Cambridge: Cambridge University Press.

Kapur, M. (2012) 'Productive failure in learning the concept of variance', *Instructional Science*, 40(4), pp. 651–672.

Kapur, M. (2011) 'A further study of productive failure in mathematical problem solving', *Instructional Science*, 39(4), pp. 561–579.

Kashaka, N.D. (2025) 'The role of folklore in modern society', *International Digital Organization for Scientific Research JOURNAL OF ARTS AND MANAGEMENT*, 10(1), pp. 32–35.

Kemmis, S. (2012) 'Phronesis, experience and the primacy of praxis', in Hager, P., Lee, A. and Reich, A. (eds.) *Practice, learning and change: Practice-theory perspectives on professional learning*. Dordrecht: Springer, pp. 147–161.

Kemmis, S., Edwards-Groves, C., Wilkinson, J. and Hardy, I. (2012) 'Ecologies of practices', in Hager, P., Lee, A. and Reich, A. (eds.) *Practice, learning and change: Practice-theory perspectives on professional learning*, Vol. 8. Dordecht: Springer, pp. 33–49.

Kessler, R. (2000) *The soul of education: Helping students find connection, compassion and character at school*. USA: ASCD.

Kierkegaard, S. (1849) *The sickness unto death*. Translated by H.V. Hong and E.H. Hong (1980). Princeton: Princeton University Press.

Kirkman, J., Long, R. and Robin-Ross, A. (2021) 'Developing excellence in music through collaborative enquiry', in Biddulph, J. and Flutter, J. (eds.) *Unlocking research: Professional learning and development in education*. Abingdon: Routledge.

Kirschner, P.A., Sweller, J. and Clark, R.E. (2006) 'Why minimal guidance during instruction does not work', *Educational Psychologist*, 41(2), pp. 75–86.

Kohlberg, L. (1981) *The philosophy of moral development*. San Francisco: Harper & Row.

Krishnamurthi, J. (1974) *Education and the significance of life*. New York and London: Harper & Brothers.

Labour, P. (2024) *Labour party manifesto 2024*. London: Labour Party.

Lantieri, L. (2001) *Schools with spirit: Nurturing the inner lives of children and teachers*. Boston: Beacon Press.

Latour, B. (2017) *Facing Gaia: Eight lectures on the new climatic regime*. Cambridge: Polity.

Layard, R. (2015) *Happiness: Lessons from a new science*. 2nd edn. London: Penguin.

Layard, R. (2020) *Can we be happier? Evidence and ethics*. London: Pelican.

Layard, R., Clark, A.E., Cornaglia, F., Powdthavee, N. and Vernoit, J. (2018) 'What predicts a successful life? A life-course model of wellbeing', *Economic Journal*, 124(580), pp. F720–F738.

Layard, R. and Hagell, A. (2015) *Wellbeing and policy*. London: LSE Centre for Economic Performance.

Layard, R. and Hagell, A. (2015a) *A good childhood: Searching for values in a competitive age*. London: Penguin.

Layard, R. and O'Donnell, G. (2015) *How's life at school? Measuring wellbeing in schools*. London: LSE.
Learning and Work Institute and The King's Trust. (2022) *Youth mental health and the labour market*. London: Learning and Work Institute.
Leopold, A. (1949) *A sand county almanac*. New York: Oxford University Press.
Locke, J. (1989) *Some thoughts concerning education*. Edited by J.W. Yolton and J.S. Yolton. Oxford: Clarendon Press. (Original work published 1693).
Lovat, T. and Toomey, R. (2009) *Values education and quality teaching: The double helix effect*. Dordrecht: Springer.
Lovat, T., Toomey, R. and Clement, N. (2009) 'Values education, quality teaching and service learning: A troika for effective teaching and teacher education', in *Values education and quality teaching: The double helix effect*. Dordrecht: Springer.
MacIntyre, A. (1981) *After virtue*. Notre Dame: University of Notre Dame Press.
Mahaffey, P. (2019) *Integrative spirituality religious pluralism, individuation, and awakening*. Abingdon: Routledge.
Marx, K. and Engels, F. (1998) *The communist manifesto*. Oxford: Oxford University Press.
Maslow, A.H. (1943) 'A theory of human motivation', *Psychological Review*, 50(4), pp. 370–396.
Maslow, A.H. (1968) *Toward a psychology of being*. 2nd edn. New York: Van Nostrand Reinhold.
Mata-McMahon, J. and Escarfuller, P. (2024) *Children's spirituality in early childhood education*. Abingdon: Routledge.
McGilchrist, I. (2009) *The master and his emissary: The divided brain and the making of the Western world*. New Haven: Yale University Press.
Mercer, N. (2019) *Language and the joint creation of knowledge*. Abingdon: Routledge.
Mercer, N. and Littleton, K. (2007) *Dialogue and the development of children's thinking: A sociocultural approach*. London: Routledge.
Mercer, N. (2021) 'Oracy and the primary curriculum: What does research tell us?', in Biddulph, J. and Flutter, J. (eds.) *Inspiring primary curriculum design*. Abingdon: Routledge, pp. 149–165.
Mercer, N., Wegerif, R. and Dawes, L. (1999) 'Children's talk and the development of reasoning in the classroom', *British Educational Research Journal*, 25(1), pp. 95–111.
Mezirow, J. (2000) *Learning as transformation: Critical perspectives on a theory in progress*. San Francisco: Jossey-Bass.
Midgley, M. (1980) *Mind and body: The theories of dualism and materialism*. London: Routledge.
Mill, J.S. (1859) *On liberty*. London: John W. Parker and Son.
Miller, J.G., et al. (2018) 'Culture and the development of self-regulation', *Annual Review of Psychology*, 69, pp. 45–69.
Miller, J.P. (1994) *The contemplative practitioner: Meditation in education and the professions*. Albany: State University of New York Press.
Miller, J.P. (2000) *Education and the soul: Toward a spiritual curriculum*. Albany: SUNY Press.
Miller, L. (2015) *The spiritual child: The new science on parenting for health and lifelong thriving*. New York: Panmacmillan.

Miller, L.J. (ed.) (2024) *The Oxford handbook of psychology and spirituality*. Oxford: Oxford University Press.

Miller, R. (2018) *Transforming the future: Anticipation in the 21st century*. Paris: UNESCO Publishing.

Mills, L. (2019) 'Growing together: spiritual development in schools and communities', in *Spiritual Development: Interpretations of Spiritual Development in the Classroom*. Available at: https://ldbs.co.uk/wp-content/uploads/2019/11/2019-Spiritual-Development-Interpretations-of-spiritual-developments-in-the-classroom.pdf (Accessed 29 Apr. 2024).

Mischel, W., Ebbesen, E.B. and Raskoff Zeiss, A. (1972) 'Cognitive and attentional mechanisms in delay of gratification', *Journal of Personality and Social Psychology*, 21(2), pp. 204–218.

Moberg, D.O. (2002) 'Assessing and measuring spirituality: Confronting dilemmas of universal and particular evaluative criteria', *Journal of Adult Development*, 9(1), pp. 47–60.

Moore, A. (2013) *Teaching and learning: Pedagogy, curriculum and culture*. 2nd edn. London: Routledge.

Moran, R. (2022) 'The philosophical retreat to the here and now: Notes on living in time', *Philosophy*, 97(4), pp. 413–433.

Muijs, D., Reynolds, D. and Kyriakides, L. (2014) *The dynamics of educational effectiveness*. London: Routledge.

Muller, W. (1992) *Legacy of The heart: The spiritual advantages of a painful childhood*. USA: Simon and Schuster.

Naess, A. (1973) 'The shallow and the deep, long-range ecology movement', *Inquiry*, 16(1–4), pp. 95–100.

Nakata, M. (2007) *Disciplining the savages, savaging the disciplines*. Canberra: Aboriginal Studies Press.

Nash, H.M. and Snowling, M.J. (2006) 'Teaching new words to children with poor existing vocabulary knowledge', *Journal of Child Psychology and Psychiatry*, 47(5), pp. 532–540.

Newberg, A. and Waldman, M.R. (2009) *How God changes your brain: Breakthrough findings from a leading neuroscientist*. New York: Ballantine Books.

Nietzsche, F. (1889) *Twilight of the idols*. Translated by R.J. Hollingdale (1990). London: Penguin.

Noddings, N. (2003) *Caring: A feminine approach to ethics and moral education*. 2nd edn. Berkeley: University of California Press.

Noddings, N. (2005) *The challenge to care in schools: An alternative approach to education*. 2nd edn. New York: Teachers College Press.

Noddings, N. (2013) *Happiness and education*. Cambridge: Cambridge University Press.

Nussbaum, M. (1997) *Cultivating humanity: A classical defense of reform in liberal education*. Cambridge: Harvard University Press.

Nussbaum, M.C. (2010) *Not for profit: Why democracy needs the humanities*. Princeton: Princeton University Press.

O'Reilley, M.R. (1993) *The peaceable classroom*. Portsmouth: Boynton/Cook Publishers.

OECD. (2015) *Students, computers and learning: Making the connection*. Paris: OECD Publishing.

OECD. (2018) *The future of education and skills*. Paris: OECD Publishing. Available at: https://www.oecd.org/content/dam/oecd/en/about/projects/edu/education-2040/position-paper/PositionPaper.pdf.

Olivelle, P. (2010) *Upanisads*. Oxford: Oxford University Press.

Orr, D.W. (2004) *Earth in mind: On education, environment, and the human prospect*. 2nd edn. Washington: Island Press.

Oxford English Dictionary. (2024) *Soul and spirit*. [online] Oxford University Press. Available at: https://www.oed.com (Accessed 31 July 2025).

Palmer, P.J. (2007) *The courage to teach: Exploring the inner landscape of a teacher's life*. 10th anniversary edn. San Francisco: Jossey-Bass.

Panadero, E. (2017) 'A review of self-regulated learning: Six models and four directions for research', *Frontiers in Psychology*, 8, pp. 422–438.

Parentkind. (2025) The national parent survey 2025. Available at: https://nationalparentsurvey.parentkind.org (Accessed 4 October 2025).

Park, C.L. (2013) 'The Meaning Making Model: A Framework for Understanding Meaning, Spirituality, and Stress-Related Growth in Health Psychology.' *The European Health Psychologist*, 15, 40–47. https://www.ehps.net/ehp/index.php/contents/article/view/ehp.v15.i2.p40/1041

Parker J. Palmer (1998) 'Evoking the spirit in public education', Educational Leadership, 56(4), pp. 6–11. Available at: ASCD *Educational Leadership* article (Accessed: 13 June 2026).

Peacock, A. (2016) *Assessment for learning without limits*. Maidenhead: Open University Press.

Pearce, C.L., et al. (2013) 'Association between purpose in life and health behaviours', *Psychosomatic Medicine*, 75(7), pp. 706–712.

Pennebaker, J.W. and Seagal, J.D. (1999) 'Forming a story: The health benefits of narrative', *Journal of Clinical Psychology*, 55(10), pp. 1243–1254.

Peterson, A., Lexmond, J., Hallgarten, J. and Kerr, D. (2014) *Schools with soul: A new approach to spiritual, moral, social and cultural education (SMSC)*. London: Royal Society for the Encouragement of Arts, Manufactures and Commerce (RSA).

Piedmont, R. and Wilkins, T. (2020) *Understanding the psychological soul of spirituality*. Abingdon: Routledge.

Plato. (2007) *Republic*. Translated by R. Waterfield. Oxford: Oxford University Press. (Original work published c. 380 BCE).

Poore, J. and Nemecek, T. (2018) 'Reducing food's environmental impacts through producers and consumers', *Science*, 360(6392), pp. 987–992.

Postman, N. (1985) *Amusing ourselves to death: Public discourse in the age of show business*. New York: Penguin.

Praetorius, A.-K., Klieme, E., Herbert, B. and Pinger, P. (2018) 'Generic dimensions of teaching quality', *Educational Assessment, Evaluation and Accountability*, 30(4), pp. 407–426.

Prince of Wales, H.R.H., Juniper, T. and Skelly, I. (2010) *Harmony: A new way of looking at our world*. London: HarperCollins.

Pritchett, L. (1996) *Where has all the education gone?*. Policy Research Working Paper 1581. Washington: World Bank.

Quigley, A. (2018) *Closing the vocabulary gap*. London: Routledge.

Quigley, A., Muijs, D. and Stringer, E. (2018) *Metacognition and self-regulated learning*. London: Education Endowment Foundation.

Radhakrishnan, S. (2006) *The principal upanisads*. India: Harper Collins.

Reay, D. (2017) *Miseducation: Inequality, education and the working classes*. Bristol: Policy Press.

Reeve, J., Jang, H., Carrell, D., Jeon, S. and Barch, J. (2004) 'Enhancing students' engagement by increasing teachers' autonomy support', *Motivation and Emotion*, 28(2), pp. 147–169.

Riveros, A. and Immordino-Yang, M.H. (2023) *Affective neuroscience and education: Theory, research, and applications*. New York: Routledge.

Roeser, R.W., Skinner, E., Beers, J. and Jennings, P.A. (2013) 'Mindfulness training and teachers' professional development: An emerging area of research and practice', *Child Development Perspectives*, 6(2), pp. 167–173.

Rogers, C. (1957) 'The necessary and sufficient conditions of therapeutic personality change', *Journal of Consulting Psychology*, 21(2), pp. 95–103.

Rolls, L. and Seleznyov, S. (2021) 'Lesson study as professional learning: Building collaborative inquiry', in Hargreaves, E. and Rolls, L. (eds.) *Unlocking research: Professional learning and development in education*. Abingdon: Routledge.

Rosenshine, B. (2010) 'Principles of instruction', *American Educator*, 36(1), pp. 12–39.

Rotter, J.B. (1966) 'Generalized expectancies for internal versus external control of reinforcement', *Psychological Monographs*, 80(1), pp. 1–28.

Rousseau, J.-J. (1979) *Émile, or on education*. Translated by A. Bloom. New York: Basic Books.

Ryan, R.M. and Deci, E.L. (2020) *Self-determination theory: Basic psychological needs in motivation, development, and wellness*. New York: Guilford Press.

Ryff, C.D. (1989) 'Happiness is everything, or is it? Explorations on the meaning of psychological well-being', *Journal of Personality and Social Psychology*, 57(6), pp. 1069–1081.

Ryff, C.D. and Keyes, C.L.M. (1995) 'The structure of psychological well-being revisited', *Journal of Personality and Social Psychology*, 69(4), pp. 719–727.

Sartre, J.-P. (1946) *Existentialism is a humanism*. Translated by C. Macomber (1977). New Haven: Yale University Press.

Schleicher, A. (2018) 'Foreword', in OECD (ed.) *The future of education and skills*. Paris: OECD Publishing. Available at: https://www.oecd.org/content/dam/oecd/en/about/projects/edu/education-2040/position-paper/PositionPaper.pdf. (Accessed 2 December 2025).

Schön, D.A. (1983) *The reflective practitioner: How professionals think in action*. New York: Basic Books.

Schwartz, B. (2004) *The paradox of choice: Why more is less*. New York: HarperCollins.

Schweig, G. and Gor, N. (2021) 'Education as the embracing of a loving universe: Designing an inclusive curriculum', in Biddulph, J. and Flutter, J. (eds.) *Inspiring primary curriculum design*. Abingdon: Routledge, pp. 107–120.

Schweig, G.M. (2010) *The Rig Veda: An English translation*. New York: HarperOne.

Scott, D. (1998) 'Listening to spiritual narratives', in Scott, D. (ed.) *Storytelling, voice and qualitative research*. London: Falmer Press.

Scott, D. (2001) 'Storytelling, voice and qualitative research: Spirituality as a site of ambiguity and difficulty', in Erricker, J., Ota, C., and Erricker, C. (eds.) *Spiritual education: Cultural, religious and social differences – New perspectives for the 21st century*. Brighton: Sussex Academic Press.

Scott Webster, R. (2018) *Understanding curriculum: The Australian context*. Cambridge: Cambridge University Press.

Seaton, C.L. and Beaumont, S.L. (2015) 'Individual differences in parenting styles and their associations with psychological needs, well-being and academic motivation', *Learning and Individual Differences*, 37, pp. 118–126.

Seldon, A. *Examined Life Podcast* with Kenny Primrose. Retrieved from YouTube. https://www.youtube.com/watch?v=COF5tUKzRdl

Seldon, A. (2016) *Beyond happiness: How to find lasting meaning and contentment*. London: Yellow Kite.

Seldon, A. (2019) *The fourth education revolution*. London: University of Buckingham Press.

Seligman, M.E.P. (2011) *Flourish*. New York: Free Press.

Sen, A. (1981) *Poverty and famines: An essay on entitlement and deprivation*. Oxford: Oxford University Press.

Sen, A. (1999) *Development as freedom*. Oxford: Oxford University Press.

Shaban, M.S. (2008) 'Spiritual values beyond the West: Jordan', in Bresler, L. (ed.) *International handbook of research in arts education*. Dordrecht: Springer, pp. 1493–1494.

Sheldrake, R. (2017) *Science and spiritual practices: Reconnecting through direct experience*. London: Bloomsbury.

Shields, C.M. (2004) 'Dialogic leadership for social justice: Overcoming pathologies of silence', *Educational Administration Quarterly*, 40(1), pp. 109–132.

Shirley, D. and Hargreaves, A. (2023) *The age of identity: Who do our kids think they are … and how do we help them belong?* Thousand Oaks: Corwin.

Shonkoff, J.P. and Phillips, D.A. (eds) (2000) *From neurons to neighborhoods: The science of early childhood development*. Washington, DC: National Academies Press.

Siegel, D.J., Payne Bryson, T. and Siegel, A. (2016) No-drama discipline: The whole-brain way to calm the chaos and nurture your child's developing mind. London: Scribe.

Slavin, R.E. (2014) *Cooperative learning*. 2nd edn. Boston: Allyn & Bacon.

Snaza, N., Sonu, D., Truman, S.E. and Zaliwska, Z. (eds.) (2014) *Posthumanism and educational research*. New York: Routledge.

Soderstrom, N.C. and Bjork, R.A. (2015) 'Learning versus performance: An integrative review', *Perspectives on Psychological Science*, 10(2), pp. 176–199.

Stahl, G. (2015) *Identity, neoliberalism and aspiration: Educating white working-class boys*. London: Routledge.

Starratt, R.J. (2000) *The drama of leadership*. London: Falmer Press.

Sterling, S. (2001) *Sustainable education: Re-visioning learning and change*. Totnes: Green Books.

Strong-Wilson, T. and Ellis, J. (2007) 'Children and place: Reggio Emilia's environment as third teacher', *Theory Into Practice*, 46(1), pp. 40–47.

Stubbs, M. (2003) *Ahead of the class*. London: John Murray.

Svendsen, L. (2023) *A philosophy of Hope*. Glasgow: Reaktion Books Ltd.

Swami, S. and Steinborn, M. (2025) 'Fueled from within: How meditation forges the inner tools required for change meditation's contribution to solving current social, economic, and ecological crises', in Schüz, M. (ed.) *Transdisciplinary thinking and acting, transdisciplinary management of ecological and social crises*, Netherlands: Springer.

Swami, B.C. (2025) *The art of dying: The way to immortality*. India: ISKCON Ujjain.

Swann, M., Peacock, A., Hart, S. and Drummond, M.J. (2012) *Creating learning without limits*. Maidenhead: McGraw-Hill International.

Tagore, R. (1929) *The religion of man*. London: Allen & Unwin.

Taylor, B. and Hodgen, J., 2026, 'Higher attaining maths pupils do better when grouped by attainment' (retrieved on 17th May 2026 https://www.ucl.ac.uk/news/2026/apr/high-attaining-maths-pupils-do-better-when-grouped-attainment

Thakura, B. (2017) *Śrī Caitanya Śikṣāmṛta*. Translated by Sarvabhavana Dasa. Kolkata: Sree Gaudiya Math.

Thomson, P. (2017) *Education, schooling and social justice*. London: Routledge.

Thoreau, H.D. (1995) *Walden; Or, life in the woods*. London: J.M. Dent & Sons.

Tillich, P. (1951) *Systematic theology. Volume 1*. Chicago: University of Chicago Press.

TIMSS-SA. (2024) 'Education election manifestos: anything new?', *TIMSS-SA Blog*. Available at: https://www.timss-sa.org/blog/education-election-manifestos-anything-new (Accessed 4 October 2025).

Tisdell, E. (2003) *Exploring spirituality and culture in adult and higher education*. San Francisco: Jossey-Bass.

Tolstoy, L. (1967) *On popular education*. Moscow: Posrednik.

Tolstoy, L. (2000) *Anna Karenina*. Translated by Richard Pevear and Larissa Volokhonsky. New York: Penguin.

Toomey, R. (2010) 'Values education and quality teaching: The double helix effect', *Australian Journal of Education*, 54(2), pp. 165–179.

Toomey, R. and Lovat, T. (2007) *Values education and quality teaching: The double helix effect*. Sydney: David Barlow Publishing.

Trump, D. (2025) *Executive order on education policy*. Washington: The White House.

Turkle, S. (2011) *Alone together: Why we expect more from technology and less from each other*. New York: Basic Books.

Twenge, J. (2017) *iGen: Why Today's super-connected kids are growing up less rebellious, more tolerant, less happy—and completely unprepared for adulthood*. New York: Atria.

UNESCO. (2015) *Rethinking education: Towards a global common good?* Paris: UNESCO Publishing.

UNESCO. (2021) *Reimagining our futures together: A new social contract for education*. Paris: United Nations Educational, Scientific and Cultural Organization.

VanderWeele, T.J. (2017) 'On the promotion of human flourishing', *Proceedings of the National Academy of Sciences*, 114(31), pp. 8148–8156.

van Gennep, A. (1960) *The rites of passage*. Chicago: University of Chicago Press.

Vansteenkiste, M., Simons, J., Lens, W., Sheldon, K.M. and Deci, E.L. (2004) 'Motivating learning, performance, and persistence', *Journal of Personality and Social Psychology*, 87(2), pp. 246–260.

Vickery, S. (2019) 'Recognising spiritual development in a primary context', in *Spiritual development: Interpretations of spiritual development in the classroom*. Available at: https://ldbs.co.uk/wp-content/uploads/2019/11/2019-Spiritual-Development-Interpretations-of-spiritual-developments-in-the-classroom.pdf (Accessed 29 Apr. 2024).

Volpe, M.R. and Chandler, D. (2001) 'Resolving and managing conflicts in academic communities: The emerging role of the 'Pracademic', *Negotiation Journal*, 17(3), pp. 245–255.

Walton, E. and Marais, C. (2023) 'Language matters', in Black-Hawkins, K. and Grinham-Smith, A. (eds.) *Expanding possibilities for inclusive learning*. Abingdon: Routledge, pp. 14–29.

Waters, T.E.A., Bosmans, G. and Vandevivere, E. (2015) 'Secure base representations in middle childhood across two Western cultures', *Developmental Psychology*, 51(7), pp. 1013–1025.

Wegerif, R. (2017) *The dialogic imagination in education*. Cambridge: Cambridge University Press.

Wegerif, R., Li, L. and Kaufman, J.C. (eds.) (2017) *The Routledge international handbook of research on teaching thinking*. London: Routledge.

Wenger, E. (1998) *Communities of practice: Learning, meaning, and identity*. Cambridge: Cambridge University Press.

Whitebread, D. (2019) *The importance of play: A handbook for practitioners and policy makers*. London: Routledge.

Whitebread, D. and Coltman, P. (2016) 'Ensuring developmentally appropriate practice in the early years of primary schooling', in Gronn, P. and Biddulph, J. (eds.) *A University's Challenge: Cambridge's Primary School for the Nation*. Cambridge: Cambridge University Press, pp. 119–139.

Wilber, K. (2000) *Integral psychology*. Boston: Shambhala.

Wiliam, D. (2011) *Embedded formative assessment*. Bloomington: Solution Tree Press.

Wiliam, D. (2017) 'Evaluating education and improving it', *Impact: Journal of the Chartered College of Teaching*. Available at: https://my.chartered.college/impact_article/editorial-evaluating-education-and-improving-it/(Accessed 29 Apr. 2024).

Wills, R. (2011) 'Music, spirituality and the creative Self', in Adams, K. (ed.) *Spirituality and education*. London: Routledge, pp. 103–107.

Wilson, E.O. (1984) *Biophilia*. Cambridge: Harvard University Press.

Wolf, A., Smith, C., Harford, L. and Lacey, M. (2021) 'Vision-driven curriculum practices: "Deeply Christian, serving the common good"', in Biddulph, J. and Flutter, J. (eds.) *Inspiring primary curriculum design*. Abingdon: Routledge, pp. 131–147.

World Health Organization. (2021) Adolescent mental health. Available at: https://www.who.int/news-room/fact-sheets/detail/adolescent-mental-health

Wright, A. (2000) *Spirituality and education*. London: RoutledgeFalmer.

Yolton, J.W. (1961) *John Locke and the way of ideas*. Oxford: Oxford University Press.

Yonker, J.E., Schnabelrauch, C.A. and DeHaan, L.G. (2012) 'The relationship between spirituality and religiosity on psychological outcomes in adolescents and emerging adults', *Journal of Adolescence*, 35(2), pp. 299–314.

Young, I.M. (1990) *Justice and the politics of difference*. Princeton: Princeton University Press.

Zajonc, A. (2009) *Meditation as contemplative inquiry: When knowing becomes love*. Great Barrington: Lindisfarne Books.

Zenner, C., Herrnleben-Kurz, S. and Walach, H. (2014) 'Mindfulness-based interventions in schools—A systematic review and meta-analysis', *Frontiers in Psychology*, 5, p. 603.

Zhao, Y. (2012) *World class learners: Educating creative and entrepreneurial students*. Thousand Oaks: Corwin Press.

Zimbardo, P. (2007) *The lucifer effect: Understanding how good people turn evil*. New York: Random House.

Zuboff, S. (2019) *The age of surveillance capitalism*. London: Profile Books.

Index

Note: *Italicized* and **bold** pages refer to figures and tables, respectively; and page numbers followed by "n" refer to notes.

For Product Safety Concerns and Information please contact our EU
representative GPSR@taylorandfrancis.com
Taylor & Francis Verlag GmbH, Kaufingerstraße 24, 80331 München, Germany

www.ingramcontent.com/pod-product-compliance
Lightning Source LLC
LaVergne TN
LVHW051458140826
845706LV00026B/311

9781032783918